RACIAL SPECTACLES

Explorations in Media, Race, and Justice

Jonathan Markovitz

Routledge
Taylor & Francis Group

NEW YORK AND LONDON

First published 2011
by Routledge
711 Third Avenue, New York, NY 10017

Simultaneously published in the UK
by Routledge
2 Park Square, Milton Park, Abingdon, Oxon OX14 4RN

Routledge is an imprint of the Taylor & Francis Group, an informa business

© 2011 Taylor & Francis

Typeset in Bembo and Stone Sans
by Florence Production Ltd, Stoodleigh, Devon
Printed and bound in the United States of America on acid-free paper
by Walsworth Publishing Company, Marceline, MO

Library of Congress Cataloging in Publication Data
  Markovitz, Jonathan.
  Racial spectacles : case studies in media, race, and justice / Jonathan Markovitz.
    p. cm.
  Includes bibliographical references and index.
  1. Mass media and minorities—United States. 2. Minorities in mass media.
  3. Mass media and race relations—United States. 4. Mass media—Objectivity—
  United States. 5. Mass media and criminal justice—United States. 6. African
  Americans in mass media—United States. I. Title.
  P94.5.M552U652 2011
  302.23089'00973—dc22   2010042048

ISBN13: 978-0-415-88345-0 (hbk)
ISBN13: 978-0-415-88383-2 (pbk)
ISBN13: 978-0-203-84321-5 (ebk)

RACIAL SPECTACLES

Racial Spectacles: Explorations in Media, Race, and Justice examines the crucial role the media has played in circulating and shaping national dialogues about race through representations of crime and racialized violence. Jonathan Markovitz argues that mass media "racial spectacles" often work to shore up racist stereotypes, but that they also provide opportunities to challenge prevalent conceptions of race, and can be seized upon as vehicles for social protest. This book explores a series of mass media spectacles revolving around the news, prime-time television, Hollywood cinema, and the internet that have either relied upon, reconfigured, or helped to construct collective memories of race, crime, and (in)justice. The case studies explored include the Scottsboro interracial rape case of the 1930s, the Kobe Bryant rape case, the Los Angeles Police Department's "Rampart scandal," the Abu Ghraib photographs, and a series of racist incidents at the University of California.

This book will prove to be important not only for courses on race and media, but also for any reader interested in issues of the media's role in social justice.

Jonathan Markovitz is a lecturer in the departments of Communication at the University of California, San Diego and at California State University, San Marcos. He received his PhD in Sociology from UCSD in 1999. He has published articles on race relations in the United States, collective memory, film, gender, and popular culture. He is the author of *Legacies of Lynching: Racial Violence and Memory* (University of Minnesota Press, 2004).

For Christie

CONTENTS

List of Figures		*viii*
Acknowledgements		*x*
	Introduction	1
1	"Exploding the Myth of the Black Rapist": Collective Memory and the Scottsboro Nine	19
2	Anatomy of a Spectacle: Race, Gender, and Memory in the Kobe Bryant Rape Case	49
3	Framing Police Corruption: The LAPD Rampart Scandal in the News	74
4	Reel Bad Cops: Hollywood's Appropriation of the Rampart Scandal	96
5	Racial Spectacles under an Anti-Racist Gaze: New Media and Abu Ghraib	124
	Conclusion: Lessons from a Campus Movement	159
	Works Cited	*169*
	Notes	*181*
	Index	*221*

FIGURES

i.1   U.S. Servicemen and Others Hunting Down Latino and
African American "Zoot-Suiters" in East Los Angeles.
June 8, 1943   2

1.1   International Labor Defense (ILD) Assessment Stamp, 1931   22

1.2   From Left: Eugene Williams, Samuel Leibowitz,
Willie Roberson, Roy Wright and Olin Montgomery.
New York City, July 26, 1937   37

1.3   Scottsboro Limited by Prentiss Taylor   39

1.4   "The Scottsboro Boys" Program Guide   41

2.1   Sports Illustrated, July 28, 2003: Kobe Bryant Mugshot   50

2.2   Hank Willis Thomas, 2008. "Hang Time Circa 1923."   56

2.3   Vogue, April 2008: LeBron James as King Kong   72

2.4   "Destroy this Mad Brute," H.R. Hopps, 1917. World War I
Propaganda Poster   72

4.1   Training Day DVD Cover, 2001   103

4.2   The Shield DVD Cover, 2002   112

5.1   "Q: And Babies? A: And Babies." Artists Poster Committee of
Art Workers Coalition: Frazier Dougherty, Jon Hendricks and
Irving Petlin. Photographer: R. L. Haeberle   139

5.2   Sabrina Harman Standing Over the Body of Manadel al-Jamadi   144

5.3   Salaheddin Sallat's Abu Ghraib Mural in the al-Sadr District of
Baghdad. May 27, 2004   150

5.4   Giuseppe Di Bella, from the series Abu Ghraib 2004/2006.
"USA Stamp Sheet."   152

5.5   Giuseppe Di Bella, from the series Abu Ghraib 2004/2006.
"Postcard."   153

5.6   Giuseppe Di Bella, from the series Abu Ghraib 2004/2006.
      "Postcard Back."   153
5.7   Daniel Heyman, from the Amman Watercolor Series, 2006:
      Edition 30. "When I Saw My Sons Dead."   157
5.8   Daniel Heyman, Istanbul: August 2008. "The Broomstick Was
      Metal," Gouache on Nishinoushi Paper   157

ACKNOWLEDGEMENTS

I have been working on this book for much of the past decade, and have relied on the assistance and support of many people over the years. This project grew out of research that I completed while writing my dissertation at the University of California, San Diego, and my dissertation committee members remained steadfast in their support as I was working on this book. Thanks to Bennetta Jules-Rosette, Steve Epstein, George Lipsitz, and Rosaura Sánchez. Ivan Evans was not on my committee, but has also been an important source of support at UCSD.

I have been lucky enough to have had the chance to present much of the research for this book at academic conferences. I thank the organizers of those conferences, and the audience members of the panels that I presented on. I am also very appreciative of travel grants that I received from the professional development funds from the lecturer's union at UCSD, and from the California State University, San Marcos faculty center. This kind of grant has become particularly important as higher education has become increasingly reliant upon contingent faculty.

I benefitted from the valuable feedback of colleagues and editors. Alexander Tristan Riley first encouraged me to write about Kobe Bryant, and presented a paper on the case with me at the American Sociological Association's annual conference. Susan Willis's comments on my Abu Ghraib chapter helped me to develop a deeper understanding of racial spectacles. The reviewers for Routledge offered careful and helpful criticism, as did reviewers at two other presses. Matthew Byrnie thought of this as a valuable project from the moment that I mentioned it to him, and I appreciate everything that he has done to help see it through to fruition. Stan Spring was a pleasure to work with when he was at Routledge, and Carolann Madden has done everything possible to make the publication process as smooth as it could be.

One of the reasons that my research is so important to me is that it gives me new things to talk about in the classroom. One of the benefits to life as a lecturer is that I have had the chance to teach an incredible array of courses at a variety of institutions. This has given me the opportunity to discuss the ideas in this book with thousands of students, and I am extremely appreciative of their willingness to grapple with what can be very difficult subject matter. I thank my students from UCSD, Pitzer College, National University, and CSUSM. While some of the ideas in this book have found their way into pretty much every course that I've taught over the past ten years, the students in my course on "Representations of Race and Violence" have really worked to make much of this material their own. I thank Dan Hallin and the Communication department at UCSD for the opportunity to develop and teach this course. Thanks to Peter Nardi and the rest of the Sociology field group for the chance to teach similar kinds of classes at Pitzer.

Because so much of this book deals with representations of race, it was important to be able to include some of the images that I write about. Giuseppe Di Bella, Daniel Heyman, Jon Hendricks, and Hank Willis Thomas were all incredibly generous in allowing me to reproduce their work in these pages. Thanks too to Roderick S. Quiroz and the Prentiss Taylor estate for permission to include "Scottsboro Limited." Giuseppe Di Bella and Daniel Heyman were also extremely generous in offering to read my work and let me know more about their own. Their comments made me think about art and Abu Ghraib in new ways. Elisa Marquez at AP Images, and Alena Barrios and Joy Novak at the Center for the Study of Political Graphics went far out of their way to help me track down and secure artwork and permissions.

Writing and research can be rather solitary activities. The support I received from family and friends ensured that I never felt isolated as I was working on this book. Thanks especially to Julie Berman, David Cutler, Alexandra Halkias, Doug Krasnoff, Susan Markens, Joe and Emily Navetta, Marni Port and Joseph and Susana Schroeder. Amy Markovitz has been a constant source of encouragement, and has always tried to motivate me, wanting to know how I was doing on the next chapter. David Weinstein writes on topics that, at first blush, seem quite far removed from the kinds of issues that I deal with, but one of the real pleasures of this work has been the chance to talk with him about parallels between our projects. Kevin Reardon, Lenny Markovitz, Ruth Markovitz, and Christie Photinos read every chapter of the manuscript. They offered fair criticism and welcome praise, and they helped me to think through my arguments in much more interesting ways than I would have if left to my own devices. Whatever problems may remain, this is a better book because of their efforts.

INTRODUCTION

In June, 1943, thousands of white sailors and other U.S. military servicemen gathered in east Los Angeles in order to hunt down, beat, and strip young Mexican American "zoot suiters." When the *Los Angeles Times* chose to taunt the victims by running photographs of the brutality under banner headlines such as "Zoot-Suit Fans Find that Life's Getting Tough," images of the "Zoot Suit Riots" became weapons in xenophobic efforts to delimit the boundaries of American national identity.[1]

In the summer of 1955, fourteen-year-old Emmett Till was lynched in the dead of night at the dawn of the modern civil rights movement, his body dumped in the Tallahatchie River near Glendora, Mississippi. Till's mother, Mamie Till Bradley, insisted on an open casket funeral, inviting "all the world to see" the mangled and unrecognizable corpse of her son. Photographs of his body, published in *Jet* magazine and African American newspapers around the country, galvanized national audiences and helped to define the nature of a racist society for a generation.

The events of March 3rd, 1991 helped to define racist brutality for members of a later generation. That night, an amateur videographer turned his lens upon a group of white police officers raining down baton strike after baton strike on the prone body of a black man named Rodney King, while dozens of other officers looked on. George Holliday's video footage of the attack was broadcast repeatedly on television stations around the world. The evidence of racist police brutality was so stark that when the officers who beat King were acquitted in a criminal trial the following year, the city erupted in violence and protest. The Los Angeles "riots," "rebellion," or "uprising" resulted in fifty-three deaths, over two thousand injuries, and nearly a billion dollars in financial damages.

In the early evening of June 17, 1994, the skies of Los Angeles were filled with news helicopters shadowing a white Ford Bronco driving along a California highway. The car was followed in a slow-speed chase by a half dozen police cars as it transported its passenger, an African American former football star and accused murderer, to his home. O.J. Simpson would become one of the most galvanizing figures in recent memory, and public responses to the "trial of the century" would lead to new understandings of the depths of racial divisions in the post-civil rights era.

Mass media spectacles involving race, violence and the law have generated some of the most indelible images in American culture. These images have been seared into collective memory and serve as common reference points for broad sectors of the public who may not agree on their relevance or meaning. Racial spectacles, or massive media events in which virtually every type of communication technology and every sector of popular culture is involved in disseminating influential representations of race to national audiences, function as instruments of socialization: They provide the occasion for the closest thing we have to national

FIGURE i.1 U.S. Servicemen and Others Hunting Down Latino and African American "Zoot-Suiters" in East Los Angeles. June 8, 1943. The *Los Angeles Times* ran the photo under the banner "Zoot-Suit Fans Find that Life's Getting Tough."

Source: Courtesy AP Images.

dialogues about race, and therefore play a central role in national processes of "racial formation," in which categories of race are continually contested and reconstructed. Mass media spectacles of race, violence, and crime often become rallying points for aggrieved communities, at the same time that they can be seized upon by elected officials looking to score political points by demonstrating sensitivity to matters of public concern. They might, at times, work to shore up racist stereotypes, but they also create opportunities for critiquing prevalent conceptions of race, and can be used to mobilize political activists.

Racial spectacles are not merely part of the imagery of contemporary life, nor simply a part of a conversation. Instead, they matter materially because they work to shape popular understandings of the social world that can affect how people lead their daily lives. They can influence the kinds of evidence that jurors will deem credible in criminal trials or that the electorate will find relevant in political debates. They can motivate people to support, or oppose, repressive anti-crime legislation. Racial spectacles might foster a cultural climate in which presidential candidates become compelled to embrace, or distance themselves from, an anti-war platform. Alternatively, they might prod the Supreme Court to intervene in the ordinary workings of the criminal justice system. Since they are ever changing and always open to challenge, racial spectacles present opportunities to contest common sense understandings of powerful institutions and social structures, and they frequently allow for the emergence of critical voices into popular discourse. They are, consequently, important sites of struggle for social change.

This book presents an extended investigation into the nature of racial spectacles, and argues that public responses to such spectacles are fundamentally shaped by past struggles and social movements. Collective memories, or shared understandings of the past, help to structure contemporary social identities and determine how various constituencies make sense of racial spectacles as they unfold on a national or international stage. Because our understandings of the past shape the way that we make sense of the present, and can help determine the ways that we think about such issues as group affiliation, state legitimacy, and social injustice, struggles over collective memory have extremely high political stakes. In order to assess these stakes, the case studies in this book involve examinations of the ways in which state actors and social movements have constructed narratives of the past and enlisted those narratives in political struggles. My case studies address a series of mass media spectacles that either relied upon, reconfigured or worked to construct collective memories of race, crime and (in)justice. The racial spectacles under consideration in this volume galvanized mass audiences around the world, prompted international protest campaigns, or simply forced people to rethink taken-for-granted assumptions about race, gender, and sexuality. I examine the impact that these spectacles have had on national processes of racial formation, and look to the ways that government actors and social movements have mobilized around them. The central concern of the book is to better understand the ways that racial spectacles are made to matter. The remainder of this introductory chapter expands upon the theoretical framework that guides my analyses of racial spectacles, and describes the organization of the book.

Racial Spectacle and Racial Formation

Guy Debord's *Society of the Spectacle* is a key text in the study of spectacles, and while my conceptualization of spectacles is different from Debord's, his work provides a valuable point of entry for thinking about the social significance of spectacular imagery. Debord generally conceptualizes the spectacle in singular terms: "the spectacle" is not one mass mediated event, but the defining feature of a society, and the "society of the spectacle" is a society in which lived experiences have given way to representations.[2] Debord's work highlights the politics of representation, even while noting that spectacle cannot be reduced to imagery. The spectacle itself is not merely a set of widely disseminated images, but a social relationship in which imagery forms the basis for social interaction, meaning-making and identity formation. "The spectacle," Debord says, "is not a collection of images, but a social relation among people, mediated by images."[3] Thus, analysis of the spectacle can never look to representations alone, but must instead consider the ways that imagery is linked to social structures and political power. The most important role played by the spectacle is that of obfuscation, since the spectacle is, above all, a "permanent opium war" that distracts people from material reality as it conditions them to identify as consumers and to take pleasure and satisfaction in the accumulation of commodities.[4] Beyond encouraging passivity and consumerism, the spectacle is important for what it says about common sense belief systems and social norms, as the spectacle is "a Weltanschauung which has become actual, materially translated. It is a world vision which has become objectified."[5] Analysis of the spectacle, then, must contend not only with methods of social control, but also with the entanglement of those methods with prevalent ideologies (or, for Debord, with capitalist ideology broadly speaking).

Some of the most important contemporary media and cultural studies critics who borrow from Debord have rejected the notion of "the" spectacle in favor of close examinations of specific spectacles, moving the analysis away from a generalized critique of a particular stage of advanced capitalism, and towards more specific readings of "spectacularized" media events. Debord has been faulted for developing a model of spectacle that is not only monolithic but also totalizing, in that it fails to provide a clear theoretical basis for the possibility of resistance. For Debord, the spectacle always serves the interests of power and capital. It is "the existing order's uninterrupted discourse about itself, its laudatory monologue," and there is no sense that its meanings might be multiple or contested.[6] The sense that the spectacle provides insight into dominant ideology has been pursued by numerous critics, though the idea that it expresses only a singular world view has been challenged by theorists drawing upon cultural studies traditions that understand hegemonic ideology as always in flux and subject to resistance.[7]

Still, Debord's work has been extremely influential in encouraging critics to examine mass media spectacles for the lessons they provide about social worldviews, and for the ways in which they have been used to support or challenge systems of power. Most notably, Douglas Kellner has examined the role that spectacles play in processes of socialization, arguing that "media spectacles are those phenomena of media culture that embody contemporary society's basic values, serve to initiate individuals into its way of life, and dramatize its conventions and struggles, as well as its modes of conflict resolution."[8] Kellner takes issue with Debord's understanding of the *spectator* as a passive consumer of capitalist ideology, easily lulled into conformity, and distracted from real social needs. He instead emphasizes the notion of an active audience that is able to grapple with the imagery that is presented to it, and that is capable of forging resistant meanings. For him, "spectacle itself [is] contested terrain," and the role of the cultural theorist is to assess the "conflicting meanings and effects" of mass spectacles, which should be seen as constituting "a field of domination and resistance."[9] There are moments where Kellner, too, appears to favor an understanding of spectacles as playing an unambiguous role in maintaining systems of social control and stratification (as when he writes that "the media spectacles that I interrogate are key cultural phenomena that naturalize and idealize the given social system"), but he is consistently attentive to the variety of forces at play in constructing and challenging the meanings of various spectacles.[10] Most intriguingly, Kellner is interested in what he refers to as the "contradictions and reversals of the spectacle," or the ways in which spectacles that start off supporting existing social arrangements can wind up being used to challenge the status quo.[11]

The idea that spectacles do not have inherent meaning, but can be interpreted in varying ways, and used for contradictory political purposes, is important for my own work, though I think that Kellner's critique needs to be taken just a bit farther. In his study of the U.S. "war on terror," Kellner discusses the 2003 U.S. invasion of Iraq as explicitly a war of spectacle, intended, in the words of George W. Bush, as a policy of "shock and awe."[12] He goes on to argue, though, that the invasion may have contributed to the revival of Al Qaeda and to the growth of anti–American sentiment, and concludes that the politics of spectacle "are thus highly unstable, subject to multiple interpretations, and often generate unanticipated effects . . . Media spectacles are subject to dialectical reversal as positive images give way to negative ones."[13] The point about the instability of the politics of spectacle is important for this study, but the notion of dialectical reversals here is problematic, since it suggests that, at any given moment in time, it is possible to assess whether the imagery of spectacles is "positive" or "negative." Instead, I would suggest that the meanings of spectacles are always, at every moment, contested. It may well be that the "shock and awe" doctrine and the devastating assault in the first days of the invasion of Iraq initially appeared to some audiences as a necessary spectacle of military might and a testament to American determination, and that those audiences eventually started to see it instead as a spectacle of American brutality and savagery. But it is also clearly the case that, for some audiences, this was never a spectacle with a "positive" valence, just as there remain audiences who see nothing "negative" about American military policies in the region. Still, while I think that the notion of reversibility is probably too neat to capture the complexity of the contests waged over the meaning of spectacles, the idea that the meanings of spectacles can shift over time, and can vary according to context, is central to this study.

My interest in spectacles has to do with their importance for what Michael Omi and Howard Winant have called "racial formation," or "the sociohistorical process by which racial categories are created, inhabited, transformed, and destroyed."[14] Racial formation is a process deeply shaped by social movements and political struggles, and I examine racial spectacles as central sites in these struggles. Debord's understanding of the spectacle as not merely a collection of images, but as images that are part of social processes, resonates strongly with Omi and Winant's argument that, while racial categories are social constructions, they nevertheless have heft and consequence. For Omi and Winant, as for Debord, representations are never *simply* representations. In order to point to the ways that particular understandings of race can be mobilized for political purposes, Omi and Winant have coined the term "racial project," which they define as "simultaneously an interpretation, representation, or explanation of racial dynamics, and an effort to reorganize and redistribute resources along particular racial lines."[15] Racial projects link the meanings of racial categories to social structures and political practices. One of my concerns throughout this book is to investigate the ways in which racial spectacles can work as part of racial projects, and to examine the material consequences of spectacularized deployments of racialized imagery.

Historical Background: Lynching as Template for Later Racial Spectacles

Every racial spectacle is unique, and, as I discuss below, there is an endless number of racial spectacles that might have been addressed in this volume. One set of racial spectacles, however, merits special attention. Perhaps the most dramatic examples of racial spectacles as racial projects come from the history of lynching and the antilynching movement of the late nineteenth and early twentieth centuries. This history provides a central part of the foundation for all of the racial spectacles discussed in this book, from Scottsboro to Abu Ghraib. Lynching has provided a lens—a way of seeing and making sense out of—all of the spectacles addressed in the following chapters. The history of lynching and antilynching struggles influences the ways in which later racial spectacles are understood, while helping to shape the ways those spectacles have unfolded over time. There are long histories of vigilante violence in the United States and lynch mobs have targeted people of every race and many ethnicities, but the lynchings that became massive public spectacles involving hundreds or thousands of spectator-participants only started to become routinized in the late 1800s, as African Americans became the primary victims of the mob.[16] These are the lynchings that set the stage for so many racial spectacles to come.

Lynching rates of African Americans in the South started to rise dramatically during the post-Reconstruction era, at a moment in time where the social status associated with "whiteness" and "blackness" had become at least potentially unstable. Lynching worked to reify racial distinctions and to reinforce the privileges associated with whiteness at precisely the moment that these distinctions and privileges had been threatened juridically. For black viewers who witnessed the "'strange fruit' abandoned at roadsides," lynching sent powerful messages about the ways in which their actions and movements were being monitored by a surveillant society intent upon maintaining the color line.[17] For lynching's white spectators/participants, "these violent spectacles offered a sense of control over racial signification."[18] In helping to ensure white control of the meanings of racial categories, the spectacle of lynching worked as a racial project that was at the core of maintaining white supremacy.

Public lynchings by mass mobs, or "spectacle lynchings" involved virtually every form of modern technology in the early decades of the twentieth century.[19] These lynchings could draw hundreds or thousands of participant/spectators, and were announced in advance in newspapers, by telegraph and even on radio. Mob members would drive to the site of a lynching, or would travel on trains that were chartered for the occasion. They might buy postcard photographs of the lynching, taken by professional photographers, as souvenirs of the event, or they might take their own photographs on their new Kodak cameras.[20] There were variations in the form that spectacle lynchings took, but standard routines, involving the hunt for the accused, the public airing of the charges and announcement of the site of the upcoming lynching, and a number of kinds of physical punishment and torture leading to death, quickly emerged.[21] While lynching rates started to decline after the 1890s, spectacle lynchings ensured the continuing power of lynching as a cultural force, since people who hadn't attended a lynching could still be made aware of it, and of the messages it sent about the costs of violating tenets of white supremacy, through its representations. Because lynchings could lead to white-led race riots that could result in substantial damage to white communities as businesses and homes were burned, and because increasing numbers of white elites started to develop economic ties outside of the South after the 1930s and were therefore sensitive to critiques of lynching coming from other regions, the opportunity to celebrate the practice of lynching from a distance was increasingly appealing for many white southerners, for whom "representations of lynching had become better than lynchings themselves."[22] The representational force of spectacle lynchings was sufficient to help maintain a culture of segregation and racial terrorism while fostering a sense of white unity, even as the practice of lynching was on the wane.

Mass lynchings thus provide especially stark examples of spectacles as racist racial projects. And yet, the meaning of spectacle lynchings was never straightforward or unambiguous. Nor was their political impact. While narratives of spectacle lynchings, as presented in white newspapers, novels, and radio broadcasts, were increasingly standardized starting in the 1890s, they were also vigorously critiqued by the black press and the antilynching movement. When apologists for the mob presented lynching as a necessary method of punishing black men who raped white women, anti-racist activists countered that lynching was instead a barbaric crime based on racist stereotypes intended to support an unjust system of racial stratification.[23] Antilynching narratives of lynching "became a hybrid sort of spectacle lynching as well: [these narratives] circulated publicly and bumped against the narrative most white southerners had learned to tell so well."[24] In fact, as black northern migration and the modernization of southern agriculture began to erode the economic foundation of lynching, and as the infamous Scottsboro trials of the 1930s (discussed in Chapter 1) brought increasing national and international scrutiny to southern race relations, the antilynching movement saw so much *anti*-racist potential in the widespread dissemination of representations of lynching that they actively sought to *create* spectacles out of lynchings that might otherwise have gone unnoticed by national audiences.

Grace Elizabeth Hale discusses the 1934 lynching of Claude Neal in Marianna Florida as the event that "signaled the end of the gruesome southern practice of spectacle lynchings," noting that from this moment on, "the NAACP worked to capture the cultural power inherent in sensationalized, gruesomely voyeuristic stories and even more grisly pictures for the anti–lynching crusade."[25] While the lynching was acknowledged in the white press, neither local nor national papers published many details of the killing, which was carried out in the backwoods, rather than in a city center. The NAACP, however, investigated the lynching, and published 15,000 copies of a pamphlet titled "Lynching of Claude Neal" which included a photograph of Neal's mutilated body, and a narrative of southern white barbarism. The NAACP's efforts to publicize, or to spectacularize, the lynching of Claude Neal were successful, and helped secure political support for the organization's efforts to pass federal antilynching legislation. The NAACP subsequently attempted to create a variety of other spectacles revolving around lynching, as they supported an antilynching art exhibition and started to use photographs of lynch mobs and victims in fundraising drives and on antilynching petitions. The success of this use of lynching imagery leads Hale to conclude that the "lynching spectacle, then, had given way to the growing antilynching crusade's attempt to make a spectacle of lynching."[26]

At first glance, the antilynching movement's success in creating spectacles of lynching appears to be a perfect example of Kellner's argument that the meaning of spectacles can be reversed. After all, imagery that was used to support a system of white supremacy had eventually proven useful in challenging racial terrorism. Hale argues, though, that lynching had worked to create white unity and a sense of black otherness, and writes that the appropriation of lynching imagery by the antilynching movement did not challenge this state of affairs:

> the NAACP's capture of the lynching narrative, its impact on national interpretations of lynching's meaning, did not disrupt the cultural work of the spectacle. . . . the image of the "black beast rapist," providing a foundation for the culture of segregation beyond the reach of rational discussion remained.[27]

I think that Hale overstates the case here. It is true that the mythical black rapist that was used to justify lynching and to rationalize segregation remained powerful even as lynching started to fade. Indeed, the myth is still powerful enough that politicians have been able to gain ground by invoking it during senatorial and presidential campaigns. But this is also a myth that was battered by decades of anti-racist struggle, and, by the mid-1930s, it had lost much of its potency.[28] The anti-racist spectacles that Hale refers to were critical in disrupting the power of this myth, and, therefore, in opening the doors to challenges to segregation and white supremacy as a whole. These spectacles provided parts of the foundation for later anti-racist struggles, and were essential for the eventual emergence of the modern civil rights movement.

If Hale is overly pessimistic about the possibility of challenging the cultural logic of spectacle lynchings, her concerns nevertheless provide an important note of caution in thinking that the racist spectacle of lynching could so neatly become its inverse and perform in an unambiguously anti-racist manner. To the extent that antilynching organizations' efforts to spectacularize aspects of lynching furthered a sense of whites and blacks as fundamentally at odds, and to the extent that the NAACP's circulation of lynching imagery reinforced the dehumanizing reduction of African Americans to the status of abject victims, these efforts might well have upheld precisely the logic they were meant to critique. Moreover, the interpretations of lynching put forward by the antilynching movement in the 1930s and 1940s were far from uniformly embraced. Southern editors and politicians were considerably more likely during this time to condemn lynching than they had been just a decade earlier, but it was not difficult to find people who would argue that lynching continued to perform valuable roles in protecting white womanhood, and in the maintenance of a civilized society. Even today, while most visitors to the travelling "Without Sanctuary" exhibit of lynching photography see the photos in the way that the NAACP would have intended— as graphic evidence of the barbarism of white supremacy—some commentators on the exhibition's web site have celebrated the torture and killing depicted in the photographs.[29] The dominant reading of lynching has clearly shifted, but there has never been a moment where the spectacle of lynching could be read in only one way.

The terrifying power, frequency and routinization of spectacle lynchings mark them as a unique form of racial spectacle, at the same time as these characteristics secure the status of spectacle lynchings as templates for later racial spectacles. Spectacle lynchings became a defining feature of race relations in the post-Reconstruction South and remain a common reference point and point of comparison for contemporary audiences trying to make sense of newly emerging racial spectacles. Spectacle lynchings can also be seen as models that provide lessons for the analysis and interpretation of later racial spectacles. As racial projects that worked to shore up the power of white supremacy, spectacle lynchings alert us to the potential material stakes of racial spectacles at the same time that antilynching efforts to resist dominant narratives of lynching highlight the role of racial spectacles as sites of political struggle. The antilynching movement's efforts to *create* anti-racist spectacles out of the lynching of Claude Neal and other spectacle lynchings belie conceptions of spectacles as purely hegemonic mass media events that always and only serve the interests of capital and power. Above all, the history of spectacle lynchings provides an important note of caution for anyone seeking to determine *the* meaning or stakes of racial spectacles, suggesting instead that racial spectacles are always contested, their meanings always in flux.

Collective Memory and Racial Spectacles

The antilynching movement's resistance to traditional lynching narratives can be seen as an effort to challenge the ways in which lynching would be understood and remembered. The struggle over collective memories of lynching had life-or-death stakes during the "lynching era" at the turn of the twentieth century, since these memories were invoked in political and legislative debates about local and federal antilynching legislation and in editorials that might provide cover for local authorities faced with the decision about whether or not to prosecute members of lynch mobs. Public support for lynching was dependent upon understanding and remembering lynching as a key tool in punishing black rapists and protecting white southern womanhood, and not as a barbaric instrument of intimidation and terror, defensible only through reliance upon vicious racist stereotypes.[30] Several of the case studies in this book address ways that struggles over collective memories of lynching continue to reverberate decades later, as lynching has come to provide a reference point for a variety of commentators trying to come to terms with contemporary racial spectacles. More generally, I argue throughout the book that struggles over collective memory are inextricably bound up with national processes of racial formation, and strongly influence the ways that various audiences make sense of and respond to racial spectacles.

My use of the term "collective memory" draws upon a scholarly tradition that can be traced back to Maurice Halbwachs's efforts to see the social basis for all memory, and to his claim that "the past is not preserved but it is reconstructed on the basis of the present."[31] There are problems with Halbwachs's conception of collective memory: he can be faulted for a tendency to think of collective memory in monolithic terms, speaking about the ways "society" as a whole remembers;[32] he was largely inattentive to the contested nature of collective memory, and to the ways in which discourses of power could influence the construction of narratives of the past; and his focus on the importance of contemporary needs in shaping understandings of the past has caused some critics to worry about his influence upon "radical social constructionists" who neglect the constraining influences of history (or of what actually happened in the past), and who would suggest that the past can be created at will "according to the dictates of power, person, and privilege."[33] But Halbwachs's interest in the links between collective memory and individual and group identity, and in the process of socially constructing collective memory, has provided a starting point even for theorists who are quite critical of his work. For scholars such as Marita Sturken, Barbie Zelizer, and Ron Eyreman, decisions over what and how to remember and forget are always open to contest. Contests over collective memory are integral components of broader political struggles, and one of the goals of this book is to explore what is at stake as political leaders and members of various social movements clash over how racial spectacles should be understood and remembered.

While I am interested in the ways that people make use of the past in order to understand the world around them, I follow Iwona Irwin-Zarecka's suggestion that the task for an analyst of collective memory is not necessarily to look to "the minds of individuals" (which might involve, for example, collecting survey data or conducting interviews to determine what people are actually thinking about the past), but instead entails assessing shared cultural resources, or widely disseminated versions of the past.[34] The notion of "shared" resources is, however, a bit fuzzy, and raises questions about who exactly is exposed to, or can tap into, these resources, and to what end. It is also important to note that even when people have access to the same cultural resources, there is no guarantee that they will understand them in the same way. Indeed, the racial spectacles discussed in this book all rely upon constructions of the past that are recognizable and familiar to large segments of the American public, but that are nevertheless hotly debated. These debates become particularly salient when considering highly charged racial spectacles that strike at the heart of national identity, raising fundamental questions about American racial and gender dynamics, and about the nature of U.S. foreign policy. Analysis of collective memory, then, must be careful to avoid assuming that people who are exposed to mass mediated historical narratives accept those narratives at face value. Instead, efforts must be made to assess the possibilities for different audiences to interact with, challenge, and make sense of those narratives.

There is no single site to examine when trying to figure out what aspects of the past are collectively remembered, and how. The question of where to look for the content of collective memory is complicated by the fact that collective memory is multiple. Different people, and different groups of people, remember different things in different ways. This multiplicity of collective memories is not, however, an obstacle. Rather, it supplies an important analytic tool, providing a clue about disparate reactions to contemporary social dramas. If people's collective memories help shape the ways that they make sense of such dramas, then it makes sense to think that differences in collective memory might lead to, and help explain, differences in public opinion and reactions to racial spectacles. But because people have innumerable resources at their disposal when trying to make sense of the past, and, perhaps more importantly, when trying to use the past to help make sense of the present, there is also a crucially important analytic concession to make: Analysts of collective memory must acknowledge from the outset that any investigation of collective memory will be partial.

But this does not mean that we can't put forward some propositions about how collective memories are constructed and used. One important starting point for many studies of collective memory is the mass media. The Popular Memory Group notes that the mass media "are a principal source of historical constructions," which "select, amplify and transform constructions of the past produced elsewhere. . . . [Access to the mass media] may often be decisive in gaining currency for an historical account."[35] Carolyn Kitch elaborates by observing that "popular media are a primary source of what most people know about history."[36] Alison Landsberg has argued that, beyond disseminating knowledge about the past, technologies of modernity have created a new form of memory (what she terms "prosthetic memory") that makes it possible for people to interact with mass mediated versions of the past and not "simply apprehend a historical narrative" but instead take on "a more personal, deeply felt memory of a past event through which he or she did not live."[37] People engage with the electronic media in particular in such a visceral way that it can become impossible to clearly distinguish between memories that are lived and individual, and memories that are experienced and constructed indirectly and collectively. Analysis of the mass media can provide only a very rough proxy of what people actually think about the past,[38] but examining the struggles over mass mediated accounts of the past can serve at least as a starting point for theoretical investigations of the ways that people engage with the past when seeking to contextualize important events in the present.

My interest in the mass media and popular culture as arenas in which collective memory is constructed, reconfigured and challenged is indebted to Pierre Bourdieu's arguments about symbolic struggles "where what is at stake is the very representation of the social world."[39] For Bourdieu, because symbolic struggles help to shape the basic categories that we use when producing knowledge about the social world, the stakes at issue in such struggles involve "the power to conserve or transform the social world by conserving or transforming the categories through which it is perceived."[40] This formulation has much in common with Debord's understanding of spectacle as a social relation mediated by images, and with Omi and Winant's notion of "racial projects" as efforts to link racial meanings with social structures and political practices. Each of these theoretical endeavors seeks to explicate the material stakes of representational politics. My goal in this project is to bring these concerns together in a study of memory and racial spectacle.

Throughout the book, I try to better understand the ways that racialized differences in collective memory affect the approaches that various audiences take in making sense of unfolding racial spectacles. My understanding of the racialization of collective memory is similar to Darnell Hunt's notion of "raced ways of seeing." In his work on the O.J. Simpson case and the 1992 Los Angeles "riots," Hunt has argued that racialized differences in understandings of racial spectacles are partly dependent upon "intertextual memory."[41] For Hunt, understandings of the past act as a "prism that refracts the content of media texts in ways that resonate with the 'real' and mediated experiences of individuals."[42] These intertextual memories, which are open to contest and negotiation, are often dependent upon social location, and can therefore vary by race, class, gender, and sexuality. Different social locations can lead to differences in the ways that memories are invoked when coming to terms with contemporary media events. Alison Landsberg complicates this discussion a bit by arguing that "prosthetic memory" in a mass-mediated age has greatly impacted the notion of social location. She writes that

> the cinema and other mass cultural technologies have the capacity to create shared social frameworks for people who inhabit, literally and figuratively, different social spaces, practices, and beliefs. As a result, these technologies can structure "imagined communities" that are not necessarily geographically or nationally bounded.[43]

The notion of racialized collective memory in an age of prosthetic memory has to be thought of as fluid and non-essentialist, given the fact that "a commodified mass culture opens up the possibility that people who share little in the way of cultural or ethnic background might come to share certain memories."[44] Collective memories can help to structure the patterns that people look to when attempting to understand the present, but these memories can be racialized in non-predictable ways. For example, people who are aware of long histories of lynching and the role that racist stereotypes have played in unjust convictions of black defendants might have a historical sensibility that shapes the ways that they evaluate evidence and credibility in the O.J. Simpson or Kobe Bryant cases. This would be a racialized collective memory, in that it is a collective memory shaped by very specific understandings of American racial dynamics. But, while African Americans might be more likely to have developed this kind of historical sensibility, or to share this particular set of racialized collective memories, there is no reason to think that these memories cannot cross racial lines, or, conversely, to think that they would be shared by all African Americans. As this discussion suggests, even an anti-racist collective memory could be shared by people in dominant racial groups.

The collective memory literature has been centrally concerned with the importance of collective memory for individual and group identity, but very little has been said about the ways that people rely upon collective memory when making sense of events such as racialized and gendered mass media spectacles as they unfold on a national and international scale. Looking at racial formation and collective memory together provides a richer sense of the ways that racial categories and collective identities are constructed over time. It has become not just accepted, but almost a truism, to say that race and gender *are* social constructions, and, more than that, that they are social constructions that evolve over time. So contemporary understandings of race might be very different from understandings of race in the nineteenth century, for example. But I think that the idea of an evolution or "transformation" of racial categories might run the risk of suggesting that contemporary understandings of race are simpler, and more discrete and clearly separable from older understandings than is truly the case.

I am wary of a sense, found in much of the social construction literature, that categories of race and gender from the past have been replaced by new categories. Instead, this volume starts with the premise that contemporary understandings of race and gender are highly complex and historically layered. The notion of collective memory is valuable in helping to conceptualize the construction of race and gender as processes that are fundamentally dependent upon historical sensibilities, and shaped by social struggle. Contemporary understandings of such categories as "whiteness" or "blackness" incorporate understandings of what those categories have meant in the past, and of struggles over those meanings. A key concern running throughout this work is to investigate those historical understandings: what "sense of the past" do people use to understand mass media spectacles involving race and gender as they are unfolding? How are those historical sensibilities shaped and contested? How are they invoked? Under what circumstances do they come into play, and to what effect? These are the central questions motivating each of my case studies.

Organization of the Book

There is no shortage of racial spectacles that I might have chosen for analysis in this book. Readers may notice that some of the most important and dramatic racial spectacles in American history, including those that I mention in the opening section of this introduction (the "Zoot Suit Riots," the lynching of Emmett Till, the beating of Rodney King and the 1992 Los Angeles "riots" or "uprising," and the O.J. Simpson trials), are not addressed at length in this volume.[45] If the task of the book were to provide anything approaching a comprehensive overview of racial spectacles, it would be difficult to know where to begin, and it would be impossible to discuss any of the spectacles with depth or complexity. My goals, therefore, are considerably more modest. I hope to offer useful and provocative ways of thinking about a set of theoretical issues that are important when considering racial spectacles. To this end, I have chosen a series of case studies that lend themselves particularly well to an exploration of the ways that racial spectacles draw upon and reconfigure collective memory, play into national processes of racial formation, and serve as focal points for social struggles.[46]

Chapter 1 addresses a racial spectacle from the 1930s that, like spectacle lynchings, has provided a reference point and point of comparison for many other spectacles in later decades, especially those involving charges of interracial rape. The Scottsboro case involves nine young black men and boys who were charged with raping two white women near Scottsboro, Alabama in 1931. In a series of trials, all of the defendants were convicted on the basis of little more than the often blatantly contradictory testimony of their accusers, one of whom eventually recanted, becoming a witness for the defense. While the Supreme Court twice overturned the convictions, it was not until 1950 that all of the defendants were freed. This chapter argues that the domestic and international movement to free the Scottsboro defendants provided a crucial bridge between the antilynching movement of the turn of the twentieth century and the better-known civil rights movement of the 1950s and 1960s.

While the remainder of my case studies involve the fairly recent past, the Scottsboro case allows for an investigation of the ways that racial spectacles enter into collective memory over a sustained period of time. The chapter traces the construction and elaboration of collective memories of Scottsboro over several decades, assessing the ways that these memories have been invoked and contested by later generations. The initial trials of the Scottsboro defendants provided an opportunity for the southern press to function in much the same way that it did while reporting on spectacle lynchings—as an extension of the mob, disseminating images of monstrously horrific black brute rapists while reinforcing narratives about the strength of white supremacy. Over time, however, what had started as an apparently straightforward racist spectacle (and one likely to end with the deaths of innocent black defendants) took center stage in a new phase of anti-racist activism. In the process, it became possible to think of Scottsboro as one of the most important *anti*-racist spectacles in American history. As the movement to free the defendants grew, and as the guilty verdicts were repeatedly overturned and the weakness of the case exposed to ever wider audiences, media coverage of Scottsboro provided activists with an important new weapon in the battle against racist stereotypes. This battle helped to change popular understandings of race and continues to reverberate to this day. Its echoes can be heard in public responses to later racial spectacles, including the Kobe Bryant rape case.

The Kobe Bryant rape case is the subject of Chapter 2, and provides the first opportunity for a discussion of the contemporary media environment. When Bryant, an African American star of the Los Angeles Lakers, was charged with raping a white woman in Eagle, Colorado, in June of 2003, the allegations and legal proceedings immediately became the subject of what Kellner might call a "megaspectacle," as it was covered simultaneously in the entertainment, business, news, and sports pages of local, national, and international newspapers; dissected on prime-time television; and endlessly debated in every kind of internet forum from fan blogs to white supremacist websites. This was the most closely followed case involving a professional athlete and the criminal justice system since the O.J. Simpson murder trial, and it was one of the most closely watched cases involving interracial sexuality and allegations of violence in the post-civil rights era. This chapter examines the social divisions revealed by public responses to the case, arguing that contemporary understandings of race, gender and crime are indebted to social struggles and rhetorical battles fought long ago, and that invocations of, and contests over, collective memory can help to determine how various audiences make sense of public dramas unfolding in the mass media.

While the first two case studies examine the role of the news media in shaping collective memories and understandings of racial spectacles, Chapters 3 and 4 move to a discussion of the relationship between journalistic accounts of racial spectacles and the re-imagination of those accounts within popular culture, as I examine televisual and cinematic constructions of collective memories of police corruption and racist police brutality. The Los Angeles Police Department's "Rampart scandal" in the late 1990s and early 2000s was one of the most dramatic American police brutality and corruption scandals in the past fifty years. The scandal received a great deal of media coverage, but without any defining visual imagery, it never quite rose to the level of spectacle until it was appropriated in fictionalized form by the entertainment industries. Chapter 3 addresses the dynamics of the scandal itself before going on to examine journalistic representations of the case. I discuss the criminal justice system as a central site of American racialization, and argue that news coverage of Rampart provided extraordinary opportunities for otherwise marginalized critics to address the race and class-based inequities of this system.

Public perceptions of the criminal justice system can have significant consequences, since they can help to determine the fate of public policies involving race and crime, including draconian anti-crime measures such as "three-strikes" legislation and related laws. The fact that anti-racist critics of the criminal justice system were granted greater access to the news media during the Rampart scandal can therefore be read as a hopeful sign for meaningful challenges to at least some of the most damaging aspects of what has been called "the prison industrial complex." The absence of defining visual evidence of the scandal meant, however, that journalistic narratives of the case were unlikely to play a decisive role in changing the ways that mass audiences understood matters of race, crime, and the law. Because Hollywood is in the business of making its own images, it was arguably better-equipped than journalists to offer what might be taken as defining representations of police brutality and corruption in the age of Rampart.

Chapter 4 examines the ways that the case was picked up, and spectacularized, by popular culture, as I assess the 2001 film *Training Day* and the television show *The Shield*, which ran on the F/X network from 2002–2008. I examine these productions against a backdrop of decades of pop cultural images of police corruption, and ask whether Hollywood's "reel bad cops" serve to further the kinds of journalistic critiques of the criminal justice system that were characteristic of Rampart coverage, or if they instead work to shut the doors that news outlets had opened to critical voices.

Chapter 5 looks to the controversies surrounding the circulation of the digital photographs of the 2003 torture of Iraqi prisoners at the Abu Ghraib prison as an example of a distinctly contemporary racial spectacle, characteristic of the age of new media. While my opening and closing case studies consider starkly different media landscapes, my project really comes full circle here, since, at a basic level, the Abu Ghraib scandal and Scottsboro are quite similar: both cases are generally thought to have become anti-racist spectacles. That is, rather than reinforcing racist stereotypes, media attention to the cases of Abu Ghraib and Scottsboro is thought to have made spectacles of racism itself, holding it up for public scrutiny and condemnation. The Abu Ghraib photographs have been compared to lynching photographs in that their migration to new contexts is said to have transformed their meaning. The photographs therefore provide another occasion to investigate the notion of the reversibility of racial spectacles. I caution, however, against too easy and reductive a comparison between these two sets of photographs as I examine differences in the cultural climates and prevalent understandings of race and violence that were at the heart of each spectacle. One potentially decisive difference between the political uses to which each set of photographs were put concerns the role of new media technologies. It took decades before lynching photographs began to be understood as antilynching photographs, or photographs that depicted the brutality, rather than the glory, of the mob. In contrast, the easy transferability of JPEG photos taken with digital cameras, coupled with ready access to the variety of forms of distribution possible through the internet and satellite technology, meant that the Abu Ghraib photographs could move to new contexts incredibly rapidly. The mass media could therefore engage in critical discussions of the photographs very shortly after they were taken. This chapter considers the role of new media technologies in the production and critical reception of the photographs, while examining the degree to which they were used to provide a meaningful critique of U.S. foreign policy.

My concluding chapter examines campus reactions to a series of racist incidents at the University of California, San Diego in the winter of 2010, in order to offer some final thoughts about the nature of racial spectacles. The racist incidents came as some members of the UCSD community were engaged in efforts to challenge the increasing privatization of the University of California system, and were working to increase the enrollment of students of color. I argue that this background helped create a climate in which it was possible for anti-racist activists to subvert the meaning of provocative acts of racial hatred, as they managed to create an anti-racist spectacle that served as a rallying point for challenging institutionalized racism at UCSD and within the broader UC system. The anti-racist movement at UCSD highlights the potential as well as the limitations of political struggles that center around and grow out of racial spectacles. My discussion of this movement allows for a consideration of the kinds of questions that racial spectacles are unlikely to raise, and addresses the difficulties that confront activists who would like ordinary inequities to be thought of in spectacular terms.

1

"EXPLODING THE MYTH OF THE BLACK RAPIST"

Collective Memory and the Scottsboro Nine

> The Negro women of the South lay everything that happens to the members of her race at the door of the Southern white woman. . . . if the white women would take hold of the situation . . . lynching would be stopped.[1]

> Whether we like it or not, and whether it is just or not, this Scottsboro case is going to wipe out of the picture of the public mind all these other lynching investigations and the like, and by its outcome the South will be judged.[2]

In 1920, black female members of the Commission on Interracial Cooperation challenged their white counterparts by arguing that "when Southern white women get ready to stop lynching, it will be stopped and not before."[3] It is unlikely that they could have imagined that the most powerful answer to their call would come, more than a decade later, from a white woman whose fabricated claims of rape at the hands of nine black boys and young men had nearly prompted a mass lynching. Nor would this woman have appeared any more likely to answer the call just over a week after the mass lynching was averted, as a crowd of 10,000 spectators gathered outside of a courthouse in Scottsboro, Alabama, listening to a brass band playing Dixie, and cheering the guilty verdicts that would send eight of the "Scottsboro Boys" to death row. Certainly, no one who sat in the courtroom on April 6th, 1931, listening to Ruby Bates provide testimony that helped make these convictions possible, would have mistaken her for a civil rights icon. Yet it is difficult to think of any individual who had a more dramatic impact upon American understandings of race, gender and justice, or who played a more central role in the struggle for African American rights in the 1930s.

What has been widely referred to as "the Scottsboro Case" is actually a series of criminal trials, convictions, appeals, and further convictions stretching out over a seven-year period in the 1930s. The "Scottsboro Boys" (or the "Scottsboro Nine") initially came to the attention of the Jackson County sheriff's department after some of them had gotten into a fight with a group of white boys while riding the rails in northern Alabama.[4] When the white boys lost the fight and were forced to leave the train, they went to the authorities to complain. Presumably outraged at the thought of black men who had the temerity to "offload" a group of whites, Sheriff M. L. Wann ordered his deputy to stop the train outside of Paint Rock, and to "capture every negro on the train and bring them to Scottsboro."[5] The deputy enlisted the aid of every armed man in the town. When the posse searched the train, among the passengers they discovered were not only nine African Americans, but also two white women, Victoria Price and Ruby Bates, dressed in overalls and wearing men's caps.[6] Bates was seventeen years old, and Price was a married woman traveling with a man who was not her husband. The most credible historical accounts suggest that it was in order to prevent possible prosecution for vagrancy, adultery, or for violations of the Mann act (forbidding the transportation of minors across state lines for "immoral purposes"), that Price and Bates decided to claim that they had been raped.[7]

The defendants were in the Scottsboro jail, thinking that they were to be charged for "assault and attempt to murder"—charges stemming from their fight with the white boys—for several hours before being put in a line up. It was only when they were identified by Price and Bates, who were asked to "point to the boys who had 'had them'" that they realized they were to be charged with rape.[8] As the prisoners started to learn the nature of their plight, a mob was gathering outside the jail. Several hundred armed men surrounded the prison, but the crowd dissipated when they learned that the governor had called out the National Guard to provide protection for the defendants. The reprieve was brief, however, since it was only a matter of days before all of the defendants had been convicted on the basis of little more than the often blatantly contradictory testimony of Price and Bates.[9]

The convictions were overturned on three separate occasions—once by a trial judge, and twice by the United States Supreme Court. The court ruled in *Powell v. Alabama* (1932) that the defendants had been denied effective assistance of counsel. *Powell* was the first in a series of cases leading up to two of the best known criminal justice decisions by the Supreme Court, *Gideon v. Wainwright* (1963), and *Miranda v. Arizona* (1966), holding that states must provide a lawyer to all indigent suspects and defendants, and that all suspects must be informed of their rights before questioning them in custody. And in *Norris v. Alabama* (1935), the second Scottsboro case to be heard by the Supreme Court, the Court ruled that Alabama jury commissioners had illegally excluded black jurors on the basis of their race. After *Norris*, and another series of trials, the state of Alabama dropped the charges against four of the defendants, who were finally released in 1937, while the other five remained in prison for lengthy sentences.

Because of efforts by the International Labor Defense (the legal arm of the Communist Party, henceforth, the ILD) to publicize the case, Scottsboro became an international cause célèbre, and there was a mass movement devoted to freeing the Scottsboro defendants that spanned much of the duration of the 1930s. Tens of thousands of protestors gathered in Moscow's Red Square, while demonstrators condemned the verdicts in Havana, and marched on American consulates in Berlin, Leipzig, and Geneva.[10] Ada Wright, the mother of one of the defendants, went on an international speaking tour to sixteen countries in six months, speaking about the case to nearly 500,000 people.[11] According to the Communist Party, more than 300,000 protestors in over 100 American cities demanded the defendants' freedom on May 1st, 1931.[12] Prominent intellectuals, including Theodore Dreiser, Upton Sinclair, John Dos Passos, Albert Einstein, and Thomas Mann wrote letters or signed petitions opposing the convictions, referring to the case as a "legal lynching." The movement was spurred on by favorable court decisions, and by Ruby Bates's 1933 admission that she had never been raped. I will return to this admission.

Much of the battle to free the defendants was waged through a struggle over the kinds of images that would be used to define the case against them. The ILD and the African American press were particularly interested in creating an anti-racist spectacle that would draw attention to the injustice of the case. To this end, they printed thousands of political cartoons about Scottsboro, and organizations within the Scottsboro defense movement circulated artwork about the case in every way that they could.[13] The ILD incorporated the case into their fundraising, printing two million one cent stamps featuring a drawing of imprisoned men and two giant arms prying open the jail cell bars. "ILD" is written on one of the arms, and "Save the Scottsboro Boys" is printed at the top of the drawing (Figure 1.1).

The stamps were sold as the ILD collected membership dues, and they were frequently affixed to postcards (along with official U.S. postage) ensuring that U.S. postal workers, as well as the intended recipients of the postcards, would learn about the case.[14] The black and Communist presses frequently fed off of each other, sharing resources to illuminate particularly galling examples of unjust treatment for the defendants. For example, the *Daily Worker* reported, in the early days of the case, that when a judge asked an attorney for the Alabama Power Company to defend the accused, he declared that his company was "in business to sell 'juice' to 'burn Niggers' and he welcomes that sale." The *Baltimore Afro-American* picked up the story and, crediting the *Daily Worker*, ran a cartoon titled "Sells Juice to Burn Negroes" showing a grotesque, hunched-over, white man in a top hat and tails pulling the lever that would kill the black man we see sitting in an electric chair.[15] The ILD published a series of Scottsboro-related pamphlets, which invariably included artwork and photographs intended to humanize the defendants and draw attention to the power and necessity of the defense movement. Pamphlets might feature photographs of the defendants as young

FIGURE 1.1 International Labor Defense (ILD) Assessment Stamp, 1931.

Source: Collection of the Author.

children, or of their mothers or childhood homes.[16] One particularly elaborate pamphlet combined a series of sketches with narration to tell "The Story of Scottsboro in Pictures." The cover illustration depicts two broad-shouldered men swinging axes in the direction of a tree that has the word "Lynching" scrawled over its middle. The tree appears ready to topple, and the word "Scottsboro" is written underneath the men, who are presumably members of the Scottsboro defense movement, chopping away at the foundation of lynching and its attendant horrors.[17] White southerners who were either convinced of the defendants' guilt or resentful of communist and northern interference did not cede the ground of imagery, and fought back with their own cartoons, and with photographs that were chosen to highlight a variety of threats posed by the defendants. For example, a book on the case called *Scottsboro: The Firebrand of Communism* included photographs of "a sullen, menacing Haywood Patterson, with a suggestive gaping hole in the crotch of his trousers" along with photos of several of the other defendants dressed in clothes that were labeled "urban," with the suggestion that they were "financed, no doubt, by . . . liberal and Communist supporters."[18]

The interest in the case was never limited to the nine defendants and two accusers. Instead, virtually everyone involved in the case saw the alleged rapes in symbolic terms. For the prosecution and the white southern press, at least in the early stages of the case, the issue was always about protecting the southern way of life in general, and "southern womanhood" specifically. One prosecutor declared in his closing arguments that the defendants had "hurled a challenge against the laws of Alabama, the sovereignty of the State and the sanctity of white womanhood,"[19] while the prosecutor in another trial told jurors not to "quibble over the evidence," since "the womanhood of Alabama was looking to them for protection." Victoria Price, he shouted, was fighting "for the rights of the womanhood of Alabama."[20] For the Communist Party, the case provided graphic evidence of the nature of capitalist oppression and class struggle:

> Like the allegorical plays of the middle ages the characters represented not only themselves but powerful forces, gigantic forces locked in combat. The force of the Southern white ruling class, backed by their brothers all

over the capitalist world, determined to perpetuate the system on which they flourish, the system of slavery and terror, of oppression and lynching. And the force of the toiling masses, workers and farmers, of all colors and creeds, determined that the system under which they are exploited and crushed, shall be destroyed.[21]

For many members of the broader Scottsboro defense movement, and for much of the black press, the case was framed in stark racial terms. Looking back on the victories of the movement, Richard Wright wrote that

> We were able to seize nine black boys in a jail in Scottsboro, Alabama, lift them so high in our collective hands, focus such a battery of comment and interpretation upon them, that they became symbols to all the world of the plight of black folk in America.[22]

Only the NAACP, which fought with the ILD over the right to lead the defense in the case, expressed concern about the idea of seeing the principals in the case as symbols. The Association was concerned that in using the case to mount an assault upon white supremacy, or capitalism itself, the ILD was jeopardizing the lives of the defendants. *The Crisis* (the NAACP's magazine) editorialized that

> A frontal attack on Alabama and the whole southern system, with trumpets blowing, banners flaunting, and short swords gleaming bravely against the baleful glare of the Dragon Prejudice makes a fine spectacle, but in the encounter it was inevitable that the lives of the Scottsboro youths became of secondary importance in the minds of Alabamians.[23]

Later, the magazine argued that "these helpless boys did not ask to be made martyrs for the sake of the cause of Communism, or for the sake of the Negro race, or for the sake of anything. *They want to be free!*"[24] While the cost of becoming symbols was important to weigh, the publicity generated by the case was a key factor keeping the defendants out of the electric chair, and in eventually winning their release from prison.

Trying to determine when the case ends is tricky. One might point to the Alabama Supreme Court's decision to uphold the death sentence for one of the defendants, Clarence Norris, in June of 1938, or to the reduction of that sentence to life imprisonment by Alabama's Governor in July of the same year. But it might make more sense to look to June of 1950, when the last of the "Scottsboro Boys" was paroled, after the defendants had spent a combined 104 years in prison. Those looking for a sense of historical justice might turn to October, 1976, when Alabama's Governor George Wallace, having long abandoned his vow "segregation now, segregation tomorrow, segregation forever," licking his wounds after being forced to drop out of the Presidential election, and contemplating his political future, agreed to sign a pardon for Clarence Norris, in effect, according to Alabama law, declaring him innocent of all charges. But, perhaps the most appropriate place to look for an end to the case is decades earlier, in 1952, the year that marks the first death of a Scottsboro defendant. Sixteen years after he was first arrested, Haywood Patterson had finally escaped from prison in 1947. By 1950, having lived all but three years of his adult life in prison, he was back behind bars, and was eventually convicted of manslaughter in a barroom brawl. He became ill, and ultimately succumbed to cancer, dying in the Michigan state penitentiary. He was thirty-nine years old. If none of these dates seems to adequately mark the conclusion of the case, one might finally take a more philosophical stance and suggest that the case never really ended, and instead lives on as memory, reverberating throughout later struggles for racial justice and helping to shape the contemporary racial landscape in ways that I can only begin to assess in this chapter.

In the introduction to this book, I suggested that contemporary understandings of such categories as "whiteness" or "blackness" incorporate understandings of what those categories have meant in the past, and of struggles over their meanings. As a defining racial spectacle of the 1930s, the Scottsboro case has entered into collective memory in numerous ways, and, in the process, has played an important though largely overlooked role in national processes of racial formation. The case has helped to determine the ways that audiences in later decades have made sense of subsequent racial spectacles. It has influenced the criteria that people use when evaluating evidence, and in assessing the kinds of analyses that they find credible. In the discussion that follows, I present an extended investigation into the racialized and gendered dimensions of the Scottsboro case as it moved through the court system and the mass media in the 1930s. My concern, however, is ultimately not limited to the past, but instead extends to the ways that the echoes of the past reverberate in the present.

The "Threadbare Lie" and Changing Racial Discourse

If the search for a concluding date for the Scottsboro case is elusive, one might think that there would be no difficulty, at least, in pinpointing the date when it all began. After all, this is a rape case, and it makes sense to start with the date of the alleged rapes. Certainly, March 25th, 1931—the date that Victoria Price and Ruby Bates charged Olen Montgomery, Clarence Norris, Haywood Patterson, Ozzie Powell, Willie Roberson, Charlie Weems, Eugene Williams, Andy Wright, and Roy Wright with raping them on a Memphis-bound freight train—is worthy of historic note.[25] But the rape charges, and the public responses to those charges, were not simply products of what happened on that train that day. Instead, there was a historically conditioned logic to the nature of the allegations, and any effort to come to grips with the genesis of the charges, and to understand the vehement reactions they generated, requires reckoning with long histories of racial terror and anti-racist activism. For that reason, I would like to suggest that a good starting date for an investigation into the events of that fateful day in 1931 is May 21st, 1892, the day that the Memphis *Free Speech* published a particularly provocative editorial by Ida B. Wells.

Three of Wells's friends were lynched in March of 1892, and in response, Wells, who was the editor and part owner of the *Free Speech,* urged members of the African American community of Memphis to abandon the city, providing her readers with detailed reports about how they might migrate to Oklahoma. Within a few months' time, nearly 4,000 people had heeded her advice, and Wells had started to consider following suit and relocating the *Free Speech*. The decision was taken out of her hands after another series of violent attacks convinced her to condemn the violence in the pages of her paper. Her editorial of May 21st declared, in part,

> Eight Negroes lynched since last issue of the *Free Speech*. Three were charged with killing white men and five with raping white women. Nobody in this section believes the old thread-bare lie that Negro men assault white women. If Southern white men are not careful they will over-reach themselves and a conclusion will be reached which will be very damaging to the moral reputations of their women.[26]

There is no way to know if it was Wells's refutation of the rape charge that was used to justify so many lynchings, or her swipe at the assumed "purity" of white womanhood, that most enraged much of the white populace of Memphis, but in any case, the reaction was swift. A mob ransacked the office of the *Free Speech* within a week. Not realizing that Wells had written the piece, a local white paper had urged that the author of the editorial be castrated, or subjected to "a surgical operation with a pair of tailor's shears," and the mob came prepared for a lynching.[27] Fortunately, Wells had left for a trip to Philadelphia almost immediately after the article was published.[28] The following month, Wells, who had joined the staff of the *New York Age*, wrote an article titled "Exiled," denouncing the destruction of the *Free Press*. Ten thousand copies of "Exiled" were distributed nationally, and an expanded version of the article was subsequently published as *Southern Horrors*—the first in a series of antilynching pamphlets denouncing not only lynching itself, but also the cultural mythologies that helped provide ideological justification for the violence of the mob.

Wells's editorial and pamphlets set the stage for what was to become the first great anti-racist movement of the post-Reconstruction era. Activists mobilized around lynching not only because they understood it as a system of racist terrorism, but because they hoped to foster an understanding of mob violence as only the most visible example of much broader racial injustice. The challenge to lynching was also, therefore, intended as a challenge to white supremacy in general. While the most important activists and organizations in the antilynching movement, including the National Association for the Advancement of Colored

People, the Anti-Lynching Crusaders (a primarily black women's group that was an off-shoot of the NAACP), and the Commission on Interracial Cooperation, frequently disagreed about tactics, they were united in the belief that any effective battle against lynching had to contend with the racist myths that made lynching possible.[29] Chief among these was the "thread-bare lie" that Wells referred to in her *Free Speech* editorial—the idea that lynching was a method of punishing black men who raped white women.

Of the estimated 3,220 African Americans lynched in the South between 1880 and 1930, less than one-third were charged with rape.[30] Because lynch mobs failed to provide even a semblance of due process, there is generally no reason to accept the validity of the rape charges in the minority of cases where they were leveled. Still, the lack of an empirical foundation to the idea that lynching was always and only a response to black rape did nothing to deter public apologists for lynching (in the halls of the Senate, or in the editorial pages of leading papers, for example) from working to cement the association between rape and lynching in popular opinion. The most powerful expression of what is now generally recognized as the "myth of the black rapist" can be found in D.W. Griffith's 1915 film *The Birth of a Nation*, which was seen by three million people in the year it was released, and was intended to glorify the Ku Klux Klan while providing ideological support for white supremacy and lynching.[31] Ida B. Wells wrote of the rape charge that "this cry has had its effect. It has closed the heart, stifled the conscience, warped the judgment and hushed the voice of press and pulpit on the subject of lynch law throughout this 'land of liberty.'"[32] Had the antilynching movement failed to grapple with the "cry" of rape, it would never have been able to convince regional or national audiences to seriously consider its condemnation of the mob.

The strength of the perceived link between lynching and rape forced anti-lynching activists and organizations to follow the lead that Wells provided in her 1892 editorial. As they fought for antilynching legislation at the state and federal levels, or worked to have local law enforcement agencies prevent lynch mobs from gathering, or challenged politicians to take a stand against mob justice, antilynching activists regularly worked to debunk popular understandings of lynching and rape. They noted that the vast majority of lynch victims were never charged with rape; they argued that when the rape charge was invoked, it was frequently nothing more than an excuse used to cover up less honorable political or economic motivations for mob violence; and, finally, they referenced the relatively infrequent lynchings of women as the most compelling evidence that at least some lynchings could not have been prompted by rape. Consequently, by the time that the Scottsboro case made national headlines, an antilynching movement had been systematically devoted towards, as one NAACP campaigner put it, "exploding the rape myth" for nearly forty years.[33]

It is difficult to gauge how successful the antilynching movement's strategies had been by 1931. Lynching rates peaked in the 1890s, and started to decline very rapidly in the 1920s. While there had been nearly one hundred recorded lynchings a year in the late 1890s, that number had dropped to less than ten a year in 1928 and 1929.[34] But there are a number of factors that contributed to this trend. Black northern migration, sparked partly by the industrial war effort surrounding World War I, encouraged southern elites to take a stand against lynching, since a system of terrorism that they had relied upon to secure access to cheap black labor had now become a liability: lynching could work to keep blacks securely within a subordinate position within the labor force only as long as they had nowhere else to go. Eventually, the modernization of southern agriculture led to a diminished need for black labor, and for extra-legal methods of controlling black workers. Lynching also lost some of its value as a method of ensuring the stability of white supremacy as white domination was increasingly secured through other means, including Jim Crow legislation and black disenfranchisement. There is no way to disentangle cultural activism and broad socio-economic factors when figuring out how to account for the decline in lynching rates, but it is important to note that public attitudes towards lynching changed as lynching rates fell. By 1937, lynching had few public supporters and sixty-five percent of southern respondents to a Gallup poll supported federal antilynching legislation.[35] The white southern press, which had endorsed and defended lynching for decades, started to see it as an embarrassment in the 1930s, and massive spectacle lynchings, involving hundreds or even thousands of spectator/participants were largely a thing of the past. If some part of the economic and political foundation of lynching had diminished over the years, it still makes sense to think that the antilynching movement's assault upon cultural narratives of lynching can be credited with taking a toll on the public support for the practice. Which is not to say that the "cry of rape" as expressed by Victoria Price and Ruby Bates fell on deaf ears.

Scottsboro, the Press, and New Understandings of Interracial Sexuality

The southern press was the first to cover the Scottsboro case, and in its initial reporting, regional papers functioned in much the same way that they did while reporting on massive "spectacle lynchings": as an extension of the mob, powerfully disseminating images of monstrously horrific black brute rapists and sending messages about the strength of white supremacy.[36] A typical example is the *Chattanooga Times* which ran an editorial with the headline "Death Penalty Properly Demanded in Fiendish Crime of Nine Burly Negroes," while its primary reporter covering the case referred to the defendants as "beasts unfit to be called human."[37] In general, the southern press accepted the rape allegations without question, often exaggerating the charges, and agreeing that this was "the most atrocious crime ever recorded" in the South, if not in the entire country.[38] Still, from the earliest stages of the case, it was clear that there had been a notable shift in the ways that regional papers reported on allegations of interracial rape.

It would be too mild to say that the white southern press accepted the legitimacy of lynching, or that it provided the ideological cover needed to defend lynch mobs from their most vocal critics throughout the 1890s and the early years of the twentieth century. Instead, the press actively facilitated mob justice and regularly sought to increase the turnout for "lynching parties." Local papers frequently printed stories announcing the time and place for upcoming lynchings, advertising the fact that a soon-to-be victim of the mob had been captured, rehearsing details of the alleged crimes that the victim was to be lynched for, and publicizing "invitations" to join the mob.[39] But as lynching rates started to decline, and as northern opposition to lynching began to mount, urban editors in the South became concerned about cultural and political isolation, and began to oppose the practice, albeit inconsistently.[40] In some ways, the most striking aspect of initial coverage of the Scottsboro case wasn't the use of racist stereotypes, but the pride that local and regional papers took in the fact that a mass lynching had been averted. Consider, for example, the April 11, 1931 edition of the Atlanta *Constitution*, which declared that

> The governor and people of Alabama deserve the praise of the whole country for the manner in which they have handled the perpetrators of the repulsive outrage upon a couple of white girls by a band of Negro tramps on a freight train near Scottsboro several weeks ago. Not in many years has so dastardly and inflaming a wholesale crime been committed in the south. The provocation to a horrified and maddened community to take summary and deadly vengeance upon the guilty brutes was fairly irresistible, but the cool courage of the local sheriff and his influence over his fellow citizens led to the peaceable arrest and imprisonment of the doers of multiple outrages.[41]

The ready acceptance of the rape charges and the overall tone of the piece suggest that, had the defendants been lynched, the paper would have seen the killings as understandable. Still, the sense that efforts to avoid such an occurrence were admirable would have been unthinkable in a white southern paper had the defendants been charged twenty or thirty years earlier. The local *Scottsboro Progressive Age* expressed similar sentiments, writing that, while a lynching would have been excusable under the circumstances, the local populace had "saved the good name of the county and state by remaining cool and allowing the law to take its course."[42]

If the sense that lynchings were undesirable and that they could be responsible for bringing shame to southern communities owes something to the battles waged by the antilynching movement to challenge taken-for-granted understandings of lynching (battles not only to refute the myth of the black rapist, but also to ensure that lynching would be understood as a barbaric crime rather than as a necessary weapon in the defense of civilization), the Scottsboro case also provides evidence of how limited any successes of the movement may have been. For while the southern white press may have started to take pride in the law-abiding nature of its citizens, in 1931 it still took the very clear position that the defendants needed to die. While the *Charleston News and Courier* editorialized, for example, that what "took place in Scottsboro was vindication of the law" since a lynching had been averted, it had little patience for activists who were pressing for a reversal of the convictions, arguing that

> Whether the two women were good or bad, the evidence is that force was employed against them, and the law in Alabama (so it is in South Carolina, as it should be) is that a crime so done is punishable by death. . . The interferers with the courts in Alabama are the arrayed accessories and promoters of lynch law in the Southern States. They are BREEDING LYNCHERS, they care less than nothing about the poor Negroes, they would welcome the lynching of a thousand Negroes because they think it is helpful to their cause of disorder and anarchy.[43]

But if the southern white press was initially willing to accept the charges without question (and indeed this was the case for any charges of interracial rape leveled against black men), that started to change over time. As the movement to free the Scottsboro defendants grew, and as the guilty verdicts were repeatedly overturned and the weakness of the case was exposed to ever wider audiences, the case provided activists with an important new weapon in the assault against racist stereotypes. It was a weapon that southern editors could not ignore.

"I was forced to say it": A White Woman's Word and the Fate of a Myth

Ruby Bates's recantation came after the first series of convictions, and after the white press had spent a considerable amount of energy inflating her allegations. While her decision to admit that the charges were fabricated had little effect in courtroom proceedings (spectators laughed during her testimony, and the defendants were found guilty once again), she was able to command much more appreciative audiences in other forums.[44] For example, she addressed an audience of at least 5,000 people at a church in Baltimore, declaring that

> I want to tell you that the Scottsboro boys were framed by the bosses of the south and two girls. I was one of the girls and I want you to know that I am sorry I said what I did at the first trial, but I was forced to say it. Those boys did not attack me and I want to tell you all right here now that I am sorry that I caused them all this trouble for two years, and now I am willing to join hands with black and white to get them free.[45]

Organizing efforts by the Communist Party meant that Bates had the opportunity to present versions of this speech many times. Coming from one of the women whose claims of rape had occupied the front pages of papers around the world for years, Bates's recantation stands as perhaps the single most dramatic refutation of the myth of the black rapist. This was not just a spectacular moment, but a sustained campaign, repeatedly staged for groups of thousands. The decision by the trial judge to throw out the conviction in the second round of trials was an unprecedented "virtual rejection of a white woman's claim of rape against blacks in the deep south,"[46] and amplified the power of Bates's recantation. I opened this chapter by noting that black women had long taken the position that white women had a unique responsibility to stop lynching—a responsibility rooted in the fact that lynchings were often carried out in their names. Because popular justifications of lynching relied upon the argument that lynchings were a method of defending "white womanhood," white women who were willing to disavow the "protection" offered by mob justice were difficult to ignore.

Bates was hardly the only white woman to take a stand against the myth of the black rapist. Indeed, the Association of Southern Women for the Prevention of Lynching (ASWPL) was founded just a year before Bates embarked upon her journey with Victoria Price. Led by Jessie Daniel Ames, this group of white women recognized that "all lynching will be defended so long as the public generally accepts the assumption that it is for the protection of white women,"[47] and throughout its twelve year history, the organization decided that "emphasis at all times was to be placed on the repudiation of the claim that lynching is necessary to the protection of white women."[48] The ASWPL eventually gathered the signatures of 43,000 southern white women on antilynching petitions and succeeded in preventing a number of lynchings. By the late 1930s, a series of southern editorials had credited the organization with helping to turn public opinion against lynching. But as important as the Association was, no one in the organization could come close to Ruby Bates when it came to commanding the attention of the press. Bates's role as a white woman whose charges of black rape helped ignite a media firestorm ensured that her refutation of those charges would place her at center stage in regional, national, and international debates about southern racial dynamics. The ASWPL was well suited to challenge the myth of the black rapist, but Bates was alone in her ability to provide first hand testimony about the fabrication of one of the best-known examples of that myth.

The Scottsboro defense movement seized upon Bates's recantation. The ILD highlighted the testimony in its publicity materials, claiming that Bates "was the first white woman in the history of the South to defend Negroes from the charge of rape."[49] Since the ASWPL had been around for three years by this time, this claim is hyperbolic, but the sense of the importance of Bates's testimony was widely shared. This is reflected in the decision by dozens of editors around the country to move the Scottsboro story to their front pages, highlighting Bates's recantation.[50] Some national magazines that had not previously paid much attention to the case also started to cover it in greater detail.[51] Even in the South, large metropolitan papers outside of Alabama began to declare that the defendants were clearly innocent. The Richmond *News Leader* wrote that "The men are being sentenced to death primarily because they are black," and asserted that "the second trial confirmed all the suspicions aroused by the first hearing."[52] Similarly, the Chattanooga *News* declared that "we cannot conceive of a civilized community taking lives on the strength of this miserable affair."[53]

If the changes in the southern white press were limited to coverage of the Scottsboro case, they would be striking, given the role that southern white reporters and editors had played in the first stages of the case. In an early motion for a change of venue, the defense argued that the local press had acted as a social force, poisoning the climate to the degree that a fair trial was impossible. They quoted an editorial from the Decatur *Community Builder*, demonstrating that the hostility extended not only to the defendants, but also to the legal team:

> in the face of the feeling that exists at Decatur as well as throughout the Tennessee Valley . . . we suggest that it would not be well for these lawyers to again show up on any soil at any point in this valley. We do not need that type of cattle down here, and their further appearance is wholly unnecessary.[54]

The defense provided a series of examples of articles and editorials that "were calculated to and did and do arouse hostility and prejudice against your petitioners in the northern counties of the State of Alabama."[55] The local press was so committed to securing guilty verdicts that even the United States Supreme Court felt the need to challenge the editor of the *Scottsboro Progressive Age* in its *Norris* decision, noting that testimony provided by the paper's editor was not believable.[56] Given the zeal with which virtually every organ of the southern white press initially set out to secure the deaths of the Scottsboro defendants, it is remarkable that a paper like the Baton Rouge, La. *Advocate* would eventually declare that "Clearly something was wrong with the early trials," while the Birmingham, Alabama *News* could write that "Grave doubt . . . surrounded these charges. In view of this doubt, and in view of all the other circumstances, no one could be certain of where truth and justice lay."[57] This alone would suggest that the days when commentators could be confident in the assumption that when "a white woman is prepared to swear that a Negro either raped or attempted to rape her, we see to it that the Negro is executed" were, if not history, then at least fading.[58] But as the case progressed through the appeals process, the new southern editorial stance towards the Scottsboro defendants reverberated through coverage of interracial rape and lynching more broadly.

In 1938, Jessie Daniel Ames published a study of editorial treatment of lynchings, noting that regional papers that had defended lynching and helped to ward off federal antilynching legislation for decades had finally started to accept the idea that there might be some benefit to federal "interference" in the activities of lynch mobs, if only as a method of rebutting the idea that lynching was a distinctly southern phenomenon:

> if three or more men and women kill a Negro, that will be a job for the Federal government. . . . The South can forget the murder but the nation will share the lynching. The pot and the kettle can't call names—a situation greatly desired by Southern editors and their readers.[59]

While southern white papers had not reached the point where they would condemn lynching under all circumstances, Ames wrote that many "leading Southern dailies no longer condone lynchings by holding them as necessary to protect Southern womanhood. Editors to some extent have absorbed a few statistics on the alleged crimes which arouse sensitive citizens."[60] Southern papers had been unlikely to mount vigorous defenses of lynching for quite a while by the time of Ames's study, but the abandonment of the rape charge as a justification for the practice was fairly new. Ames attributed this editorial change of heart partly to the need to court northern investment, but also to the fact that editors "dare not lay themselves open to ridicule by defending lynching on the grounds of gallantry."[61]

Ames doesn't offer much of an explanation about why a defense of lynching based on claims of gallantry would be so laughable a proposition, other than to mention the "few statistics" that southern editors have "absorbed." She is perhaps too modest here, failing to note that the ASWPL had spent much of the decade publicizing the fact that only a minority of lynch victims were ever charged with rape, or that her organization had been a consistent reference point in editorials on the subject. But she also doesn't address the tremendous embarrassment caused by the Scottsboro case—a sense of embarrassment so strong that the editor of the *Montgomery Advertiser*, who had spent years defending the Alabama courts from northern interference, was ultimately moved, in 1938, to wish the case away, saying of the defendants that "I don't care what they do . . . so long as they do it in another state, preferably Ohio or New York. I don't care if they eat one another without benefit of pepper sauce."[62] It is impossible to assess the degree to which the publicity generated by the Scottsboro case contributed to the broader antilynching sentiment expressed in southern papers, but it was not until the 1955 lynching of Emmett Till that another case involving southern understandings of black masculinity, white femininity, and interracial sexuality would bring a similar degree of scrutiny and reprobation to the region's racial dynamics. That such attention might have played a role in causing southern editors to shrink in their defense of lynching seems reasonable given their concern with avoiding political and economic isolation.

Psychopathic Daydreams: Anti-racist Discourse and Sexist Stereotypes of Rape

If there is much to celebrate in the evolving coverage of Scottsboro and of lynching in the late 1930s, there is also reason to temper such celebrations, since it was not just attitudes towards black men that were changing. In an effort to explain Bates's admission, the *Raleigh Times* declared that while

> it is difficult to understand . . . how two women . . . could have gone the length of attempting to perjure away the lives of a number of innocent men . . . the phenomenon is a common experience in the pathology of women.[63]

The paper went on to declare that the case should serve "to give solemn warning to the South, all too apt to execute judicially, as well as by lynch law, when some psychopathic woman has a day dream and sticks to it on the witness stand."[64] This statement provides a clear indication of the power that the Scottsboro case had to challenge common-sense understandings of race and gender, and of the antilynching and Scottsboro defense movements' successes in refuting the myth of the black rapist, at the same time as it highlights the potentially troubling relationship between anti-racist discourse and misogynistic understandings of rape. The *Raleigh Times* wasn't alone in its declaration that rape charges could be traced to women's pathology. This can be seen, for example, in the declaration by one self-appointed expert who informed Alabama's Governor that "nine out of ten charges of rape are false and are due to a peculiar psychological condition of the woman," that women fantasized about rape, and that women asked to be raped.[65] In fact, demonization of the women's sexuality was central to Scottsboro movement rhetoric, and to the extent that the regional or national press sided with the defendants, this support was contingent upon representing their accusers as sexually deviant.

Victoria Price and Ruby Bates had lived difficult lives. They came from poor families, had little formal education, and had been working in the cotton mills of Huntsville, in northern Alabama, when work could be found, for years before moving to Chattanooga in search of more secure employment. They hopped the Memphis-bound freight only when their hopes for Chattanooga didn't pan out. James Goodman notes that their "lives mocked the white South's most sacred ideal," since they provided clear illustration of the permeability of the color line.[66] In Huntsville, they had

> lived among black people, played with them as children, roamed the streets with them as teenagers, bootlegged liquor and got drunk with them as young adults. They also went out with them, slept with them, fell in and out of love with them, apparently unaware of the widespread wishful thinking

that made it possible for many white southerners to call all sex between white women and black men rape.[67]

Until Scottsboro, few would have seen either Price or Bates as exemplars of pure white womanhood. And when the prosecution and the southern white press suggested that it was necessary to convict the defendants in order to "protect the fair womanhood"[68] of Alabama, the Scottsboro defense movement seized upon this fact, making every effort to discredit their testimony by focusing on their sexual histories. The defense team had gathered affidavits from Chattanooga claiming that Price and Bates had worked as prostitutes, and from the moment that these affidavits became public, virtually every piece of Scottsboro movement literature referenced these claims as definitive proof of the absurdity of the rape charges. For example, a 1937 pamphlet declares that

> the State of Alabama concurred in Victoria Price's perjured testimony and held her up as a glowing example of true white womanhood. Upon the words of a habitual prostitute, whose purity of womanhood and character had long passed into obscurity, the lynchers sought to snuff out the lives of nine black boys.[69]

Langston Hughes, who produced some of the most powerful writing about the case, was more succinct in his appraisal: "And who ever heard of raping a prostitute?" he sneered.[70]

Attacking the accusers' sexuality was also a central part of the legal defense strategy, and played an important role in the trial judge's decision to throw out the second conviction of Haywood Patterson. Judge Horton listed a number of factors that had caused him to come to the conclusion that Patterson was innocent, highlighting the lack of physical evidence and of credible corroborating testimony, along with Ruby Bates's recantation, but the most widely quoted part of his decision focused on the backgrounds and characters of the accusers:

> History, sacred and profane, and the common experience of mankind teach us that women of the character shown in this case are prone for selfish reasons to make false accusations both of rape and of insult upon the slightest provocation for ulterior purposes.[71]

This decision was foreshadowed by the references in Horton's jury instructions to Bates's "lack of virtue" and to Price as a "woman of easy virtue" who had given false testimony.[72] Horton's decision was seized upon by the Scottsboro defense movement, which quoted from it liberally in virtually all of its literature after 1933, and reprinted it in its entirety as a pamphlet, placing the references to the accusers' character in bold. But Horton's decision was an aberration. He was the only trial judge to seriously consider the possibility that the defendants were innocent, and the only judge to allow consideration of the accusers' sexual histories.

In general, the strategy of demonizing the sexuality of two white women did not go over well in southern courtrooms. Thus, in what might at first glance appear to be a precursor of feminist anti-rape rhetoric, the judge in one series of trials argued that a rape victim's sexual past was irrelevant in determining the validity of her charges. Judge Callahan declared that if a woman has been "unlawfully violated, she may appeal to the courts with an abiding faith that no accusing finger can be pointed to her erring past or hopeless future, as an excuse for denying her full and adequate protection of the law."[73] The judge was only echoing the 1932 Alabama Supreme Court's Scottsboro decision which declared that "previous chastity" was "not an essential element of rape," and that "rape may be committed on an unchaste woman."[74]

This stance is somewhat less heartening when we consider its racial specificity. The notion that women's sexual history is irrelevant when determining the validity of rape charges is something that 1930s-era southern courts would have held to only when considering charges leveled by white women against black men. There was no question of a similar position being taken when considering the rapes of black women, since white southern discourse continued to promote the myth of the sexually available black woman, and therefore tended to treat black women as un-rapeable, especially if their attackers happened to be white men. But even when the alleged victim was a white woman, the idea that questions of chastity or sexual history were irrelevant would have seemed absurd in southern courts had a *white* man been accused of the crime.

Still, the ease with which the campaign to discredit the myth of the black rapist was enlisted for misogynistic purposes suggests that however superficial and problematic the courts were in their refutations of sexist understandings of rape during the Scottsboro trials, it would be a mistake to dismiss such refutations out of hand as nothing more consequential than an attempt to secure white supremacist jurisprudence in one extraordinary case. The Scottsboro defense movement's reliance upon sexist stereotypes provides an important caution against uncritical praise of the discursive battles that were won by anti-racist activists in this case. Decades later, the anti-rape movement of the 1970s would confront such stereotypes head on, while focusing on the legal system as a site responsible for putting rape victims through a second assault. There were precious few legal precedents that were useful for challenging the infiltration of rape mythology into the courtroom, but some of the most notable legislative victories of 1970s-era feminism were a series of "rape-shield" laws that worked to limit evidence about rape victims' sexual pasts. To the extent that these laws build upon the kinds of arguments made in an attempt to secure guilty verdicts for the Scottsboro defendants, it is worth questioning whether they are in any way tainted by their racist lineage.

There have been a number of recent mass media spectacles where media coverage suggested that there were stark conflicts between feminism and anti-racist activism (including the O.J. Simpson trials, the Hill/Thomas hearings and the Kobe Bryant rape case, discussed at length in the next chapter). In each of these cases, feminism was widely represented as a white women's movement, while anti-racist activism was seen as incapable of addressing sexist victimization. One reason that it has been so easy to pit feminist and anti-racist discourses against each other may well be that there has been no thorough reckoning with the genealogy of these discourses, and the ways in which similar kinds of anti-sexist and anti-racist arguments were enlisted in what was to be the defining racial spectacle of the 1930s. Because contemporary understandings of race and gender build upon past struggles over the meanings of these categories, a failure to grapple with a clash of discourses in the past might produce all sorts of unforeseen consequences, not least in the realm of public opinion and race relations.

A Forgotten Spectacle? Scottsboro in Collective Memory

While the legacies of Scottsboro may be mixed, there is no doubt that the Scottsboro defense movement was crucially important in helping to debunk one of the cornerstone myths of white supremacy, generating widespread outrage about southern race relations, and ultimately helping to pave the way for the international condemnation of the lynching of Emmett Till in 1955, and for the emergence of the civil rights movement. And yet, the names of Haywood Patterson, Clarence Norris, Ozzie Powell, any of the other defendants, or even Ruby Bates or Victoria Price are not well-known. Some influential historians and journalists writing about the case appear reconciled to the idea that while Scottsboro may have been the defining racial spectacle of the 1930s, not enough has been done to secure a collective memory of the case. While advocating for the town of Scottsboro to confront its past, Dan Carter noted that "It was the story of the decade, and then 25 years later it was gone. That tells you something about selective memory."[75] Robin D.G. Kelley laments the fact that few people attended Clarence Norris's funeral in 1989, and while he says that "we cannot afford to forget Scottsboro," he also claims that by "the time the final defendants were released, the case had pretty much drifted into obscurity."[76] And, in 1994, David Oshinsky of the *New York Times* referred to the case as a "vital but largely forgotten episode."[77]

There is some truth to these claims. News coverage of the case started to drop off after the 1935 *Norris* decision, and once the press had fully covered the 1937 decision to release four of the defendants, what had been a flood of articles slowed to a trickle.[78]

Hugh T. Murray, Jr. argues that the lack of coverage after 1937 is the result of a compromise between the State of Alabama and the Scottsboro Defense Committee (a coalition of groups including the ILD, the NAACP, the ACLU, the League for Industrial Democracy, and the Methodist Federation for Social Service). Murray claims that, in return for the freedom of the four defendants,

FIGURE 1.2 From Left: Eugene Williams, Samuel Leibowitz, Willie Roberson, Roy Wright and Olin Montgomery. New York City, July 26, 1937. Once Williams, Roberson, Wright and Montgomery were released, news coverage of the Scottsboro case slowed down considerably, despite the fact that five of the defendants remained imprisoned.

Source: Courtesy AP Images.

the SDC "promised that Communists would not agitate about Scottsboro. The Communists agreed, and such agitation, propaganda, and literature virtually disappeared."[79] Once the protest movement stopped publicizing the case, the press followed suit. There appears to be little evidence for this explanation, however. It is true that the SDC and the governor's office discussed a compromise in the case, but the state broke off negotiations, and reneged on agreements to limit the prison time of the remaining five defendants once Roy Wright, Eugene Williams, Olen Montgomery and Willie Roberson were released.[80] The SDC in fact informed the governor that it would continue to criticize the state until all of the defendants were released.[81] While press accounts suggested that there had indeed been a compromise, the SDC consistently refuted these claims. In any event, immediately after the release of the four defendants, the SDC held a mass meeting of nearly 5,000 people in New York as evidence of the organization's "determination not to rest until all nine were free,"[82] and a Communist Party press rushed to put out a pamphlet titled *The Scottsboro Boys: Four Freed! Five to Go!*[83]

The more likely explanation for the decline in coverage is that, according to the routine practices of news organizations, there was little that would count as "newsworthy" once the defense had exhausted its appeals and the state had dropped its pursuit of the death penalty for the remaining defendants.[84] And, while the SDC did continue its work on behalf of the defendants, without the looming threat of the electric chair, and without hope of further intervention by the courts, the Scottsboro defense movement began to fade, and could no longer generate the massive protests that would compel the attention of the world's press. Still, there is good reason to think that a lack of continuing press coverage after the 1930s doesn't mean that the case was relegated to the realm of collective amnesia.

While coverage of the case dropped off after the 1930s, there have been a series of moments in subsequent decades when the press has looked back on the case. The deaths of the principal actors in the case have occasioned not only obituaries, but also op-ed pieces in national and regional papers.[85] And, despite the fact that the Supreme Court refused to hear the final appeal in the case in 1937, there were still events involving the legal system that the press felt bound to cover, including parole decisions and the 1976 pardon of Clarence Norris. Haywood Patterson and Clarence Norris both published autobiographies that garnered some attention, and helped keep memories of the case alive in the 1950s and 1970s.[86] There were two highly regarded histories of the case, Dan Carter's *Scottsboro: A Tragedy of the American South*, and James Goodman's *Stories of Scottsboro*. Both books were widely reviewed, and Carter's book provided the inspiration for *Judge Horton and the Scottsboro Boys*, a docudrama that aired on NBC in 1976.[87] *Judge Horton* repeated an error that Carter had made in his book—that Victoria Price was dead—and the press actively covered Price's libel suit over the next several years.[88] Carter and Goodman were key sources for *Scottsboro: An American Tragedy* (2000), an Academy Award-nominated, and Emmy-winning documentary on the case that screened at film festivals and on PBS. The docudrama and documentary each prompted dozens of reviews and retrospective analyses of the case. Shortly after the PBS airings of the documentary, the town of Scottsboro put up a plaque on the courthouse lawn marking where the first trials were held, and in February, 2010, a Scottsboro Boys Museum and Cultural Center opened in the town.[89]

Beyond direct references to the case in the mass media, Scottsboro has left a tremendous artistic and literary legacy. The *Daily Worker* published a song titled "The Scottsboro Boys Shall Not Die," which became a de-facto anthem for the Scottsboro defense movement, though there were many other Scottsboro ballads in the 1930s.[90] There were thousands of political cartoons about Scottsboro printed throughout the 1930s, and visual artists produced a series of works about the case for two antilynching exhibitions.[91] There have been several plays based on the case, including John Wexley's *They Shall Not Die* which played off-Broadway in 1934, and returned to New York in 1949, and Langston Hughes's *Scottsboro Limited*.[92] Hughes also wrote a series of essays about the case, and published the

FIGURE 1.3 Scottsboro Limited by Prentiss Taylor. In this lithograph, the Scottsboro defendants are on a box car flat. The telephone wires almost appear to be attached to the defendants, as though the pole, which is shaped like a cross, has become a lynching tree. The image presents the defendants as Christian martyrs, and implicates modern communication and transportation technologies as contributing factors in their martyrdom.

Source: Courtesy of the Library of Congress and Roderick S. Quiroz (estate of Prentiss Taylor).

play and several poems in a collection also titled *Scottsboro Limited*, illustrated by Prentiss Taylor (Figure 1.3).[93]

Don Mankiewicz published a novel titled *Trial* in 1955, which was later made into a film. While *Trial* wasn't a history of Scottsboro, the novel parallels the case in so many ways that "the book must be considered a thinly veiled and extremely partisan view of" Scottsboro.[94] Richard Wright wrote about the case in his nonfiction essays, and the character of Max, Bigger Thomas's attorney in *Native Son* is said to be based on Samuel Leibowitz, the most important Scottsboro defense attorney.[95]

More famously, Scottsboro was one of the main sources of inspiration for Harper Lee's *To Kill a Mockingbird*, and the novel is structured to parallel the case in a variety of ways. Claudia Durst Johnson writes that the

> central parallels between the trial in the novel and the Scottsboro trial are three: the threat of lynching; the issue of a southern jury's composition; and the intricate symbolic complications arising from the interweave of race and class when a lower-class white woman wrongfully accuses a black man or men. The centrality of the woman's testimony, her behavior on the witness stand, the cover-up of another crime or secret, and the important issue of her low social standing in the Scottsboro case correspond to the situation constructed by Lee.[96]

Steven Lubet adds that *Mockingbird* parallels Scottsboro in that the defense strategy in the novel involved a reliance upon misogynistic rape mythology and the demonization of the accuser's sexuality.[97] *Mockingbird* is "the most widely read twentieth-century work of fiction devoted to the issue of race,"[98] having sold more than 15 million copies by 1982.[99] The novel won the Pulitzer Prize in 1961, and Robert Mulligan's 1962 film adaptation won several academy awards, and was nominated for several others. The film was voted number 34 on the American Film Institute's survey of the 100 best films of all time.[100] While most people who are familiar with *Mockingbird* do not know of its connection to the Scottsboro case, the popularity of the novel and film suggest that the case has had a tremendous, albeit indirect, role in shaping American understandings of race, gender, and the criminal justice system.

The most dramatic recent effort to disseminate and reconstruct collective memories of the Scottsboro case came in the Spring of 2010, as the Kander and Ebb musical *The Scottsboro Boys* opened off-Broadway at the Vineyard Theater in New York. Composer John Kander and lyricist Fred Ebb were one of the most highly acclaimed songwriting teams in the history of American musical theater, having collaborated on such plays as *Cabaret* (1966), *Chicago* (1975), *Zorba* (1968) and *Kiss of the Spider Woman* (1992). Fred Ebb died in September, 2004, but he and John Kander had wanted to do a play about the Scottsboro case for years, and they completed a draft of the script for the musical before his death. *The Scottsboro Boys*, which was, as of this writing, set to move to Broadway for a Fall, 2010 opening, takes the form of a minstrel show (*Minstrel Show* was, in fact, the working title of the play in its early stages) featuring the Scottsboro defendants as cast members.[101] The decision to stage the musical as a minstrel show allows the producers to highlight the spectacular aspects of the case while suggesting that the trials worked to put black male sexuality on public display. Historically, minstrel shows provided opportunities for whites to stage and define blackness, but *The Scottsboro Boys* seeks to subvert the form as the production plays upon traditional features of the genre to very non-traditional effect.

FIGURE 1.4 "The Scottsboro Boys" Program Guide.

At first glance, the cover illustration depicting a man in flight appears to somewhat innocuously suggest the joy of musical theater. However, the body is somewhat contorted, and the lines that descend from the letters of the word "boys" might be read either as lynching ropes or prison bars. This reading is in tune with the spirit of the play, which presents the Scottsboro case as a minstrel show in which the defendants were forced to perform as part of a racist spectacle.

Most notably, in standard minstrel shows, the character of "the Interlocutor" is a white man who acts as the master of ceremonies and directs all of the action, helping to determine the kinds of blackness that will be displayed for the audience. In *The Scottsboro Boys*, the Interlocutor performs his traditional role as he commands the Scottsboro defendants to perform blackness in stereotypical ways, but the defendants are never content to passively accept the roles in which they are cast. For example, when the Interlocutor tells the defendants to "sing that old song" (a nostalgic song about the glories of the South), they slyly insert their own lyrics about white supremacy, lamenting the death of a cousin by lynch mob.[102] Throughout the production, the defendants defiantly refuse to go along with white definitions of blackness, and instead find ways to reassert their own humanity at the same time that they reveal apparently innocent representational forms as racist cultural productions. *The Scottsboro Boys* is rather thin in historical detail (there is no mention of Judge Horton or either of the Supreme Court decisions), but does clearly convey the fact that the defendants were unjustly convicted on the basis of trumped up charges and fabricated evidence.[103] The off-Broadway production of the show received mixed reviews, but garnered a considerable amount of attention, and provided the occasion for numerous media outlets to rehearse the history of the case.

Perhaps the best evidence that the Scottsboro case occupies a prominent place in a national "collective memory" of race has less to do with the amount of media attention it has received, or with its artistic and literary legacies, than with the fact that memories of the case have been powerfully institutionalized, in the form of the *Powell* and *Norris* Supreme Court decisions. The Scottsboro defendants were arrested at a time when the criminal justice system was the subject of widespread allegations of racism. (Some anti-racist activists argued that, as lynching rates were declining, extra-legal violence was no longer necessary for white supremacy, since racial domination was increasingly likely to be enforced through sham trials and lengthy prison terms.) In this context, the Supreme Court's interventions in the Scottsboro case suggested to at least some audiences that it could be possible to enlist the federal government in anti-racist struggles.

The Scottsboro case thus foreshadows the emergence of the modern civil rights movement two decades later not only because it shed light upon the nature of the mythology of interracial sexuality, thus helping to prepare a climate in which national audiences could be horrified at the lynching of Emmett Till in 1955, but also because it provided two compelling examples of the key political strategy which was to define the bulk of civil rights movement activism: For activists, the primary lesson to emerge from Scottsboro is that it was possible to pit the federal government against southern authorities when the power of a mass movement could compel the media to cover stark violations of black civil rights.[104] The Supreme Court's 1954 decision in *Brown v. Board of Education* (declaring segregated education "inherently unequal"), President Eisenhower's mobilization of the Arkansas national guard to help integrate the Little Rock school system in 1957, and the passage and enforcement of the Civil Rights act of 1964 and the 1965 Voting Rights act were all outcomes of this strategy.[105]

How Far We Have Come: Scottsboro and Racial Progress Narratives

Beyond its impact on the civil rights movement, the Scottsboro case fulfills a function in a narrative about our nation's racist past which is quite similar to the function played by slavery, lynching, or the most brutal forms of racist violence during the civil rights era. That is, Scottsboro is regularly invoked not only to show how horrific our racist past was, but also to provide what is widely thought of as indisputable evidence of how far we have come. For example, a review of James Goodman's *Stories of Scottsboro* says that the book

> is a chilling reminder of the violence and hatred that substituted for justice in the South. It shows just how much the legal system has evolved since the 1930s. In the two Scottsboro cases that reached the Supreme Court, decisions were issued that expanded the protections accorded by the due process clause of the Constitution. These protections are now taken for granted.[106]

This is a fairly typical assessment of the importance of the case, and it provides a sense of the ways in which collective memories of Scottsboro have become integral components of a narrative of national progress in race relations.

This narrative is enhanced by selective reference to Supreme Court decisions. The notion that indigent defendants have a right to counsel is based on the series of cases from *Powell* to *Gideon* and *Miranda*, and upon ignoring the ways in which the Court has undermined that right in the time since *Gideon*. The Court has held, for example, that defendants have no right to state appointed counsel before indictment, or during most appeals, and it has watered down the notion of "effective assistance of counsel" to the point where lawyers who have slept through portions of trials, used heroin or cocaine during the course of a trial, or even who have informed juries that their clients are guilty of murder, have all met the standard.[107] Similarly, *Norris v. Alabama* and several related cases have been widely understood as having largely eliminated racist processes within jury selection, despite the fact that race-based peremptory challenges (which were only ruled unconstitutional in 1986, and which have persisted under race–neutral rationale) still facilitate the selection of all white juries.[108]

None of the cases that have limited the "effective counsel" requirement or that have accepted racially based uses of the peremptory challenge have received nearly the attention of *Gideon* or *Norris*, and a progress narrative has therefore been allowed to continue largely without contest, at least within the mainstream media.[109] Narratives of racial progress were central to the Scottsboro case from the start, as local editorials proudly declared that if the case had happened anywhere else, the defendants would surely have been lynched instead of receiving a fair trial. The black press, however, refused this progress narrative from the outset. Rather than praising Alabamans for avoiding vigilante justice, the black press consistently condemned the state for engaging in a legal lynching.[110] For the *New York Amsterdam News,* the initial trials were clear evidence of southern barbarism and the rule of the mob:

> Anyone who understands the psychology of the Southern people realizes that the news of negroes alone with white girls is enough to make rape a

fact. . . . 10,000 people swarmed about the courthouse. When the death sentence was entered against these youngsters the crowd, hooting and yelling, celebrated the "victory" while a brass band played.[111]

The Portland, Oregon *Advocate* was even stronger in its condemnation of the trials, arguing that the convictions were based on the "usual lie of 'rape' on two white girls," and claiming of Alabaman authorities that the "savage lust of these bosses demanded a legal lynching, which in their opinion would cover up the crude and illegal lynching. A farcical trial was held amid the tensest mob spirit whipped up by the bosses and the city officials."[112] Even after the two favorable Supreme Court decisions, papers like the *New York Age* refused to celebrate, and instead continued to focus on the racism of the case and the plight of the defendants.[113]

Credibility Gaps and the Racialization of Collective Memory

For much of the duration of the case, in fact, it makes sense to see the black press as having been *part* of the Scottsboro defense movement. When Haywood Patterson was convicted and sentenced to death for the second time, the *New York Amsterdam News* posted a statement on its bulletin board calling for a march from Harlem to Washington to protest the verdict. By the early evening, twenty thousand people had signed a petition agreeing to take part in the march.[114] Even when black owned papers didn't organize their own protests, they could be counted upon to report on the protest activities of the Scottsboro defense movement, and on encouraging their readers to support such activities.[115] In later years, the black press has always been highly attentive to the ways that the rights secured in cases like *Norris* have been undermined. And while the mainstream press has regularly invoked Scottsboro as evidence of a bleak era in American racial dynamics that we've moved beyond, the black press consistently presents Scottsboro as a touchstone—a moment that helped set the pattern for the ways that the criminal justice system continues to deal with black men charged with sexualized crimes, especially those involving white women. Scottsboro was a regular reference point for the black press when covering the cases of Charles Stuart (a white man in Boston who murdered his pregnant wife in 1989, then told the police that she had been killed by a black assailant), Susan Smith (a white woman who killed her two sons in South Carolina in 1994, later claiming that a black man had ordered her out of her car at gunpoint, then driven away with her kids still in it), and the O.J. Simpson murder trials. Most recently, Scottsboro became the most important historical reference point for a series of stories in the black press about the decision to set aside the guilty verdicts of five teenagers from Harlem in the "central park jogger" case, once DNA evidence confirmed the confession of another man who claimed to have acted alone.[116] The point in referencing Scottsboro was seldom to suggest that the racism involved in the contemporary event would have been more predictable in another era, but instead to draw attention to what was presented as a clear continuity in American racist spectacles.[117]

In contrast, when the mainstream press addresses the racism surrounding the Scottsboro case, not only is it likely to suggest that such racism is either confined to the past or aberrational in the present, but it cannot even be counted upon to accept that the defendants were innocent.[118] A 2001 article in the *Chicago Sun-Times* notes that "many historians, including [Dan] Carter, believe they were innocent."[119] By the time this article was written, virtually *every* credible historian had come to this conclusion. It is possible that the paper felt constrained by notions of objectivity here, since it might be accused of a failure to provide balance were it to effectively declare that a state had unjustly prosecuted, and a series of juries had unjustly convicted, nine people for crimes they did not commit, without at least allowing for the state's position to be represented. But however problematic the notion of journalistic objectivity is under the best of circumstances, in this case it would be a truly absurd crutch to rely upon when failing to take even the most minimal anti-racist stance.[120] After all, this article was written a good quarter of a century after Governor Wallace had pardoned Clarence Norris, in effect declaring that all of the Scottsboro defendants were factually innocent of all charges. As far as the state of Alabama was concerned, there was no longer any other side of the story worth presenting. An even more disturbing presentation of the case can be found in a *Boston Globe* review of James Goodman's *Stories of Scottsboro*. The reviewer accepts that there "is little doubt that the Scottsboro Boys were not guilty of rape" but he goes on to say that "they were not innocents," noting that Patterson died in prison after a manslaughter conviction, that Roy Wright killed himself and his wife in 1959, and that Clarence Norris was arrested "numerous times."[121]

Of course, all of the events referred to here occurred many years after the defendants were first accused of rape, and therefore none of this information can reasonably be used to suggest that the defendants weren't "innocents" at the time they were charged and convicted. Most people reading Goodman's book would be likely to come away with the impression that many of the problems that the defendants experienced later in life, including their troubles with the criminal justice system, could be traced in part to the toll taken by the years they spent in prison for crimes that they did not commit. The impression left by the review, that the defendants were fated for at least some run-ins with the law regardless of Scottsboro or of racism, is antithetical to the thesis of Goodman's work.

This failure to offer a full and honest appraisal of one of the most glaring examples of racism within the criminal justice system is likely to mark a significant gap in the degree to which people who are aware of histories of racism are likely to accept the credibility of the mainstream press. If major papers can't acknowledge that the Scottsboro case involved a series of racist prosecutions and convictions, and if it continues to portray the defendants as something other than "innocents," then how likely are readers who are familiar with this history to trust these sources when covering contemporary racial spectacles? One reason that circulation figures for the black press jump significantly when the mass media becomes preoccupied with racial scandals may well be that the mainstream press's failures to fully reckon with the nation's racist past have given some audience members pause when it comes to their coverage of contemporary racism, and have provided them with good reason to look for alternative sources at moments where racism has again become particularly salient for national audiences.

In fact, some commentators in the mainstream press have taken note of the ways that some African Americans have drawn upon their collective memories of Scottsboro in order to frame their understandings of contemporary racial spectacles; understandings that are often at odds with versions of those spectacles that have been endorsed by the mass media. In a special section on the O.J. Simpson criminal trial, a series of commentators in the *New Republic* address an apparent racialized divide in public opinion about Simpson's possible guilt.[122] Jim Sleeper discusses the way that the Revered Al Sharpton responded to a question about whether the controversy surrounding Simpson's acquittal had to do with "differences of perception based on race." Sharpton is quoted as saying that

> It's not the perception of race; it's the experience of race in the criminal justice system where blacks have been treated so differently for so long. A long road does run from the Scottsboro Boys . . . all the way to Simi Valley, where a mostly white jury acquitted Rodney King's assailants (for reasons even more dubious than those used to acquit O.J.). Such experiences have become archetypes, seared into collective black memory.

Sleeper then adds: "But Sharpton and his own one-time attorney, Alton Maddox . . . know better than anyone how black 'perceptions of race' have sometimes distorted even their bitter experience of it." Sleeper cites a series of cases that Maddox was involved in, including the Tawana Brawley case and the acquittal of Lemrick Nelson in 1992 for the murder of Yankel Rosenbaum in Brooklyn's Crown Heights, and writes that like "Maddox, Cochran has mobilized searing black experiences of violation by white authorities to counter a lengthening list of ordinary whites' searing experiences of violation by blacks."[123] The idea that unscrupulous black attorneys can take strategic advantage of African American collective memory is seconded by Jonetta Rose Barras, who argues that Cochran

> understood that the legacy of mistreatment by the American judicial system cannot be fully divested from the individual or collective black psyche . . . Like an amnesiac flashing back to a former life, the O.J. Simpson jury recalled with remote accuracy the pain of a people too often accused of crimes they had not committed. Cochran subtly raised the specter of Emmett Till . . . He reminded the jury about the Scottsboro Boys—the

black Alabamans falsely accused of rape by two white women. He invoked the beating of Rodney King. ... The jury became deaf to closing arguments; their minds were made up. Simpson was just another African American male caught in the snares of the system.[124]

By all rights, this commentary should have been stunning. After all, Barras offers no evidence for his claims about the jury members' deliberative processes.[125] He cites no interview data that might shed light upon what, if any, historical reference points the jury members might have drawn upon. And he provides nothing more than empty assertions that the jurors ignored the closing arguments, thus failing in the duty that they were sworn to uphold.

One might have hoped that the racism apparent in the assumption that black jurors are so easily manipulated, and so blinded by collective memories of racist injustice that they are incapable of rationally evaluating the presentation of evidence arrayed against a black man in the present, would have sparked outrage from every part of the political spectrum. Instead, parts of this basic assumption were shared by one of the commentators who was clearly intended to provide a liberal perspective and political balance in the debate. Law professor Randall Kennedy claims that

> There is a paranoid, conspiracy-minded sector of the population that would honestly though irrationally have rejected the state's argument virtually without regard to the evidence. One of the things that nourishes much of this community, particularly that part comprised of African Americans, is a vivid and bitter memory of wrongful convictions of innocent black men and wrongful acquittals of guilty white men. A key example of the former were the convictions of the Scottsboro Boys in the 1930s.[126]

Kennedy also references the lynching of Emmett Till and says that

> Some readers may find it hard to believe that these despicable events of sixty and forty years ago influence the way that people now evaluate people and events. But ... many blacks recall with a pained disgust the racially motivated miscarriages of justice that they have helplessly witnessed or been told about. That recollection, refreshed occasionally by more recent outrages, prompts them to regard prosecutions against black men— especially black men accused of attacking white women—with such an intense level of skepticism that they demand more than that which should convince most reasonable people of guilt beyond a reasonable doubt.[127]

While Kennedy doesn't present collective memory or racial solidarity as the sole factor accounting for Simpson's acquittal, and doesn't presume to speak for the jurors, he accepts the premise that at least some segment of the African American population has been so wounded by histories of racial injustice that they are incapable of fair and reasoned evaluation of evidence when considering criminal charges against black men.[128]

"The past is never dead. It's not even past."[129]

It is possible, however, to argue that racialized differences in collective memory can have an impact upon contemporary understandings of race and gender without suggesting that the legacy of the past is black irrationality in the present. Because collective memories of Scottsboro have been constructed and invoked differently within the mainstream and black press, I would suggest that references to the case are likely to carry different sets of meanings, and to provide different cues about how to understand contemporary events, for audiences relying upon different media sources. Racialized differences in the construction of collective memory might play an important role in determining how various segments of the population evaluate evidence and determine credibility in highly publicized trials. Audience members of any race who have learned not only about Scottsboro itself, but about race and the criminal justice system in general, by reading the black press, would be likely to come to very different conclusions about later racialized media spectacles than would audience members who have not been exposed to these versions of events: People who are aware that there is a longstanding media fascination with, and history of inflating, allegations of black male sexual deviance and violence might be more likely to approach new media spectacles involving black masculinity with caution. And people who are familiar with the history of criminal penalties and extra-legal violence meted out to black men on the basis of evidence that was subsequently revealed to be fabricated or unreliable seem quite likely to be skeptical of new charges of interracial sexual violence, absent compelling evidence. To the extent that Scottsboro has played a role in fostering racialized differences in collective memory, the legacies of the case can be found in public responses to contemporary racial spectacles. Nowhere is this clearer than in the Kobe Bryant rape case. I turn to that case now.

2

ANATOMY OF A SPECTACLE

Race, Gender, and Memory in the Kobe Bryant Rape Case

On June 30th, 2003, Los Angeles Lakers star Kobe Bryant flew to Eagle, Colorado in order to undergo arthroscopic surgery. The next afternoon, a nineteen-year-old white woman who had been working at Bryant's hotel filed criminal charges against Bryant, reporting that he had sexually assaulted her the previous night. After initially denying that he had either raped or had sex with the woman, Bryant eventually admitted to having had consensual sex with her, but he continued to deny the rape charges.[1] These charges and the consequent legal proceedings became the subject of intense media scrutiny over the next year, only subsiding once the criminal case was dropped and a civil suit settled, in the fall of 2004. The case occasioned almost obsessive coverage from virtually every sector of the media, as hundreds of reporters from domestic and international news organizations, entertainment television, and sports shows camped out across the street from the Eagle County court house so as to be sure to capture every possible shot of Bryant or anyone else involved in the case. Bryant's mug shot, featured on the cover of *Sports Illustrated* (Figure 2.1), became ubiquitous in American popular culture.

This was the most closely followed case involving a professional athlete and the criminal justice system since the O.J. Simpson murder trial, and it was one of the most closely watched cases involving interracial sexuality and allegations of violence in the post–civil-rights era. Because there were nearly two hundred thousand victims of rape, attempted rape, or sexual assault in the United States in 2003,[2] and since there were press reports of an average of nearly one hundred cases a year of professional or college basketball and football players accused of battering or sexually assaulting a woman in the five years preceding the charges against Bryant,[3] it is worth asking why this particular case was singled out for so much attention.

FIGURE 2.1 Sports Illustrated, July 28, 2003: Kobe Bryant Mugshot.

I argue that the answer has to do with the ways in which the case worked to illuminate bitter divisions in American society, as the allegations against Bryant brought forth simmering tensions involving conceptions of black masculinity, white femininity (and mainstream feminism), and the role of sport and celebrity in public life. The questions that concern much of the media (Did he do it? Was she just out for fame? Was his "nice guy" image a façade, hiding true brutality?) are, therefore, not nearly as interesting as the more fundamental issues the case raises about the ideological forces that work to bind the culture of the United States together and that threaten to pull it apart. In order to better illuminate these forces, I suggest that the Bryant case can best be understood by taking account of a broader context of racialized and gendered mass media spectacles, as the divisions revealed by the case involve long histories of struggles by social movements and state actors over the meanings of categories of race and gender.

These struggles have influenced the ways that various segments of the American public understand history. People's understandings of the past help shape their understandings of the present, and social actors can tap into historical under-standings for strategic purposes. Contemporary understandings of race, gender and crime are very much indebted to rhetorical battles fought long ago, and invocations of collective memory can help to determine how various audiences make sense of public dramas unfolding in the mass media. Audiences who are aware of long histories of racist injustice may be appealed to, and may understand events like the Bryant case, differently than would audiences without this kind of historical knowledge. Similarly, people who are aware of the ways that sexist stereotypes have shaped mass media and legal discourse surrounding rape are likely to respond to a highly publicized rape case quite differently than would people who lack such awareness. I argue, therefore, that public responses to the Bryant case cannot be understood without considering the ways that historical sensibilities have been shaped by feminist interventions into public discourse surrounding rape, and anti-racist critiques of stereotypes of black masculinity. Ultimately, the two parties at the center of the criminal trial and civil suit should not be seen merely as individuals, but as figures who represent a variety of discourses of race, gender, and sexuality that have been constructed and refined over centuries. I suggest that one way to understand the public reaction to this case is to examine the ways these discourses have been pitted against each other.

Understandings of the Past as Guide to the Present: Racial Spectacles as Context

While the relationship between personal, collective, and national identities has been a central theme running through the collective memory literature for decades, there has been very little work seeking to explain how people can rely upon collective memory when making sense of events such as racialized and gendered mass media spectacles as they unfold on a national scale. This chapter looks to the Kobe Bryant rape case as a case study that provides some clues about how various segments of the American public might use their understandings of the past as a way to contextualize and come to terms with mass media representations of race, gender, and justice in the present.

As discussed in the introduction to this book, there is no single site that reveals which aspects of the past are collectively remembered, and how these memories are constructed. The diversity of sites of collective remembering, along with the fact that different people remember in different ways, presents a liability for analysts of collective memory, since the multiplicity of ways of remembering can call into question the degree to which such a thing as collective memory can even be said to exist. But to the extent that it makes sense to think that members of groups in society share common historical reference points and some sense of the past (at least with other group members, if not also with members of other groups), acknowledgement of the multiplicity of collective memories can provide an important analytic tool, since this multiplicity provides a clue about disparate reactions to contemporary social dramas. Because people use their past experiences and their knowledge of the past to help make sense of contemporary events, it makes sense to think that differences in collective memory might lead to, and help explain, differences in public opinion and reactions to such racialized dramas as the Bryant rape case.

One way to gain some sense of group differences in collective memory is to examine differences in the kinds of "memory resources," or materials available for constructing a sense of the past, that are shared by different groups. Again, there is no end to the kinds of resources that might be looked to, but one particularly important memory resource that can be looked to in order to begin to gauge the kinds of historical understandings that various constituencies might bring to bear when seeking to make sense of particularly potent racial spectacles is the news media. Journalism has been said to be "the first draft of history," but it might make sense to see it as the first draft of collective memory as well. Jill Edy writes that "Journalists' depictions of the past have repercussions for the ways in which a community relates to its past. It may be that journalists' work impacts whether we remember our past at all."[4]

While every part of the mass media has a role to play in the construction of collective memory, journalism may be particularly powerful since

> The documentary style of journalists' work gives them a unique authority in telling the story of the past. That authority may make for more powerful emotional connections on the part of the audience. The viewer who sits through action and horror films without difficulty may find the image of Robert Kennedy as he lay dying on the floor of a hotel kitchen far more troubling because it is "real."[5]

The emotional investment that people make in the news, and the fact that journalistic accounts often form the raw material for later accounts of events which can be dramatized in film, television, or literature, or commented upon in music or other forms of art, suggest that the news is a uniquely important site for investigations of the dynamics of collective memory. For that reason, an analysis of press coverage served as the first step in my investigation of the role of collective memory in the Kobe Bryant case.

In order to gain a sense of how differences in collective memory might play into public understandings of the Kobe Bryant case, I have analyzed the ways that a variety of news outlets reported on the case, and the ways that coverage of the charges invoked collective memory or relied upon assumed knowledge about the past.[6] Differences in the kinds of historical context that are offered by a particular kind of media outlet can play an important role in how the audience for that kind of news will approach the case. Key examples of news invocations of collective memory include efforts on the part of some African American newspapers to contextualize the charges against Bryant by referencing histories of lynching, and efforts by the mainstream press to explain concerns over public disclosure of the alleged victim's sexual history by referencing struggles waged by the anti-rape movement in the 1970s. These examples, discussed at greater length below, should suffice to demonstrate that the consumers of the African American press, no matter their own race, are provided with very different kinds of shared resources than are consumers of the mainstream press, even as there are certainly people who have access to both kinds of news sources.

My analysis of news coverage of the Bryant case seeks to provide some insight into the dynamics of collective memory, and to touch upon some of the ways that various segments of the American public might use their understandings of the past when trying to make sense of the politics of race, gender, and justice in the present. But in order to begin to assess the ways that various audiences rely upon collective memory in order to make sense of contemporary circumstances, it is necessary to look beyond coverage of those contemporary circumstances, and to begin to consider audiences' pre-existing understandings of the past.

The first part of my analysis of the case discusses the kinds of historical context that various audiences might have brought to bear when trying to come to terms with the case. To provide a sense of the kinds of collective memories that coverage of the case was likely to evoke, I build upon existing scholarship about the racial dynamics of the NBA, and about media representations of rape and of allegations of interracial sexual violence. I provide a brief discussion of some of the key racial spectacles that were often referred to explicitly in coverage of the Bryant case, and that have been at the center of a tremendous number of "memory projects," or "concerted efforts to secure presence for certain elements of the past."[7] These are events that were covered in hundreds, or thousands, of articles, that have been the subject of documentary films, or that have provided the occasion for national debates regarding the state of contemporary race relations. I suggest that it is reasonable to think that even when they are not invoked explicitly, they are the kinds of events that some segments of the population had at their disposal when looking for context to help think about the case.

Finally, I look to one other kind of "memory project" that I argue is relevant for understandings of the case. One of the most controversial aspects of the case involved the Court's treatment of the privacy interests of the alleged victim. In order to explain the privacy issues in the case, coverage frequently invoked the past, referencing struggles over rape jurisprudence in the 1970s. Since this is one of the most consequential and explicit ways that the press sought to construct and rely upon collective memory, I address this issue at length. I investigate the ways that rape-reform legislation serves as the institutional embodiment of collective memory of a sexist legal system, and of 1970s-era feminist activism. Legal scholars of "Critical Race Theory" have investigated the ways that law has worked to construct categories of race and gender.[8] My discussion of the rape shield statutes builds upon this body of scholarship, arguing that rape reform legislation has helped to shape understandings of sexualized stereotypes and privacy. Rape-reform legislation emerged as a direct response to the anti-rape movement, and contemporary media discussions of this legislation invoke memories of rape victims being tried for their sexuality and blamed for their own rapes.

This chapter suggests that an analysis of collective memory is crucially important for understanding the kinds of racialized and gendered divisions that so frequently define public reactions to racial spectacles. I argue that the Bryant case cannot be understood without grappling with ways in which collective memories of racist violence and sexist injustice were constructed and deployed within the mass media. More generally, this chapter highlights the ways that social struggles of the past continue to reverberate and work to shape understandings of race and gender in the present.

Rape Allegations and Memories of Racial Spectacles

The spectacle surrounding the Bryant rape case is, of course, inseparable from Bryant's fame as a superstar player in the National Basketball Association. Bryant was a key member of the Los Angeles Lakers team that won national championships in three consecutive years, from 2000–2002. While the Lakers had not performed particularly well during the 2002–2003 season, the team's fortunes appeared to be on the rise during the summer of 2003, since the Lakers were in the process of signing All-Star players Gary Payton and Karl Malone. Payton was considered one of the best point guards to ever play the game, while Malone was the second highest scorer in NBA history. Payton and Malone would complement Bryant and Shaquille O'Neal, who was widely considered the most dominant center in the league, if not in league history. The team would be coached by Phil Jackson, who had coached the 2000–2002 Laker teams after leading the Chicago Bulls to six championships with Michael Jordan as his star player. This array of talent led many professional sports commentators to predict another championship, and to speculate about whether the Lakers would become the next NBA "dynasty." Separately, each member of this potential dynasty was capable of drawing tremendous amounts of media attention (Gary Payton had a reputation as an extremely articulate and charismatic "trash talker"; Karl Malone, in contrast, was known as a folksy hero who still darned his own socks, despite making tens of millions of dollars a year; Shaquille O'Neal was known for his wild parties and entertaining press conferences, along with his squabbles with Phil Jackson and Kobe Bryant; Bryant was one of the most athletically gifted and dazzling players in the NBA, regularly drawing comparisons to Michael Jordan; and Phil Jackson was known not only as the winningest coach in NBA history, but also for his quirky "Zen-Master" approach to the game), but together, under the white hot spotlights of the Los Angeles media market, this new "dream team" was already fated to become a nightly spectacle of the highest order, even if the criminal allegations directed against Kobe Bryant had never surfaced. But while this particular coach and group of players was perhaps uniquely likely to attract media scrutiny, the spectacle owes something to the fact that this was not just any professional sports league, but the NBA.

Douglas Kellner describes NBA basketball as

sexy, showing glistening and well-honed male bodies in a state of semi-undress, clad in skimpy jerseys and shorts. Compared to the male gladiator body armor of football players and the nineteenth-century full body attire of baseball, basketball present[s] a mode of male beefcake, especially with TV close-ups capturing the hard and agile bodies of NBA hunks.[9]

Boyd and Shropshire also remark upon the relative vulnerability and intimacy of basketball players, writing that, as opposed to

> baseball and especially football, in basketball the player's faces are easy to see and thus easy to use in advertisements. Because of this intimacy, there is a clear identification between fans and individual players, or at least with players as we perceive them to be.[10]

The physical vulnerability and intimacy of basketball, and the heightened possibilities for fan identification with NBA players are particularly notable given the racial dynamics of a sport in which a disproportionate number of players are black, while the majority of fans are white.[11]

Alexander notes that black bodies displayed "for public consumption have been an American spectacle for centuries. This history moves from public rapes, beatings, and lynchings to the gladiatorial arenas of basketball and boxing."[12] The bodies of African American athletes from a variety of sports have been at the center of a number of mass media spectacles in recent years, most notably involving Mike Tyson and O.J. Simpson, but NBA players have been particularly likely to occupy center stage in American racial discourse. When Latrell Sprewell allegedly choked and threatened to kill his coach, the media regularly "represented the incident in ways that vilified Sprewell through the use of derogatory images of Black men," failing to consider Sprewell's claims about the coach's abusive behavior, and frequently referring to Sprewell in animalistic terms, variously characterizing him as a "garbage-picking raccoon," a "tamed lion" or other "subordinated jungle beasts."[13] Chris Webber, Allen Iverson, and Ron Artest have all received substantial media attention for violent actions, while it would be impossible to begin to quantify the amount of ink spilled documenting the sexual behavior of Dennis Rodman, Wilt Chamberlain, and Magic Johnson. Even Michael Jordan, whose dominant media representation is a perfectly tamed and commodified image of black masculinity, has been packaged as a sex object in his ads for Hanes underwear.[14] More broadly, Sarah Banet-Weiser argues that media construction of the NBA has been shaped by racist discourse, claiming that the "NBA exploits and makes exotic the racist stereotypes of the Black menace, even as it domesticates this cultural figure."[15]

Tucker sums up many of the points discussed above by noting that "in ways absent from other sports, then, the Blackness, sexuality, and the physical and emotional vulnerability of the majority of players are stamped on the face of the

FIGURE 2.2 Hank Willis Thomas, 2008. "Hang Time Circa 1923." Inkjet on Canvass.

Source: Courtesy of Jack Shainman Gallery.

game of basketball."[16] The racial dynamics of the NBA spectacle have been of immense interest for anti-racist activists and have been addressed in the work of visual artists such as Hank Willis Thomas. Willis Thomas's "Hang Time Circa 1923" (Figure 2.2) features the iconic Nike/Michael Jordan "Jumpman" logo, hanging from a noose in a tree.

"Hang time" is a term that has been used to define the moment when the most athletic basketball stars appear to float in the air after they have launched off the ground to make a shot, and after their defenders have fallen back to earth. The term was regularly applied to Michael Jordan, and, later, to Kobe Bryant. Willis Thomas's work draws his audience back to 1923, during the heart of the lynching era, in order to suggest that the contemporary fascination with black athletes cannot be easily separated from a very different understanding of what it means to "hang," while his appropriation of the Nike logo suggests that the NBA continues practices of commodifying the black male body that were central to the spectacle of lynching. "Hang Time Circa 1923" serves as a powerful reminder that NBA players are always already at the center of an eroticized and racialized mass media spectacle. For this reason, it is somewhat predictable that allegations of sexual misconduct on the part of an NBA superstar would be immediately seized upon and scrutinized for larger lessons about celebrity, gender, and racial conflict in American society. When the allegations involve charges of interracial sexual assault, as in the Bryant case, the resulting media attention can powerfully, and uncomfortably, resonate with age-old narratives of black sexuality.

Race Matters

There was notable frustration throughout the duration of the case on the part of various commentators who were unable to come to terms with people who "insisted" on seeing the case in racialized terms. These critics argued instead that the only issues of import in the case had to do with gender, celebrity, and wealth. Jessica Johnson, for example, warned Bryant's defense team that "Very few jurors will have a sympathetic ear if . . . [Bryant's lawyers provide] an attenuated recitation in court about black men who were victims of Southern white racism,"[17] while E.R. Shipp expressed concern with people who were "trapped in the time warp of race" and intent upon weighing the case down with the "nation's historical baggage."[18] And yet, opinion polls suggested that there were racialized differences in public reactions to the case. A USA *Today*/CNN/Gallup poll conducted in August of 2003 showed that white respondents were nearly twice as likely as black respondents to see the charges against Bryant as "probably true," while blacks were nearly five times more likely than whites to be "very sympathetic" towards Bryant.[19] When attempting to explain this apparently racial division in reactions to the case, it seems reasonable to suggest that understandings of history may play a role in determining how people evaluate evidence and think of media coverage. Histories of racialized spectacles might be particularly noteworthy in this regard.

In his analysis of the Bryant case, David Leonard references a contemporary and historical media "obsession with Black male sexuality and its dangerous relationship with White female sexuality"[20] to contest claims that blacks were inappropriately "infusing race" into their understandings of the case, and to demonstrate that race was, in fact, central to the quantity and content of media coverage of the case. Leonard discusses the tremendous amount of media coverage surrounding Magic Johnson's HIV positive status, and the "constant coverage of groupies/sexual appetites of Black athletes," and argues that the "mainstream media voyeuristically imagines Black male athletes as hypersexual bodies."[21] Leonard observes that the trials of white male celebrities charged with sexual crimes, including Mark Chamura, Marv Albert, and William Kennedy Smith, weren't covered nearly as extensively as were the cases of Johnson, Bryant, Mike Tyson, Michael Jackson, or O.J. Simpson.[22] While it is true that none of the white defendants that Leonard mentions were nearly as famous before facing criminal charges as their black counterparts, it is also true that sexual crimes in the United States have consistently been personified by African American men within the mass media.[23] Thus, for example, the "representative figure" for sexual harassment is Clarence Thomas,[24] while media stories surrounding Michael Jackson's alleged child molestation far outnumber the stories of any of the individual priests who were actually convicted of child abuse in the Catholic church scandals.[25]

The media template for stories highlighting allegations of black sexual excess and deviance can be traced back to the narratives that were used to justify lynching in the post-Reconstruction period. Leonard writes that "the discursive field surrounding rape allegations represents a continuation of long-standing fears, myths, and hatred of Black male bodies, all of which are wrapped up in the histories of lynchings, injustice, and state violence."[26] Lynchings, in particular, played a major role in fostering a set of symbolic connections between black masculinity and sexualized criminality. As noted in the introductory chapter, while there are many parallel histories of lynching, involving victims of different races and ethnicities, the vast majority of lynchings occurred in the southern United States after Reconstruction, and the primary victims were African American men.[27] The fact that there was seldom any factual basis for claims that lynchings were motivated by rape did nothing to diminish the power that public defenses of lynching had to shape understandings of race and gender. By the early years of the twentieth century, these defenses took the form of increasingly standardized narratives, featuring pure white women, chivalrous and heroic white male defenders, and monstrous black brute rapists. Reports of "spectacle lynchings," disseminated to national audiences by an approving white press, reinforced such narratives, while the mythical black rapist became a popular figure in virtually every arena of popular culture. The character of Gus in D.W. Griffith's *The Birth of a Nation* (1915) is only the most famous embodiment of this figure.[28]

More Than Memory: Contemporary Racial Spectacles

It would be a mistake to suggest that the racist stereotypes that were so central to the dynamics of lynching have remained static, or that their strength is undiminished. Instead, the Scottsboro defense movement (discussed in Chapter 1) and the broader antilynching movement of the late nineteenth and early twentieth centuries devoted considerable resources towards challenging these stereotypes almost from the moment of their inception.[29] Dramatic evidence of the success of the battles over lynching rhetoric can be found in the reception of Clarence Thomas's outraged declaration that he was the victim of a "high tech lynching" as he faced Anita Hill's sexual harassment allegations during his nomination process to become Associate Justice on the United States Supreme Court. After all, when Thomas explained his charge by noting that the history of lynching involved "invariably, or in many instances, a relationship with sex, and an accusation that that person cannot shake off," and argued that this history was relevant for his own circumstances, since Hill's accusations "play to the worst stereotypes we have about Black men in this country," no one countered him by suggesting that lynching really *was* a method of punishing black rapists.[30] Instead, Thomas was able to count upon the widespread recognition that lynching was a brutal crime based on racist stereotypes. The antilynching movement's claim that the rape charges in lynching narratives were myths had become, by 1991, part of a racialized common sense.[31]

Acknowledging that stereotypes of black male sexuality have changed over time does not, however, mean that they are irrelevant for understanding more recent racialized media spectacles. Indeed, there is no shortage of examples where the circulation of such stereotypes has had dramatic consequences. Thus, for example, political advertisements in the 1988 presidential election, featuring the convicted rapist William ("Willie") Horton, associated Massachusetts governor Michael Dukakis with the looming specter of black rape and played a key role in costing Dukakis the election.[32] Versions of the black beast stereotype, lacking only the explicitly sexualized dimensions, were readily accepted when invoked in 1989 by Charles Stuart, in Boston, and in 1994, by Susan Smith, in South Carolina.[33] Perhaps the most dramatic case involving stereotypes of black male sexuality in the post-civil rights era involved Trisha Meili, a white investment banker who was raped, beaten, and left for dead in New York's Central Park in 1989.

Meili (who had been identified only as "the Central Park Jogger" until revealing her identity in 2003 as part of a promotional campaign for her upcoming book tour) remembers nothing about the attack, and has never claimed to be able to identify her assailants.[34] But five teenagers from Harlem (four were black, one was Latino) were soon arrested for the crime, and they were tried and convicted the next year. There was never any forensic evidence or witness testimony tying the defendants to the attack, so they were convicted solely on the basis of confessions they later tried to retract, claiming that they had been coerced. In January of 2002, a man named Matias Reyes, who had been convicted of a series of rapes and murders, and who was serving a thirty-three and a third year to life sentence, confessed to having raped Meili, and said that he had acted alone.[35] DNA tests quickly confirmed that the semen that had been found at the crime scene matched Reyes'. In December of 2002, shortly after the final defendant had completed his term and been released from prison, the State Supreme Court set aside the guilty verdicts.

The case has been widely compared to the Scottsboro case, since both cases involve coerced confessions from innocent young black men falsely accused of interracial rape, and belated admissions on the part of the mainstream press that there had been a racist rush to judgment. While the cases are crucially different in many respects (there are, for example, no doubts that the Central Park attack occurred), the similarities suggest that there are important continuities between contemporary discourse surrounding race, sexuality, and crime, and under-standings that are commonly understood as relics of the past. The legal case against the Central Park defendants is troubling on its own, raising serious questions about possibly coercive interrogation practices and prosecutorial reliance upon questionable confessions, but equally disturbing is the news coverage of, and public reaction to, the attacks and the defendants.[36]

The attack on Meili was not the only violent crime committed in Central Park on April 19th, 1989, nor even the only violent crime that her alleged attackers were accused of.[37] Instead, there was a series of assaults in the park that night, carried out by approximately thirty teenagers from the Harlem area. The defendants in the assault upon Meili were also convicted of charges including assault, robbery, and rioting. Even as the guilty verdicts in the assault upon Meili were vacated, these convictions were let stand. From the beginning, the media frenzy surrounding the crimes in Central Park that night relied heavily upon racially coded language and stereotyping. The group of teens was consistently referred to in animalistic terms, most frequently as a "wolf pack," and a new term was coined to describe their actions that night: "wilding." The *New York Post* defined wilding as what happens when "packs of bloodthirsty teens from the tenements, bursting with boredom and rage, roam the streets getting kicks from an evening of ultra-violence."[38] The mainstream press accepted the validity of the confessions without any serious scrutiny, even when crucial elements of the confessions contradicted each other, and even when DNA evidence revealed the overall weakness of the prosecution's case.

The tone of the news coverage was echoed by public figures, as then Mayor Ed Koch regularly referred to the defendants as "monsters," while Donald Trump paid for full page ads in every daily paper in New York calling for the death penalty in the case, saying that the defendants "should be forced to suffer."[39] The hysteria generated in the case paved the way for the reinstatement of the death penalty in New York, and contributed to "rage against juvenile crime" at the national level, and to a sentiment that led, by the mid-1990s, to the passage of laws in most states providing for children to be tried as adults.[40]

Race, Memory, and Skepticism

This is an admittedly skeletal history of some of the most dramatic racialized spectacles that helped to set the stage for the Bryant case, but it should be sufficient to provide a sense of the kinds of context available to various audiences when trying to make sense of the Bryant case. Audiences who are aware that there is a longstanding media fascination with, and history of inflating, allegations of black male sexual deviance and violence might be more likely to approach new media spectacles involving black masculinity with caution. And people who are familiar with the history of criminal penalties and extra-legal violence meted out to black men on the basis of evidence that was subsequently revealed to be fabricated or unreliable seem quite likely to be skeptical of new charges of interracial sexual violence, absent compelling evidence. Indeed, Bryant's defense team tapped into this history at one point in the pre-trial maneuvering when lead attorney Pamela Mackey noted that "there is lots of history of Black men being falsely accused of this crime by White women,"[41] while the black press regularly sought to contextualize the Bryant case by referencing the kinds of history that I've outlined above. For example, the *New York Amsterdam News* claimed that

> Bryant is reliving the horrors of the Scottsboro Boys trial in medieval Alabama. No Black man, regardless of economic status, can receive a fair

trial when a white female makes a false accusation against him, especially when the allegation is rape.[42]

An article in the *Mississippi Link* expanded upon this theme, arguing that "Since the turbulent 1960s, lynchings and castrations have gone from literal to figurative. Figuratively, lynchings of high profile Blacks are done through the media, presumably to send a message to all other Blacks and to the amusement of whites."[43] The Tallahassee *Capital Outlook* used collective memory of mob violence as an explanation for reports of racialized differences in public reactions to the case:

> Few crimes, if any, draw the fear and ire of Blacks more than the alleged rape of a white woman. As recently as 50 years ago, throughout the South, Black men were subject to summary lynching for the mere accusation of sexual impropriety against a white woman. As such, when a prosecutor ignores the scientific evidence that weakens the accuser's credibility in favor of sticking to the veracity of her story, Blacks remain skeptical.[44]

Collective memory works here as a lens: it encourages readers to focus on the case in ways that require evaluating evidence quite differently than do the mass media.[45] For readers who follow the logic of such accounts, it is impossible to see the Bryant case in isolation since mass media representations of the case become understood as links in long chains of images of black men as sexually monstrous. Bryant himself cannot be seen as an individual superstar with immense wealth and privilege, but is instead connected to what Gooding-Williams would see as a vast "storehouse" of racial imagery.[46] A substantial portion of any racial divide in reactions to the Bryant case may well have to do with the fact that African Americans are more likely to have been exposed to versions of collective memory that include knowledge of spectacularized forms of racist injustice.

But if racialized differences in collective memory account for some of the hesitancy on the part of African Americans (and, it should be said, of people from other racial groups who are also familiar with the kinds of history discussed above) to accept the validity of the rape allegations in the Bryant case, memories of the past were not the only basis for a belief that the case against Bryant was tainted by racism. Instead, aspects of the racial politics directly surrounding the Bryant case itself should have been cause for serious concern. Eagle County, where the trial was to take place, is "almost 90% white, and less than .02% Black."[47] More important, the Eagle County Sheriff's department had a well-documented history of racial profiling, and had settled a lawsuit after it was revealed that deputies had stopped hundreds of black and Latino drivers, telling them that "they fit a profile of drug smugglers because each had California license plates and 'because of the color of their skin.'" Leonard argues that this "history and the fact that the lead investigator in the Bryant case was named in the racial profiling case is a testament to the ways in which race will continue to filter interpretations and understandings of the Kobe Bryant trial," although his broader point is that the bulk of commentators in the mass media were intent upon *ignoring* this history, or declaring it irrelevant.[48] Compelling evidence that the racism of the Eagle County legal establishment was not confined to the past came with the disclosure that members of the district attorney's and sheriff's offices "had ordered T-shirts depicting a stick figure being hanged" and including "derogatory statements" about Bryant.[49] Bryant's defense team characterized the t-shirts as "invocative of Klan lynching."[50] District Attorney Mark Hurlbert initially denied that anyone on his staff had ordered any of the shirts, but then issued a statement apologizing for having been unintentionally misleading, and saying that he had "disposed" of his own shirt immediately.[51] For anyone who was already wary of the possibility that Bryant might, as a black man charged with raping a white woman, be a metaphorical lynch victim facing trumped up charges, the fact that such T-shirts were owned by key members of the legal establishment that was seeking to try him could hardly have been reassuring. Thus, it is likely that, for many observers, a collective memory of lynching and other racist spectacles was bolstered by the contemporary state of racial affairs in Eagle County on the eve of Bryant's trial.[52]

The Institutionalization of Memory: Feminist Struggle and Rape Reform Legislation

If there was good reason for skepticism about the charges against Bryant on the part of people whose sensibilities and "common sense" beliefs were shaped by a knowledge and collective memory of racism, there were also ways that collective memory may have prepared other audiences to see Bryant as likely to have committed the crime. Most important to consider here are people whose understanding of rape is informed by feminism and by the anti-rape movement of the 1970s. Such people would know that false allegations of rape are rare, since women who charge rape are often subjected to brutal treatment by the legal system and generally would have very little to gain from false charges. Moreover, because a key part of the legal maneuvering in the lead up to the trial centered around the accuser's sexual and medical history, the case resonated quite strongly with decades-long feminist concerns about violations of rape victims' privacy.

White Female Sexuality on Trial

The sexual history of Bryant's accuser became an issue almost immediately after charges were filed, since Bryant's defense team wanted to argue that injuries to Bryant's accuser were a result of having had sex with someone other than Bryant. Rowe, McKay, and Miller have argued that in racial sports spectacles of the 1990s involving Magic Johnson and Mike Tyson, discourses that had figured black male athletes as powerful and invincible were transformed into discourses of black male vulnerability by refocusing the discussion and invoking stereotypes of "active" female sexuality. They write that "In this way, the body of the Black male elite athlete is protected from racist discourses that seek to reduce it to no more than blind sexual urges—only by projecting such identity upon the bodies of women."[53]

The notion of linking representations of black male monstrosity with images of white women's sexual excess can also be traced back to lynching narratives and the discourse of chivalry. Black men may have been the most direct targets of the racist discourse surrounding lynching, but because lynchings were defended in the name of white women, lynching narratives also worked to place limits upon white women's sexual freedom. As Hall has argued, "the right of the southern lady to protection presupposed her obligation to obey."[54] While lynching has been widely understood as a method of terrorizing African American communities and enforcing racialized hierarchies, stereotypes of black sexual monstrosity worked to create a "legacy of terror"[55] that reinforced white women's dependency upon white men. White women who failed to live up to the standards of behavior suggested by the stereotype of the "pure white woman" that was so central to lynching narratives were demonized as "fallen women."[56] This stereotype was fully in play during the Kobe Bryant criminal proceedings, but was not uncontested. Instead, use of this stereotype provided the opportunity for the prosecution and the press to discuss the importance of rape reform legislation, and, in the process, to invoke collective memories of a sexist legal system and of feminist activism.

The strategy of representing Bryant's accuser as excessively sexually active was on display in the preliminary hearing, when the lead defense attorney asked the detective who had interviewed Bryant's accuser if the accuser's injuries might be consistent with having had "sex with three men in three days."[57] This question set the tone for the defense strategy throughout the case. The prosecution argued that this defense strategy conflicted with Colorado's rape shield law, that was intended to provide victims of sexual assault with "greater protection from humiliating and embarrassing 'fishing expeditions' into their past sexual conduct, without a preliminary showing that evidence thus elicited will be relevant to some issue in the pending case."[58] The defense argued that there was no conflict, since the evidence they were looking for was directly relevant to the question of whether the victim's injuries were sustained through the violent act that Bryant was accused of. The judge in the case agreed with the defense, allowing limited evidence about the sexual activity of the alleged victim, but this decision only came after a series of blunders on the part of the court that catapulted the issues of rape victims' privacy and rape shield laws to a national stage.

The court twice released Bryant's accuser's name on its website, citing "clerical errors," and mistakenly emailed copies of the transcripts from a closed-door session regarding the admissibility of evidence about the accuser's sexual history to members of a variety of news organizations. The trial judge apologized to the accuser and ordered the news organizations not to publish any information contained in the transcripts,[59] but the apologies did little to reassure the accuser or her family, who decided to stop cooperating with the prosecution, thus effectively ending the criminal case. Advocates for rape victims saw the decision to allow evidence about the accuser's sexual experiences into trial, along with the court's errors, as potentially chilling. A spokesperson for the Colorado Coalition Against Sexual Assault reacted to the court's actions by saying "no wonder women are so afraid to go to police when they are raped . . . . Not only do you have to relive the rape, but the defense lawyers try to broadcast every other aspect of your private life."[60] But while rape victim advocates were critical of the court's actions, they tended to argue that the most serious breaches of the alleged victim's privacy were beyond the ability of the court to prevent. As the media searched relentlessly for every detail of the alleged victim's personal life, not only exposing her name but also speculating about her mental health and providing information about her sexual past, the case exposed the limits to the protection that rape shield laws could provide.[61] In an opinion piece for the *New York Times*, Dahlia Lithwick summed up some of the problems with contemporary rape jurisprudence, observing that rape shield statutes were written with "stranger rape" cases in mind, and that "The legal system is inadequate to the task of resolving acquaintance rape cases, and the media actually exacerbates the original injustice—be that a rape, or a false accusation of rape." By the time that the district attorney dropped the criminal charges against Bryant, Lithwick's conclusion that "rape shield laws don't work, particularly in high-profile cases" was widely shared.[62]

Rape shield laws were a direct response to arguments made by the anti-rape movement of the 1970s that the practice of allowing testimony about a rape victim's sexual history into evidence was a key factor in the underreporting of rape, as it ensured that legal proceedings surrounding rape worked to place the victim, and her sexuality, on trial. The ordeal faced by rape victims in the courtroom, often referred to as "a second rape," could be a powerful deterrent when considering filing charges. In addition, the anti-rape movement argued that allowing irrelevant information about a victim's sexuality into legal proceedings worked to seriously taint the legal notion of "consent," which is central in determining whether a rape has been committed. For example, in her analysis of rape reforms, Ireland notes that "'consent' in a rape case has been found in the manner of the victim's dress, in her presence at a bar, or in her previous sexual conduct."[63] The rape reform movement achieved some of the most notable legislative victories of 1970s-era feminism, and by 1980, forty-five states had rewritten their rape laws to limit the admissibility of evidence about an alleged rape victim's sexual history.[64] I would suggest that the rape shield statutes can be seen as the institutionalized embodiment of collective memories of sexist treatment of rape victims, and of feminist efforts to challenge such treatment, since these laws point to the problems of the past that account for their origin: presumably, no one would have bothered to write such laws if the treatment of rape victims within the criminal justice system hadn't been seen as a serious problem.

Law As Memory

The Colorado rape shield statute, enacted in 1977, held that "except in certain instances, in rape and sexual assault cases, evidence of the victim's prior or subsequent sexual conduct is presumed to be irrelevant."[65] Collective memories of the conditions that prompted rape shield laws have been constructed and reinforced every time the laws have been invoked or contested within the criminal justice system. For example, a 1978 Colorado Supreme Court decision reflects upon the genesis of the Colorado law, noting that before the statute was enacted

> defense counsel in a rape case was accorded wide latitude in cross-examining the prosecutrix. Since her credibility was placed in issue when she testified, her prior sexual conduct was considered admissible to undermine her credibility . . . [but] it has become apparent that in many instances a rape victim's past sexual conduct may have no bearing at all on either her credibility or the issue of consent. In fact in many cases, cross-examination probing her sexual history has served only to put her on trial instead of the defendant.[66]

Since I am juxtaposing histories and memories of the sexist treatment that rape victims have faced at the hands of the legal system with histories and memories of racist spectacles centering upon unfounded allegations of black male sexual deviance and violence, it is worth noting that there is no parallel construction of spectacle and causes célèbres. While images of lynch victims and of lynch mobs have been circulated widely enough to have been seared into a mainstream anti-racist consciousness (they have appeared in documentaries on American race relations, in high school textbooks, and even in rap videos and Hollywood movies), and while the name Emmett Till has achieved a place alongside Rosa Parks and Martin Luther King Jr. in collective memory of the civil rights era, there is no similar iconic and widely disseminated history of rape victims' treatment at the hands of a sexist legal system: there is no case where the mere mention of an individual's name would conjure up images and memories of a legal system that turned the tables on rape victims, trying them for their sexuality. But collective memories of this kind of treatment *are* kept alive not only through the invocation of the rape-shield statutes, but also through news reports about these laws. When rape shield laws were discussed in the coverage of the Bryant case, the media addressed not only the contemporary relevance of these laws, but also the social conditions that prompted them. Recht and Kornfeld write, for example, that decades ago, courts admitted evidence in sexual assault cases of the alleged victim's character and reputation for chastity, i.e., whether she was sexually active. The Rape Shield Statute, passed in Colorado (and in many other states) in the 1970s, was appropriately enacted to change that situation.[67]

Similarly, an op-ed piece in the Denver *Rocky Mountain News* notes that "In the 1970s, legislatures across the country enacted 'rape shield laws' to help protect rape victims from the re-victimization they suffered as a matter of course when they had the courage to report what happened to them."[68] News coverage of the legal maneuvering surrounding the Bryant case thus provided a centrally important opportunity for tapping into and shoring up collective memories of the sexist treatment accorded rape victims by the legal system in the 1970s, at the precise moment that the prosecution was relying upon the successes of 1970s-era feminist activism by invoking the rape shield statute in an effort to defend the interests of Bryant's accuser.

Privacy and the Limits of the Law

The media's obsession with every detail of the life of the alleged victim in the Bryant case demonstrated that, at least in high-profile cases, rape shield statutes were incapable of fully protecting privacy rights, since the kinds of abuse that state legislatures were concerned with could happen outside of the courtroom. A good deal of the potentially embarrassing information in the Bryant case was, however, gathered by the defense team and contained in the documents that the court mistakenly released to the press. So, when the judge attempted to prevent publication of the leaked information, the goal was to prevent the court's actions from contributing unnecessarily to a climate outside the courtroom that could become even more emotionally abusive.[69] Still, the media organizations that were told not to publish the leaked transcripts immediately appealed the order. The Colorado Supreme Court heard the case and decided that while there is generally a "heavy presumption" against the constitutional validity of any form of prior restraint (any effort on the part of the state to prevent publication of any statement), Colorado's rape shield statute addressed a state interest of the "highest order," and prior restraint could be justified as a method of securing this interest. The Court allowed the decision to ban disclosure of the contents of the transcripts. The media organizations appealed the Colorado Supreme Court's ruling, asking the United States Supreme Court to rule that the ban on publication was unconstitutional. Justice Stephen Breyer weighed in, refusing to overturn the ban, but saying that the news organizations could re-file their petition after waiting two days, since "a brief delay will permit the state courts to clarify, perhaps avoid, the controversy at issue here."[70] The trial judge ordered the prosecution and defense to produce an edited version of the transcripts that could be released to the media. Rather than risk an unfavorable ruling from the Supreme Court that might be a major setback for first amendment principles, the news organizations appear to have made a tactical decision to end the appeals process.[71]

The prior restraint issues were of major concern to the media, and provided the occasion for dozens of articles weighing the need to protect rape victims' privacy with the public need to be informed. The bulk of articles that I examined that discussed the legal strategies in the case focused on the rape shield statutes. The need for and history behind such statutes was addressed frequently. Analysis of the rape shield laws often entailed discussions of whether particular pieces of information about the victim's sexuality or mental health were relevant in determining her credibility, and whether the rape shield laws might exclude information that was necessary for Bryant's legal team to mount an appropriate defense. Press accounts often misinterpreted the Colorado rape shield law by suggesting that it ruled out *any* evidence about an alleged victim's sexual past.[72] In fact, while it was true that the law created a legal presumption that such evidence was irrelevant, a number of exceptions to that presumption were provided for by the statute. Bryant's defense team was thus regularly mischaracterized as challenging the rape shield statute. [73] Instead, the strategy that proved most successful for the defense was to argue that evidence of the alleged victim's sexual activity in the time period surrounding the alleged assault should be seen as falling within the exceptions carved out by the law.[74] This mischaracterization was not inconsequential. Because the media regularly focused on the rape shield laws, representing them, appropriately, as the legislative embodiment of the 1970s anti-rape movement,[75] the notion that Bryant's defense was in conflict with these laws made it possible to see the prosecution as a surrogate for feminism, and to see Bryant's defense as having to overcome not the claims of one woman, but the institutionalized force of an entire social movement.[76]

A Clash of Discourses and Contests Over Memory

For some commentators whose skepticism about the charges against Bryant was rooted in collective memories of lynching and knowledge of past racist spectacles, the specter of a feminist movement pitted against a black man was all too familiar. For anti-racist activists, allegations of white women's victimization at the hands of black men have long required a great deal of care and scrutiny because such allegations were central to the dynamics of lynching and the maintenance of white supremacy. Hutchinson writes that

> there's a reason many blacks buy Bryant's racial victim claim. For decades, the Klan used white fears of black men raping white women to terrorize blacks. Older blacks still have vivid and painful memories of the lynch murders of fourteen year old Emmett Till for allegedly whistling at a white woman in 1955 in Mississippi, and Mack Charles Parker for the alleged rape of a white woman in 1959 in Louisiana.[77]

The anti-rape movement of the 1970s was a largely white women's movement, and it has been long criticized for reliance upon racist stereotypes. Angela Davis's well-known analysis of the anti-rape movement's rhetoric concludes that the foundational texts of the movement, including Susan Brownmiller's 1975 book *Against Our Will*, "have facilitated the resurrection of the timeworn myth of the Black rapist."[78]

The often unacknowledged racist legacies of the anti-rape movement leave contemporary feminist rhetoric particularly vulnerable to claims of racism. For example, one way to explain the ease with which supporters of Clarence Thomas were able to dismiss Anita Hill's allegations of sexual harassment is that the legal strategies animating her charges were a product of the same 1970s-era activism indicted by Davis, and were thus possible to represent as tainted by "white women's feminism." Feminist supporters of Bryant's accuser found themselves dealing with a similar dynamic. For example, Ishmael Reed writes about the Bryant case as part of an ongoing "war against Black men," and sees what he refers to as the "Ku Klux Feminists" of CNN, including Naomi Wolf and Wendy Murphy, as important soldiers in this war.[79] Reed goes on to argue that Susan Brownmiller "and other well known feminists have an irrational hatred of Black men."[80] The comparison to the Klan is a clear indication that Reed's rhetoric is exceptionally inflammatory, but he is not alone in his assessment of the Bryant case as being marked by feminist complicity in the metaphorical lynching of a black man.

Conclusion

In the fall of 2004, after the dismissal of the criminal charges in the Bryant case, the *Los Angeles Times* ran an article titled "Kobe's Second Act: It All Worked Out for Him: No Shaq, No Phil, No Prison. But Have We Worked Out Our Feelings About Him?"[81] The article rehearses some of the details of Bryant's career, and asks, "knowing what we now know, should we root for him?" A similar article focuses on Los Angeles Laker fans and parents, who were said to be "torn over Kobe," "disillusioned by the sexual assault charges," and wrestling with "rooting for one of their favorites."[82] The explanations that are offered in these articles for the conflicted feelings that people have when considering the Bryant case are fairly superficial, revolving around notions of celebrity, the costs of fame, and the inability to know the person beneath the image of the sports hero. But the question of whether to sympathize with Kobe Bryant is a vexing one for anyone concerned with the dynamics of race, gender, and violence as represented within popular culture and the mass media. No doubt there are many reasons that people might be "torn over Kobe," but one set of tensions is never addressed in the media coverage. For audiences who are concerned with a variety of oppressive forces, and whose sensibilities and collective memories are shaped by recognition of the value of struggles for social justice, coming to terms with the Bryant case is no simple matter. As common sense belief systems shaped by anti-racist struggle conflict sharply with common sense belief systems shaped by feminist politics and the anti-rape movement of the 1970s, the question of what, exactly, it means to root for Kobe Bryant remains. Is this possible without trivializing not only the suffering of his alleged victim, but also rape itself? Alternatively, what does it mean to withdraw support from a black man charged with interracial rape, especially once the criminal charges have been dropped? Can this be done without falling prey to some of the most corrosive and enduring racist stereotypes in American society? Rowe et al. argue that the

> difficulty of disentangling assumptions of guilt or innocence of an appalling sexual crime from preexisting racist and sexist discourses—not to mention the knowing exploitation of those discourses by both prosecution and defense—reveals the extent to which ideologies of power are ever-present in the practice of everyday life and in the conduct of cultural politics.[83]

It is not just difficult but impossible to separate thoughts about guilt and innocence from ages-old narratives of race and gender in cases like these and the question of whether or not to root for Kobe Bryant is implicated in, and inseparable from, a clash of discourses. An anti-sexist discourse that would highlight the privacy rights of rape victims clashes with an anti-racist discourse that seeks to link Bryant to victims of a racist legal system, and to victims of extra-legal violence.

In her discussion of racial discourse surrounding the O.J. Simpson case, Kimberlé Crenshaw argues that inadequate attention to the ways that categories of gender and race intersect led to a dominant framing of the case that pitted feminists against anti-racist activists and suggested that "race and gender were locked in a zero-sum game in which a win for Blacks was a loss for women, and vice versa."[84] Crenshaw's point about the perils of failing to account for the complexities of intersecting forms of oppression provides an important note of caution for anyone trying to come to terms with the Bryant case. As long as the case is seen in "he said/she said" terms, or as long as the framing suggests that there are two clearly distinct sides, and that one must be worthy of support and the other of condemnation, it is impossible to more fully assess the complexities of the racial and gendered dynamics in play. More specifically, the "zero-sum" game that Crenshaw refers to obscures the need for critical assessment of the ways that the case resonates with ages-old stereotypes of race *and* gender.

Crenshaw argues that the Simpson case and other cases "involving such vexed categories as race, gender, and class" call for "an intersectional politics that merges feminist and antiracist critiques of institutional racism and sexism."[85] Of course, figuring out how to develop and mobilize such an intersectional politics is far from clear. McDonald credits anti-racist activists and feminists for their critiques of the ways that media coverage can work to determine dominant understandings of sexualized violence, yet she notes that anti-racist and feminist arguments have gained little traction within the mass media, and that media attention to "violent actions does not necessarily translate into critical understanding."[86] Crenshaw is similarly concerned with the inability of activists to intervene in unfolding sports spectacles in politically useful ways. She notes that the kinds of issues surrounding sexual violence and racial injustice that played out in the Simpson case have been usefully analyzed by feminists and anti-racist activists, but she argues that, as the case unfolded, "there was no readily accessible framework that allowed the critiques to be aligned in a complementary rather than implicitly oppositional fashion."[87] As the Kobe Bryant case unfolded more than a decade later, very little appeared to have changed. Collective memories of racist spectacles and of sexist treatment of rape victims at the hands of the legal system were mobilized in order to garner support for particular parties involved in the case, but there were few signs of an organized "feminist antiracist"[88] response that was simultaneously attentive to the sexist and racist dimensions of the case.

One indication of the lack of an effective feminist anti-racist intervention into the Bryant case is that the case has so thoroughly faded from public discourse, even as Bryant himself continues to capture tremendous amounts of media attention. The Lakers were in disarray during the spring of 2005, as the civil suit settlement was being negotiated, and they failed to make the playoffs for the first time in over a decade. When the suit was settled, Bryant received a good amount of bad press, though criticisms tended to center around basketball and not the rape allegations. (He was frequently accused of being a selfish player, and of creating an atmosphere that led Shaquille O'Neal to leave the Lakers, for example.) In subsequent years, however, Bryant experienced a resurgence in his professional career. He was the NBA's leading scorer in the 2005–2006 season, and scored 81 points, the second highest total in NBA history, in a game in January, 2006. He won the NBA's league Most Valuable Player (MVP) award in 2008, and led his team to the NBA finals that spring, before losing to the Boston Celtics. He was a key player for the gold medal-winning U.S. Olympic basketball team in 2008, and, as the Lakers won the NBA championships in 2009 and 2010, he was twice voted the MVP of the finals. Bryant's professional accomplishments led to dozens of profiles in the national and international press, but the rape case was generally relegated to the status of a footnote, when it was mentioned at all. The combination of Bryant's success on the basketball court and the dwindling attention to the rape case might help to explain how a Harris interactive poll could report that Bryant had become tied with Tiger Woods as the most popular sports figure in the United States by July, 2010. [89]

It might be reasonable to suggest that basic journalistic conventions determined that the rape case would recede from view, since once the civil suit was settled, there was very little news to report. But this would not explain why retrospective pieces on Bryant's life and career had so little to say about the case, or why the *New York Times* was able to refer to him as a "savior" of the NBA as early as 2006, just a year after the settlement was announced.[90] The more plausible explanation for media silence about the case in recent years is that, in the final analysis, the press cared far more about winning than about rape. Violence against women has rarely received sustained coverage in the mass media as an issue of concern in its own right, and instead tends to garner media attention only when coupled with issues of race and/or celebrity. Once the spectacle of the rape allegations had played its way through the court system, the alleged victim faded back into obscurity as Bryant remained in the spotlight.

If the amount of media attention devoted to rape victims and sexist rape mythology in the Bryant case was a historical anomaly, fascination with threatening interracial sexuality remains an unbroken tradition for the mass media and popular culture. Almost before news of the civil settlement in the Bryant case could be digested, the media turned its attention to the Duke Lacrosse case, which I have argued (in Chapter 1) was inappropriately discussed as a contemporary inversion of the Scottsboro case. The 2008 election season ushered in a new round of media scandals involving interracial sexuality, most famously including an advertisement during the Tennessee Senate race that demonized Representative Harold Ford (the Democratic candidate who was hoping to become the first African American southern Senator since reconstruction) by playing upon fears that black men were sexually desirous of white women.[91] Throughout all of this, the NBA continued to pump out images of blackness on a nightly basis, and, as the cover of the April, 2008 issue of Vogue magazine (Figure 2.3) suggests, the Bryant case is unlikely to be the last time that the public will be presented with representations of black NBA players who exhibit a dangerous sexual interest in white women.

The cover of the magazine shows African American NBA star LeBron James, slightly hunched over in a somewhat simian pose, baring his teeth and dribbling a basketball with one hand, while the other arm is wrapped around the waist of Gisele Bundchen, a white model. The Annie Leibovitz photograph, in which James appears ready to hoist Bundchen off of the ground, is reminiscent of a racist World War I propaganda poster that is thought to have been the inspiration for *King Kong* (see Figure 2.4).[92] (The photo also invokes later movie posters of King Kong and Fay Wray.)

James is regularly talked about as the player next in line to inherit the mantle of the "best player in the league" from Bryant, and in featuring Bryant's successor, the Vogue cover suggests that the NBA remains an ever-ready source of potential racial spectacle and scandal even as the Bryant case itself fades into the recesses of collective memory.

Iwona Irwin-Zarecka writes that collective memory "is best located not in the minds of individuals, but in the resources they share."[93] At one level, this is just a definition of collective memory, but it is also a methodological claim indicating that the way to assess the nature of collective memory is not necessarily to conduct interviews or to accumulate survey data to determine how people are thinking about the past. Instead, Irwin-Zarecka's claim suggests that the task for the analyst of collective memory is to look to shared resources, or to the cultural

FIGURE 2.3
Vogue, April 2008: LeBron
James as King Kong.

FIGURE 2.4
"Destroy this Mad Brute,"
H.R. Hopps, 1917. World
War I Propaganda Poster.

production of widely disseminated versions of the past. Clearly, I have taken this suggestion to heart, looking not to "the minds of individuals" but to the media and the legal system as sites where collective memory is constructed and deployed. Still, an analysis of cultural production can ultimately only provide clues as to how people might make use of their understandings of the past in making sense of the present. Irwin-Zarecka cautions that

> an abundance of resources does not guarantee that people actually use them ... As we look at a collective memory, at what it offers and at how its offerings change, we ought to remain modest in our claims. Individuals are perfectly capable of ignoring even the best told stories, of injecting their own, subversive meanings into even the most rhetorically accomplished "texts"—and of attending to only those ways of making sense of the past that fit their own.[94]

In order to determine how, and whether, "people actually use" the cultural resources and kinds of collective memory that I have discussed in this chapter when following racialized and gendered spectacles, it would be necessary to conduct research into "the minds of individuals." Empirical research along these lines might involve interviews or surveys that seek to measure what exactly people knew about histories of racist injustice before the allegations against Bryant surfaced, or whether and how people thought about history and memory as the case unfolded. The theoretical investigation into the dynamics of collective memory that I have conducted in this chapter is necessarily speculative and only one step in a larger process of assessing the ways that collective memory can influence public responses to contemporary events.

The question of whether or not Bryant is guilty of rape is beyond the scope of this chapter, but I do hope to have provided some of the conceptual tools necessary to make sense of the ways that memories of racialized spectacles and memories of sexist practices surrounding treatment of rape victims were pitted against each other in what became a clash of anti-racist and anti-sexist discourses. As members of various constituencies approach unfolding racialized and gendered spectacles, the understandings that they come to are not generated whole cloth on the spot, but are instead informed by collective memories that have been constructed as products of long histories of political struggle. In an attempt to understand the social nature of individual consciousness, Antonio Gramsci argued that it was necessary to take on the task "of 'knowing thyself' as a product of the historical process to date, which has deposited in you an infinity of traces, without leaving an inventory." In order to achieve this kind of self-knowledge, "it is imperative at the outset to compile such an inventory."[95] This chapter highlights the value of such a compilation project—only by reckoning with the traces or collective memories of struggles over race and gender is it possible to begin to come to terms with the nature of the disparate reactions to the Kobe Bryant rape case or other racial spectacles.

3

FRAMING POLICE CORRUPTION

The LAPD Rampart Scandal in The News

Introduction

On the night of March 3rd, 1991, George Holliday aimed his video camera out of his Lake View Terrace apartment window in Los Angeles and recorded several members of the Los Angeles police department beating a thirty-five-year-old African American man named Rodney King as approximately a dozen other law enforcement officers looked on. King had been pulled over for speeding and reckless driving, and had already been tasered twice before Holliday started filming. Holliday's video captures fifty-six steel baton strikes and six kicks that left Rodney King with a fractured skull and eye socket, a broken ankle, internal injuries, and, according to a civil lawsuit, possibly permanent brain damage.[1] While the four officers who were tried for the beating were famously acquitted in a criminal trial, Sergeant Stacey Koon and officer Laurence Powell were eventually convicted on federal civil rights charges. King was awarded $3.8 million in a civil suit against the city of Los Angeles.[2]

Five and a half years after King was beaten, a nineteen-year-old Honduran immigrant named Javier Ovando was shot four times in the neck and chest by Raphael Perez and Nino Durden, two Los Angeles police officers who were members of the LAPD's Rampart Division's CRASH (Community Resources Against Street Hoodlums) anti-gang unit. Perez and Durden claimed to have fired in self-defense as Ovando, armed with a semiautomatic pistol, burst into a room that they were using to monitor gang activity on the street below. Ovando was paralyzed from the waist down, and was convicted of assaulting the officers. He was sentenced to twenty-three years in prison. In September, 1999, Ovando was released from prison, having served two and a half years of his sentence, after Perez recanted his testimony, admitting that all of the charges against Ovando had been fabricated, and that he and Durden had planted the gun that was discovered next to Ovando's body. In November, 2000, Ovando was awarded $15 million in the largest police misconduct settlement in Los Angeles history. Perez recanted as part of the testimony he provided to secure a plea bargain after he was caught stealing over a million dollars worth of cocaine from a police evidence locker, with intent to deal.[3] His testimony helped to initiate an investigation that led to what has been called "the most consequential police corruption scandal in Los Angeles history."[4] By July, 2006, the "Rampart scandal" had resulted in guilty pleas by five police officers, nearly 400 Administrative Complaints involving almost 100 officers, approximately $70 million paid to settle 187 lawsuits, and more than 150 felony convictions dismissed or overturned due to tainted testimony by corrupt police officers. The Los Angeles Police Department was also forced to agree to a series of reform measures and to enter into a consent decree allowing for federal oversight, in order to settle a lawsuit by the United States Department of Justice alleging that the LAPD was "engaging in a pattern or practice of excessive force, false arrests, and unreasonable searches and seizures in violation of the Fourth and Fourteenth Amendments to the Constitution."[5]

It would not be productive to rank the relative suffering of Rodney King and Javier Ovando, nor to suggest that one was subjected to a more horrendous or meaningful form of violence. I do, however, want to call attention to the fact that, while Rodney King has become an internationally recognized icon, used to define the very nature of American police brutality and racist victimization, Javier Ovando has never become a household name, even within southern California. The entire Rampart scandal has received a small fraction of the attention devoted to Rodney King, and only a small part of the media attention to Rampart has focused on Ovando. While Rodney King played a central role in what was to become one of the most important and dramatic series of racial spectacles in recent memory (aside from the videotape of his own victimization, images of the "Los Angeles riots" or the "L.A. rebellion" that came in the wake of the acquittal of the officers who beat King have circulated around the world and continue to circulate nearly two decades later), Ovando and Perez became central figures in a polarizing scandal that never quite rose to the level of spectacle, at least until it was taken up in fictionalized form by Hollywood. The story of Rodney King is, rightly, well-known. Despite a tremendous amount of coverage in the print media, the story of Rampart, like that of most cases of widespread police corruption and violence, has been largely obscured, and is deserving of greater attention.[6] This chapter presents an assessment of the nature of this scandal and of ways that it unfolded in the press, while Chapter 4 addresses the ways that memories of the scandal have been drawn upon and reconfigured within the realm of popular culture. I argue that press coverage and fictionalized appropriations of the scandal had the potential to help change popular under-standings of race and the criminal justice system while providing opportunities for political elites, activists, and ordinary people to mobilize around and resist institutionalized racism within the "prison industrial complex." Together, these chapters offer analyses of the Rampart scandal and of Hollywood's "reel bad cops" that consider the extent to which this potential was fulfilled.

Police Scandals, the Criminal Justice System, and Racial Formation

The central difference between the shooting of Javier Ovando and the beating of Rodney King has less to do with the extent of the violence, of course, than with the fact that only one of these incidents was filmed. The lack of dramatic video imagery goes a long way towards explaining why the Rampart scandal never became the kind of spectacle that developed around Rodney King. And it's worth noting that, as horrifying as the beating of Rodney King was, the primary thing that separated it from other instances of police brutality was, again, George Holliday's video. While much of the nation was shocked by the raw footage, many area residents and anti-racist activists argued that the kind of brutality that the tape depicted was ubiquitous in poor communities of color, in Los Angeles and in many other parts of the country. Indeed, in the year before Rodney King was beaten, the city of Los Angeles had paid out $11 million to settle claims of police brutality.[7] Without video evidence, the vast majority of the cases that led to these settlements never received any noticeable media attention, and never made a dent in public consciousness. Still, it is not enough to say that the difference between the beating of King and the shooting of Ovando is George Holliday's video, since it is worth inquiring into the question of *why* there is such explosive footage of Rodney King, and nothing similar for Rampart.

Clearly, the most direct answer to this question has to do with luck and circumstance. George Holliday was a plumber trying out a new purchase, not a journalist seeking out stories of racist state violence, and it was pure chance that he was awakened that night in March, 1991, by the sounds of a police beating. But, as stark as the victimization of Rodney King was, this was not the only incident of police brutality to be caught on tape. Holliday's actions were prefigured by "Copwatch," an organization founded in Berkeley in 1990 to monitor police activity. In the past two decades, numerous unaffiliated "copwatch" organizations around the country have relied upon amateur video to publicize incidents of police activity, and these videos have become something akin to their own genre. A March, 2010 YouTube search for "police brutality" yielded over 14,000 hits, and while not all of these hits correspond to separate cases of police brutality, the number that do is overwhelming. Few of these incidents were as stark or involved as much brutality as was evident in the video of the beating of Rodney King, which might help explain why they were never as widely publicized.[8] One incident that arguably did have a similar potential to shock audiences, and that might have been seen as equally newsworthy, was the 2009 New Year's Day killing, in Oakland California, of

Oscar Grant, a twenty-two-year-old African American man. Grant, who had been detained after reports of a fight on a Bay Area Rapid Transit train, was lying face down when a white BART officer named Johannes Mehserle shot him in the back. This killing was captured on at least four cell phone cameras, and the footage was played on the local television station KTVU, and viewed by hundreds of thousands of people on YouTube and on KTVU's website.[9] There were mass protests and incidents of violence that have been referred to as "riots" in response to the killing, and in response to the fact that it initially appeared that officer Mehserle would not be charged with a crime.[10] While the story was picked up around the country, the extent of the coverage never approached that of the King case. Ironically, it might be the fact that the video was *so* stark that kept it from receiving greater attention, since few stations are comfortable airing footage of dead bodies.

What all of these incidents have in common with the King case is not simply that they were filmed, but that they involve a kind of "simple" brutality, and that the resulting videos can be fairly easily read as depicting the isolated actions of a few bad cops. Taken together, it's not difficult to look at these cases and discern a troubling national pattern of police brutality and racism, but these cases are rarely taken together, at least by the mass media. Again, most of these cases have not received much media attention, and when they are covered by the local or national press, they tend to be discussed as relatively discrete events. In contrast, the victimization of Javier Ovando goes beyond the fact that he was shot, and extends instead into the ways that he was framed and tried, which involve a kind of corruption and systemic inequality that is not easily photographed and that does not easily lend itself to the politics of spectacle. Police are unlikely to plant evidence in public view, and underfunded and overworked public defenders are not the stuff of high drama.

Ovando and King were both the victims of a kind of crime that strikes at the very fabric of the criminal justice system and American national identity. When the people who are charged with enforcing the laws of the land brutalize and prey upon those they are sworn to protect, none of the rights afforded by the Constitution can be counted upon, and the entire notion of due process becomes suspect. And when it becomes clear that there is a pattern of such violations regularly following racial lines, it becomes plausible to argue that people of color are being violently excluded from the "imagined community"[11] of the nation. It is perhaps because illegal and unjust acts of police violence pose such a direct threat to the belief in order and formal equality that they are so readily seized upon not only by activists seeking to expose the workings of an unjust system, but also by ordinary people who might otherwise be willing to give that system the benefit of the doubt. Widespread outrage at such actions accounts for much of the resulting media attention, and helps to explain why so many recent racial spectacles revolve around cases of police brutality. And yet for all of the ways that the cases of Rodney King and Javier Ovando indicate profound problems with the politics of race and crime in the contemporary United States, Jean Baudrillard's warning that "denunciation of scandal pays homage to the law"[12] is important to consider here, since the most serious aspects of racial inequality within the criminal justice system are not at all spectacular, at least by traditional measures. The risk of devoting too much attention to cases of extreme police brutality is that mundane and systemic patterns of oppression can be obscured by the glare of media spotlights.

Racial disparities within the criminal justice system have been well-documented, and for several decades some of the most important anti-racist social struggles have revolved around challenging the inequities of what has been called the "prison industrial complex" or the entire set of institutions supporting the police, the courts, the prison system and corporations that are involved in constructing and supplying technologies to prisons.[13] There are over 2.3 million prisoners in the United States, and another 5 million people on probation or parole. People of color are imprisoned in grossly disproportionate numbers. African Americans and Latinos each represent under 16 percent of the population, but constitute 40 percent and 20 percent of inmates, respectively, while non-Hispanic whites, who represent over 65 percent of the population are just over 33 percent of the prison population.[14] Black men are incarcerated at nearly 7 times the rate of white men,[15] and have more than a 1 in 4 chance of going to prison during their lifetimes.[16] According to the Department of Justice, "more than a third of the young African-American men aged 18–34 in some of our major cities are either in prison or under some form of criminal justice supervision."[17]

Policing strategies and sentencing guidelines account for a good deal of the problem. Racial profiling has become so common that the phrase "DWB" or "Driving while Black (or Brown)" is commonly used within popular culture without any need for explanation, and human rights groups like Amnesty International have long criticized racial discrepancies in prosecutions for capital offenses.[18] Perhaps the greatest source of concern for anti-racist activists involves the so-called "war on drugs" and federal sentencing guidelines that, until recently, called for the same prison term for someone selling 5 grams of crack cocaine as for someone selling 500 grams of powder cocaine. This legislation appears race-neutral on its face, but nearly 90 percent of crack cocaine defendants are black, and, according to estimates by the U.S. Sentencing Commission, 65 percent of crack cocaine users are white.[19] Conversely, whites are much more likely than blacks to be arrested and convicted for powder cocaine crimes that involve dramatically lower criminal penalties, even though there is substantial evidence that the effects of crack and powdered cocaine are similar.[20] In March of 2010, the Senate passed the "Fair Sentencing Act of 2010" that would reduce the disparity in amounts of crack vs. powder cocaine needed to secure a variety of felony convictions to an 18:1 ratio. The only way this can look like progress is by considering that the previous ratio was 100:1.[21]

When thinking about racial disparities in the criminal justice system, it is the impact upon African Americans that has received the bulk of scholarly and popular attention. The Rampart scandal, however, sheds light upon the growing targeting of Latino communities.[22] Tom Hayden has said that the Rampart scandal was inevitable, given the LAPD's engagement in "gang profiling," which is a form of racial profiling that was given legal sanction by a 1998 California anti-terrorism law that "legalizes a dragnet approach to anyone who looks like a gang member."[23] The law identifies gang members and "associates" on the basis of such criteria as not only admitting membership or associating with gang members, but also "corresponding with gang members," having tattoos, writing graffiti, or wearing "gang clothing." Hayden notes that the majority of people who are arrested under this legislation are not gang members at all, and he quotes an INS agent saying that "the real target is a 'whole race of people.'"[24] While this practice is particularly acute in California and the rest of the southwest, racial profiling of Latinos as gang members or undocumented immigrants is a problem of national scope. Mary Romero has argued that under immigration law, citizenship "appears embodied in skin color (that is brown skin absent a police or border patrol uniform) serving as an indicator of illegal status" and that one result is that "Mexican Americans and other racialized Latino citizens and legal residents are subjected to insults, questions, unnecessary stops, and searches."[25] Until recently, there were mild checks on some of these varieties of profiling and abuse, since the Department of Justice had long held that local and state law enforcement agencies did not have the power to enforce civil immigration violations, but in the wake of the September 11, 2001 attacks, the DOJ withdrew its earlier position, concluding that states did have the power to make arrests for violations of both civil and criminal immigration laws.[26] Local authorities have also increasingly started to enter into Memorandum of Agreements with the Justice Department in order to receive federal training and authorization to enforce immigration law.[27] As local law enforcement authorities start to take on greater immigration enforcement powers and responsibilities, the potential for profiling increases exponentially.[28] At the federal level, increased rates of illegal immigration and harsher enforcement of immigration laws have led to dramatic changes in incarceration rates of Latinos. In 2007, 40 percent of all federally sentenced offenders were Latino (more than three times their proportion of the population), while immigration offenses counted for 24 percent of all federal convictions.[29]

Beyond the direct toll that racial inequities within the criminal justice system take on people of color, the "prison industrial complex" works as a major force of racialization in the United States, helping to maintain and further other structures of institutionalized racism while drawing upon and reinforcing a host of racist stereotypes. The disproportionate numbers of African Americans and Latinos in prison can be traced not only to racist policing strategies and sentencing guidelines, but also to waves of economic disruptions that have ravaged poor communities of color. Even before the recent and ongoing "great recession," free trade agreements had facilitated the movement of capital overseas, leading to massive deindustrialization in the United States at the same time that government spending for education and social services had been cut to the bone. The resulting economic desperation turns people who live in the most affected communities into "perfect candidates for prison."[30]

Popular understandings of crime as solely a matter of individual responsibility obscure these underlying social conditions, and prisons help to sweep aside any concern with the relationship between crime and economic devastation. Angela Davis writes that

> Because of the tendency to view it as an abstract site into which all manner of undesirables are deposited, the prison is the perfect site for the simultaneous production and concealment of racism. The abstract character of the public perception of prisons militates against an engagement with the real issues afflicting the communities from which prisoners are drawn in such disproportionate numbers. This is the ideological work that the prison performs—it relieves us of the responsibility of seriously engaging with the problems of late capitalism, of transnational capitalism.[31]

Prison construction and "tough on crime" policies rely upon racialized appeals to fear, as images of Latino "gang bangers" (a modified version of the decades-old stereotype of "the bandido") and what Katheryn Russell calls the "criminal-blackman"[32] (stereotypes of black criminality that are ubiquitous enough that each of the characteristics here—"criminal," "black," and "man" run together in popular culture, breathlessly) regularly surface to generate public support for measures such as California's "three-strikes" legislation. Racist stereotypes thus provide the ideological foundation for repressive anti-crime measures and prison funding, while the very existence of prisons deflects attention from the root causes of black and Latino crime.

Because so much of the public discourse surrounding the beating of Rodney King revolved around the question of how to explain the images captured in Holliday's video, it became possible to frame questions of racism and police brutality in fairly narrow terms. Questions tended to center around the extent of police brutality as a local or national problem and, later, around the inability of the court system to convict police officers who were so clearly guilty of extreme and unjustified violence, while news reports generally avoided touching upon the broader issues that I've discussed above. In contrast, the extent of the Rampart scandal made such avoidance more difficult, and Rampart thus had the potential to open up more extensive examinations of the role of institutionalized racism within the criminal justice system. In the remaining sections of this chapter, I examine the extent to which this potential was fulfilled in news accounts of the case. First, I discuss the nature of the scandal itself in greater detail.

On Men and Monsters: The Nature of the "Scandal"

> Whoever chases monsters should see to it that in the process he does not become a monster himself.
>
> Rafael Perez[33]

> They knew, of course, that it would have been very comforting indeed to believe that Eichmann was a monster.
>
> Hannah Arendt, *Eichmann in Jerusalem*[34]

Hannah Arendt did not doubt that Adolph Eichmann was guilty of crimes against humanity, that his crimes were monstrous, or that he deserved to be executed for committing them. Her reason for resisting portrayals of Eichmann as a monster (for insisting that he was "not Iago and not Macbeth"),[35] and for painting him instead as an example, in her famous phrase, of the "banality of evil" is, ultimately, that monster tales are too easy. Monsters are isolated figures whose evil requires no explanation—it simply is. When used to explain crime, monster stories tend to present clear divisions between monster and society, and thus miss the opportunity to examine the root causes or social production of monstrosity. Just as the "bad apple" explanations for Abu Ghraib (discussed in Chapter 5) fail to address the broader structures and policies that made torture possible, stories of criminality that focus only on the figure of the criminal, or the monster, capture only a small part of the picture.[36] The story of Rampart is not a monster tale, even if, as suggested in the quote that I've used to open this section, the monster would disagree.

The Rampart Division of the LAPD covers a 7.9 mile area with the greatest population density in Los Angeles, with nearly 34,000 residents per square mile. Rampart is not a neighborhood or a district, but a patrol area that cuts across ten communities, the best-known of which include Echo Park, Westlake, and Koreatown. The median income in the Rampart patrol area in 1990 (just a few years before key events in the "Rampart scandal" were starting to unfold) was just over $21,000, as compared to about $43,000 for Los Angeles as a whole. Thirty-seven percent of the population in the area earned under $15,000 a year, as opposed to 22 percent of the population in the city of Los Angeles. And, while Latinos made up 48 percent of the Los Angeles population, 79 percent of the Rampart precinct was Latino in 1990.[37] As the LAPD declared war on gangs in the late 1980s, this population of disproportionately poor and Latino residents (including many recent immigrants from Central America) was heavily targeted. As a young Honduran immigrant who spoke little English, Javier Ovando represents a fairly typical Rampart victim.

The shooting and framing of Javier Ovando is just the best-known incident of police brutality and corruption in what I have been referring to as the "Rampart scandal." I should mention that I am following what has become the conventional terminology to refer to these events, but that I do so advisedly, keeping Baudrillard's caution in mind. The real danger in accepting the idea that the events I am discussing are "scandalous" is, however, probably not one of paying homage to the law, but of failing to adequately take their measure. And taking the measure of the nature of the law as embodied by the LAPD and related institutions, and as revealed by Rampart, turns out to be nearly impossible. The brief summary that I have provided begins to lay out the toll of the scandal, but there is much that remains unsaid and unknown.

As one of the most far reaching corruption scandals in the history not only of the LAPD but of American police departments in general, the Rampart scandal has been studied extensively. At least five major reports on Rampart have been issued, including internal reports commissioned by the LAPD itself, a report requested by the Los Angeles Police Commission, and an independent analysis of the initial LAPD "board of inquiry" report, requested by the police protective league. The United States Justice Department also thoroughly assessed the nature of the Rampart scandal in order to bring the suit that led to the consent decree. While the LAPD's board of inquiry report has been criticized as a whitewash that minimized the severity of the scandal and refused to allocate responsibility in a meaningful way, the rest of the reports are extremely thorough and far reaching.[38] These reports pulled no punches and, when looking for possible solutions to entrenched problems within the LAPD, or when seeking to allocate responsibility, they have not hesitated to point to the highest levels of city and state government and to the systemic inequalities that are at the heart of the criminal justice system. And, yet, there is agreement that none of these reports can begin to provide a full assessment of the nature of the scandal. The obstacles to a full accounting begin, but do not end, with Rafael Perez.

While Javier Ovando may be the most famous victim of Rampart (he is, in fact, the only victim who is regularly mentioned in news accounts of the scandal), the central figure in the scandal is Rafael Perez. If Perez had not been caught stealing cocaine, and had not agreed to provide evidence about other "dirty cops" as part of a plea agreement, it is not clear that any of the events that constitute what has become known as the "Rampart scandal" would have come to light. Over the course of more than a year, in dozens of interview sessions, Perez provided over four thousand transcript pages of testimony about a staggering variety of kinds of police misconduct. The testimony suggested not only that the population in the Rampart patrol district was at the mercy of a band of corrupt cops who thought nothing of shooting unarmed and innocent people, lying in court to obtain convictions on the basis of fabricated evidence, violating department policy by turning immigrants over to the Immigration and Naturalization Service for deportation, and "indiscriminately beating any youth they encountered,"[39] but also that this kind of corruption and brutality was not confined to Rampart, and instead extended to every CRASH unit, and, in some measure, to the rest of the LAPD. The difficulty with relying upon this testimony to gain insight into the nature of the scandal is, of course, that it came from a lying, murderous and drug dealing officer who had every reason to say whatever his interrogators wanted to hear if it would help him to avoid a longer prison term. Still, much of Perez's testimony was corroborated, and, as noted in the introduction to this chapter, a number of other officers eventually pleaded guilty to a series of crimes. For all of the reasons to be skeptical of Perez's testimony, his lack of reliability is not the real obstacle in assessing the scope of the Rampart scandal.

Much of the difficulty in coming to terms with Rampart can be traced to the LAPD's initial investigation into Perez's charges. Part of the problem here has to do with the kinds of questions that were asked in preparing the LAPD's Board of Inquiry Report, and in how the report chose to allocate responsibility. In his independent evaluation of the report, requested by the Police Protective League, law professor and former chair of the Los Angeles Charter Reform Commission Erwin Chemerinsky acknowledges that the report was far-ranging, noting that it "is 362 pages; it contains 108 recommendations," but he goes on to say that "the Report, for all of its length and detail ignores the real problems in the department and therefore fails to provide meaningful solutions."[40] Chemerinsky faults the report for holding only middle and low ranked personnel responsible for the scandal, and for failing to call for any structural changes. He writes that

> Crucial, basic questions must be answered in appraising the extent of the Rampart scandal and the magnitude of the problems confronting the Los Angeles Police Department. How many officers in the Rampart Division CRASH unit participated in illegal activities? How many officers in this unit and in the Rampart Division knew of illegal activity and were complicit by their silence? How high within the Department was there some knowledge of illegal activities by Rampart officers? Was there similar illegal activity in other CRASH units, in other specialized units, and in other divisions? The Board of Inquiry report provides no answer to these questions.[41]

Six years after Chemerinsky's evaluation, a report by the "Blue Ribbon Rampart Review Panel" (requested by then police Chief William J. Bratton and the Police Commission, and chaired by Constance Rice) echoed Chemerinsky's analysis, noting that "the scope of CRASH corruption remains unknown" since "no public entity conducted an independent investigation with the capacity, authority and resources to definitively vet the extent of the CRASH corruption or its causes."[42] While this report praises the LAPD for substantial reforms, it is scathing in its critique of efforts to explore the nature of the scandal, claiming that "if obscuring the extent of the corruption were the goal, it is hard to imagine a better game plan."[43] Neither of these reports goes so far as to claim that there was an intentional cover-up, but they do suggest that the reasons for inadequate examinations on the part of the LAPD and the city of Los Angeles had to do with more than a lack of investigative ability.

Even if the LAPD or the city had desired an investigation that could have revealed the full scope of the scandal, it would have been difficult to overcome the "code of silence" that is at the heart of Los Angeles police culture. This code has been a part of the LAPD for generations, and was highlighted in the "Christopher Commission report," which was commissioned to provide an examination of the structure of the LAPD in the wake of the Rodney King beating. That earlier report cited the "unwritten code of silence" as perhaps "the greatest single barrier to the effective investigation and adjudication of complaints."[44] Chemerinsky and Rice both found that the code remains a major force in the LAPD, and that it is reinforced by department policies that provide disincentives for officers to come forward with knowledge of misconduct. Chemerinsky concluded that, as a general practice, "the Department punishes whistleblowers and those who expose the wrongdoing of others."[45] The Blue Ribbon review panel found that when it came to the Rampart scandal specifically, "Whistleblowers who intercepted and challenged rampart CRASH officers were punished or ignored."[46]

Beyond implementing what had become fairly standard ways of enforcing the department's code of silence, there appear to have been notable efforts on the part of some members of the LAPD to obstruct investigations into police misconduct. Even before Perez was caught in the evidence room, there had been numerous community complaints about Rampart division officers. When then California Senator Tom Hayden held a community meeting to address these complaints in the mid-1990s, "Rampart CRASH officers lined the walls of the meeting and tried to take down the names of everyone in attendance. The Department took no action in response to the hearing."[47] Some of the criminal investigations into the Rampart scandal itself were undermined by LAPD investigators who refused to follow up on any of Perez's testimony, assistant district attorneys who were reluctant to sign warrants for investigations, and, more troubling, LAPD command staff members who provided advance warnings about search warrants to the defense attorneys of officers who were under investigation.[48] Leaking information about a search warrant would ordinarily be prosecuted as obstruction of justice or for creating a risk to the safety of others, but there was no penalty for these staff members. The Department also regularly failed to turn witness names over to the court in a timely manner, so these witnesses were prevented from providing testimony in officers' trials.[49]

Even more damaging than low-level efforts to hinder the investigation was an apparent lack of political will, at the highest levels of the LAPD, to expose the full extent of the scandal. District attorney Gil Garcetti accused police chief Bernard Parks of obstructing the investigation into the scandal by ordering LAPD detectives to block prosecutors' access to reports on the investigation. The Police Commission found Parks not-guilty of misconduct on a 3–2 vote, but there were other problems with the way that Parks handled the investigation. Most notably, he made it clear that any officer who had known about misconduct but remained silent would be fired. At first blush, this sounds like a relatively hard-line stance in opposition to the code of silence. The effect, however, was that officers now had a powerful disincentive to come forward with any information about past crimes. Other police departments, faced with similar kinds of scandals, have been able to mount successful prosecutions by offering administrative leniency or immunity to police officers who could provide information about more serious cases of misconduct or crimes. Gerald Chaleff, the former president of the Los Angeles Police Commission sums up the issue:

> Do I think that we know the full extent of what happened? No. Do I think we'll ever know the full extent? No. I think one of the problems we had is Chief Parks' refusal to allow any kind of amnesty or immunity for officers coming forward for wrongdoing that may have occurred in the past that they now wanted to talk about. And they are fearful of being punished, because of L.A.P.D.'s rule about if you fail to report a misconduct, you're guilty of misconduct. That inhibited the ability to have officers come forward.[50]

Without full cooperation between the chief of police and the district attorney, and without more meaningful testimony from other officers, it was never possible to determine just how widespread the corruption in Rampart and in the larger LAPD was. The Blue Ribbon review panel refers to the "Rampart Rorschach Test" as a way to indicate that the question of how to define the nature of the scandal is very much in the eye of the beholder.[51] Still, even without knowing the full extent of the corruption, some sense of the likely scale can be gleaned from the convictions and guilty pleas of a number of officers, the parts of Perez's testimony that were corroborated, and the lawsuits against the city and the LAPD that were settled. We know, for example, that the Rampart CRASH unit had a culture that celebrated police violence, awarding plaques for every officer-involved shooting, with mounted shell casings corresponding with the number of times the suspect was shot. There were more prestigious plaques awarded when the suspect was killed.[52] We not only know the names of specific people who were shot and framed by Rampart officers, but also that the practice of carrying "drop guns," or weapons that were confiscated from criminals but not checked into evidence, and that could be planted on suspects, appears to have been fairly widespread.[53] Most important, we know that the problems of Rampart extend to the rest of the criminal justice system, since it is clear that "many innocent people plead guilty to crimes that they did not commit because of their fear of far longer sentences if they went to trial and were convicted."[54] This is not just a matter of a few defendants facing overwhelming odds because of particularly clever framing jobs. Instead, public defenders often pressure their clients to accept a plea regardless of guilt, knowing that the system imposes especially harsh sentences when defendants demand trials, thereby taxing the limited resources of the court system. At the same time, prosecutors press for guilty pleas before public defenders have a chance to do any meaningful investigation into the allegations their clients face, while judges, who also have massive caseloads, are notoriously reluctant to pursue suspicions of police perjury.[55] Ultimately, it is clear that the corrupt Rampart officers could not have acted alone: they were able to rely upon the aid of a system that rendered the victims of misconduct powerless. In the words of the Blue Ribbon review panel, this was a case of "total systems failure."[56] Once again, Rafael Perez's actions may have been monstrous, but this is not a monster story.

Bad Apples or Contaminated Orchard?: Press Coverage of Rampart

Of course, my insistence that the Rampart scandal is not a monster story is proscriptive: what I really mean to say is that Rampart *should* not be presented as a monster story, since too strong of a focus on the monster would preclude an examination of the root causes and social forces that produce monstrous actions. I've mentioned, though, that the press tends to present incidents of police brutality or corruption as isolated cases, traceable only to the actions of the officers directly responsible for the violence or misconduct. When reporting on "bad cops," monster stories are the norm for the mainstream press. And yet, there are exceptions.

In her study of media and police brutality, Regina Lawrence notes that there are strong cultural presumptions in the United States that make it difficult for news outlets to suggest that police misconduct is a serious social problem.[57] Dominant understandings of the United States as a meritocracy, and of the criminal justice system as an arena in which equal justice is guaranteed for all, are put to the test by stories of brutal and corrupt cops, especially when those stories present the actions of these officers as indicative of a broader problem. Lawrence writes that to "suggest that a particular community—or, especially, the nation as a whole—has a systemic brutality problem is to raise a host of serious and difficult questions about crime, justice, and, often, race."[58] News stories that depict police brutality as aberrational avoid these "difficult questions," and represent the path of least resistance for the press. Reporters who wish to explore far-reaching questions about systemic inequalities are not only likely to alienate readers, but would also generally be hampered by journalistic conventions that require reliance upon official sources, since such sources tend to reject systemic explanations for police misconduct.[59] Lawrence argues, however, that particularly dramatic stories involving "accidental events" (unpredictable events that "violate standard assumptions about the way things are and ought to be") have the potential to generate coverage that relies upon different kinds of sources and that gives voice to otherwise marginalized perspectives.[60]

Lawrence identifies a series of "critical story cues" that can help to legitimize a systemic frame and encourage journalists to rely upon non-traditional sources. When, for example, a case of brutality sparks protests or investigations, when legal proceedings are initiated, when reform measures are implemented, or when a pattern of misconduct becomes apparent, reporters have more freedom to veer from or challenge news frames that are sponsored by public officials.[61] Lawrence's primary example of an accidental event is the Rodney King case, in which all of these story cues were available. Coverage of the King beating immediately escaped the control of the LAPD, as local, national, and international news rejected explanations of the beating as an "aberration."[62] The King case was exceptional, even as an accidental event, in that many official sources "broke ranks" and quickly began offering their own versions of systemic critiques that news accounts could draw upon.[63] These conditions were closely paralleled as details of the Rampart scandal began to emerge.[64]

From the moment that the shooting of Javier Ovando hit the headlines, it would already have been difficult for the press to present the story as aberrational, since the case came to light during a press conference during which then LAPD Chief Bernard C. Parks announced not only that Rafael Perez had implicated himself and his partner in the shooting, but also that an ongoing investigation had led to twelve other officers either being fired or placed on modified duty.[65] Unlike most brutality cases, there was no effort on the part of any official to suggest that the victim had done anything to bring the case on himself, and there was no attempt to isolate responsibility by blaming only the officers directly involved in the shooting.[66] Instead, the earliest coverage of the case tends to rely upon not only members of the LAPD who are willing to look within the department for further signs of corruption, but also on non-traditional sources offering more far ranging critiques. Thus, one of the first articles in the *Los Angeles Times* follows a reference to Chief Park's announcement that he expected additional officers to be indicted in the coming days by quoting Elizabeth Schroeder from the American Civil Liberties Union (ACLU) saying that "the Rampart scandal is indicative of a larger problem within CRASH units citywide."[67] A similar article in the *Philadelphia Inquirer* quotes a spokesperson for an organization called "Police Watch" saying that "this type of conduct can be found across the entire LAPD—certainly in all the CRASH units."[68] Even in the first days of coverage, there was official sponsorship for some version of a systemic frame, as then Mayor Richard Riordan announced that Rafael Perez's charges had cast "a dark shadow over the entire police department."[69] *Newsweek* reported on Riordan's assessment of the scandal, and echoed his point, noting that "the question is how deep the scandal runs."[70] *Newsweek* expressed no doubt that the scandal would indeed run deep, and no one in the press suggested that the problems in the LAPD began or ended with Perez and Durden. This is not to say, however, that there were not attempts to minimize the importance and extent of the scandal.

In a scandal as extensive as Rampart, it is possible to resist a "bad apple" narrative while still failing to fully assess the nature of the problem. When complaints are leveled against dozens of officers, and hundreds of lawsuits are filed as evidence emerges that suggests that thousands of convictions might have been obtained on the basis of tainted testimony, it is not terribly meaningful to say that this was not simply the work of a few bad cops. With this in mind, it is important to note that the same type of critiques that appeared to be far-reaching when raised in the context of a case like the Rodney King beating can actually work to deflect attention from more serious issues when raised to help explain Rampart. Lawrence argues that the King case stood out from most cases of police brutality because coverage of the case often involved systemic claims, but she defines such claims as critiques that "cast brutality as an endemic and patterned problem arising from poor police management, inadequate police accountability, a hostile police subculture, or a racist culture more generally."[71] While this kind of systemic critique is important in resisting narratives of isolated brutal cops, it does not generally involve critiques of anything beyond the level of the police department, or even of problems *within* police departments that go beyond brutality. This notion of "systemic critique" does not entail consideration of such things as racist policing strategies, inequities built into the court system, or any other broader social factors, except insofar as these things are captured by the phrase "a racist culture more generally." The "systemic" critique offered by most news outlets in coverage of King's beating generally involved only the first few items in Lawrence's list, as reporters looked to sources who found considerable fault within the leadership and culture of the LAPD, but who rarely raised broader questions about social inequalities or the nature of the criminal justice system. A similar failure to look beyond the LAPD itself in order to explain Rampart would lead to coverage that could not begin to address the variety of issues that were central to the scandal, even if this coverage might still be seen as providing a systemic critique. The relevant questions about coverage of Rampart, then, do not concern whether the press chose to offer a systemic critique or to frame the case as one of a few bad apples. Instead, it is necessary to consider the *kinds* of systemic critiques that were offered.

The *Newsweek* story that I mention above provides some sense of the ways that the press chose to cover the Rampart scandal early on. The story refuses a "bad apple" frame, but even when quoting an ACLU spokesperson, it does not provide any indication that the problems revolving around the Rampart district might extend beyond the LAPD. This was a fairly typical way to frame the case. To the extent that there were any substantial differences in how the case was presented in the first few months of coverage, they centered around the question of whether the Rampart corruption, brutality, and command issues were confined to one precinct, typical of CRASH units in general, or something to be concerned about when considering the LAPD as a whole. While this kind of questioning might indicate a robust debate, only rarely did reporters look beyond the police department itself to point to broader problems. For example, a *New York Times* story about Los Angeles's decision to disband the CRASH units similarly refers to "widespread corruption," noting that "It is not clear yet whether the problems extend to the Crash units outside the Rampart area."[72] Not only does the article fail to consider that "the problems" might extend to the criminal justice system more broadly, it also suggests that, even within the LAPD itself, issues of concern are limited to the CRASH units. As the extent of the corruption started to become clearer, however, and as federal authorities became more interested in the scandal, more far-reaching critiques became common.

While no prominent representatives of the LAPD or of the city of Los Angeles ever sought to limit blame for the Rampart scandal to Perez and Durden, some early efforts by members of the LAPD did suggest that stories of corruption had been blown out of proportion. For example, in March, 2000, about six months after the Ovando shooting was first brought to light, Chief Parks drew attention to the fact that relatively few officers had thus far been charged with any crimes, and went on to minimize the scandal by suggesting that declining public support for the police department could be traced to such problems as sloppy police work and minor violations of procedural rules.[73] Ordinarily, this kind of claim might be taken at face value as representing a reasoned, if potentially self-interested, assessment. Parks's statement came, however, as the City was actively negotiating with the Justice Department over the terms of a consent decree that would constitute a virtual admission that excessive force and constitutional violations were widespread within the department. These negotiations rendered Parks's position thoroughly untenable, and traditional journalistic deference to official sources was nowhere to be found.[74] Parks's comments were covered in the same paper that had recently reported that the public defender had failed to notify 4,000 convicted felons that their cases might have been tainted by police misconduct.[75] Revelations such as this were coming to light on a regular basis, and in this context, Parks came across as a willful obstructionist. Thus, when Parks later claimed that "what you have to realize is where that claim about being the biggest scandal in history came from—the two reporters who started this story in the *Los Angeles Times*," he was held up for ridicule by the paper's Steve Lopez, who noted that "nobody with a steady pulse and two active brain cells can possibly believe the entire Rampart story has been told."[76] The consent decree and consequent reform and investigative measures opened the doors for the press to entertain perspectives that challenged virtually every part of the criminal justice system.

Some of the most important criticism in coverage of the scandal came from people who were involved in preparing reports about the scandal for the city or for the police. Because the city had been forced to look for outside experts to help shed light upon the nature of the scandal, a group of otherwise non-traditional sources were now invested with something akin to state authority. Thus, prominent civil rights and civil liberties lawyers and law professors such as Constance Rice and Erwin Chemerinsky were regularly asked to comment on

Rampart throughout the duration of the case. In a 2003 op-ed piece in the *Los Angeles Times*, Chemerinsky wrote that "going after the police is not enough. When innocent people are not just arrested but tried, convicted and imprisoned, the entire justice system must be reevaluated,"[77] while Rice had earlier challenged the "bad apple" framing head-on, noting that "we're talking the barrel, the tree and the whole orchard."[78]

Critics were not content to define the orchard abstractly. Instead, major papers and news magazines provided regular indictments of very specific and extensive problems. The *Christian Science Monitor* quoted a past chair of the American Bar Association's Criminal Justice section, charging that "Every part of [Los Angeles's criminal justice system]—prosecutors, defense counsel, judges, juries—has played a role in the miscarriages of justice,"[79] while the *Los Angeles Times* frequently presented examples from Rampart to make broader points about unequal justice. For example, one article highlighted the case of Ruben Rojas, who had pleaded no contest to "what are probably fabricated drug charges" so that he would receive a six year sentence rather than the twenty-five year sentence that he would likely have received had the case gone to trial. The article uses this case to support the claim that "The Rampart cases reveal a sorry truth about L.A. law: Using entirely lawful threats, the state can make even the innocent plead guilty." The paper suggests, moreover, that this situation is not unique to Los Angeles, since the vast majority of criminal cases in the country are decided by plea bargains, and "Nationwide, only 1 out of every 10 criminal cases goes to trial."[80] The plea bargain system was, in fact, a regular target of the press. One of the first extensive pieces on the case, in the *New York Times*, noted that the system made it more difficult to uncover police misconduct, since corrupt cops are aware that few cases come to trial, and can therefore count on being able to avoid cross-examination. Thus, guilty pleas reduced "the chances of officers getting caught in lies."[81] An op-ed piece by Tamar Toister, Javier Ovando's original public defender, noted that "truly innocent people are afraid to go to trial because they know they don't have a chance with cops who lie, prosecutors who defer to the cops and judges who defer to the prosecutors. The problem is that innocent people are afraid to go to trial because they know they will be punished with the maximum sentence if they lose."[82]

Some international coverage was even more scathing in its criticism than the American press. The London *Independent*, for example, discusses the killing of Juan Manuel Saldana, and claims that in

> a corruption scandal of monstrous proportions, this episode was hardly unusual. It was just another day's work for a unit that routinely shot people without justification, framed them for crimes they did not commit, and got away with it because their superiors did not care.[83]

The Australian offers a wider perspective, noting that "The scandal has spread to the Federal Bureau of Investigation and the Immigration and Naturalization

Service, which allegedly co-operated with Rampart units. It will possibly reach into other units and agencies. No one knows where it will end."[84] Scotland's national paper summed up much of the international sentiment with a headline noting simply "Stench of Corruption Chokes City of Angels."[85]

It was only in the later years of the scandal that the press began to quote officials trying to minimize the extent of the corruption or misconduct. Even then, the press presented such quotes only rarely, and when such quotes were presented, they tended to be accompanied by contradictory information that served to seriously undermine their credibility. For example, a 2005 *New York Times* article quoted the Los Angeles City Attorney Rocky Delgadillo attributing the scandal to "a handful of rogue officers," but then quotes Joe Domanick, from the Institute for Justice and Journalism, who notes that one effect of the city's decision to settle so many Rampart-related cases was that investigations were cut short and many officers who had committed crimes were never charged. Domanick charges that "If any of these cases had gone to trial under a federal judge and discovery had taken place . . . it would have blown the city's entire criminal justice system apart and shown the rot that was there." Non-traditional sources with expertise in police brutality and civil liberties were not only relied upon regularly, but were frequently given the final word.

In addition to allowing for the emergence of otherwise marginalized sources, the Rampart scandal appears to have created opportunities for coverage of a variety of misconduct stories that might otherwise have gone unnoticed. An October, 2000, *Los Angeles Times* piece presented a detailed examination of the failure to prosecute police officers who had been accused of police brutality or other crimes. The article notes that, over a five year period, the LAPD had referred "hundreds of potential criminal cases against its own officers to the district attorney, but only a fraction of those officers actually have been prosecuted." Nearly one hundred of those cases involved allegations of excessive force, but there was only one criminal prosecution for brutality. Moreover, the article reports that prosecutors declined to file criminal charges in "dozens of cases in which there was compelling evidence that the accused officer did commit a crime," including a case where the city agreed to pay $160,000 to settle a civil suit in which a videotape had captured an officer "approaching a man from behind and striking him over the head with his metal flashlight, apparently without provocation," and another case in which an officer "detained his paperboy and the young man's father at gunpoint after the morning newspaper errantly struck the officer's car, which was parked in his driveway." The influence of the Rampart scandal is clear, since the article sums up the current state of the LAPD by relying upon the criminal defense lawyer that was hired by the Superior Court to ensure that the rights of Rampart victims were not being abridged. Gigi Gordon is quoted as saying that "police officers in Los Angeles are immune from prosecution."[86] Other misconduct stories that appear to have been prompted by Rampart include an article addressing the unlawful deportation of "at least 160 people from the Latino community who witnessed police abuses,"[87] and an op-ed piece decrying increasing complaints of police brutality by African American and Latino residents of Los Angeles.[88]

The Rampart scandal continued to provide opportunities for detailed explorations of race and crime even as reform measures started to be enacted and as the corruption and brutality that was at the heart of the scandal began to recede into the past. In the months leading up to and immediately following the decision by the federal government to lift the consent decree in July, 2009, the press devoted considerable attention to assessing changes in the LAPD over the past ten years. Much of the coverage praised the department and the city for enacting meaningful changes and making real progress. Nevertheless, there was a consistent and sustained focus on lingering problems. A *Los Angeles Times* op-ed piece argues that "progress does not mean that all necessary reforms have been accomplished," and refers to data from the LAPD that shows that "racial disparities in how people are treated when stopped have increased, rather than declined, over the last five years."[89] Another op-ed, by Tom Hayden, paints an even dimmer picture of the contemporary state of the LAPD. Hayden, writing just after the consent decree was lifted, asks "why the decree was lifted now, before a number of critical reforms were achieved," and draws upon a 2009 study of the department's reform measures in order to suggest that the watchdog function performed by the federal government was still necessary. Hayden highlights a number of issues, including a "17% increase in the use of nonlethal force" in the department's Central Bureau over the past three years, a "troubling pattern" of subjecting African Americans to use of force out of proportion to their rates of contact with the LAPD, and the fact that the department had rejected every one of the 1,200 complaints of racial profiling that had been filed over the previous five year period.[90] Even straight news articles about the end of the consent decree tended to draw upon critical sources. For example, a fairly typical article quoted the legal director of the Southern California ACLU saying that there is "still too much evidence that skin color makes a difference in who is stopped, questioned and arrested by the LAPD."[91]

The Power of the Press: Public Perceptions of Rampart and Evolving Standards for Coverage of Police Corruption

The above examples provide some sense of the truly extraordinary kinds of coverage and critique that were generated in response to the Rampart scandal. There is some indication that this coverage had some (possibly ephemeral) impact on popular understandings of race, crime, and brutality, particularly in Los Angeles. From the beginning, the scandal captured the attention of most city residents. A *Los Angeles Times* poll conducted in April, 2000, provided some sense of the extent of the interest in the case, revealing that "three quarters of Los Angelenos have been following this scandal closely."[92] This interest could be felt in criminal trials, for as early as December, 1999, the scandal had started to undermine police credibility for Los Angeles jury members. In an op-ed piece for the *Los Angeles Times*, Pat Morrison wrote that "Already, in the noxious wake of the Rampart bad-cop scandal, the L.A. city attorney's office is noting an uptick in acquittals and hung juries, a few more jurors telling prosecutors they just didn't believe the cops in the witness box."[93] The *Philadelphia Inquirer* made a similar point, quoting the supervising judge of the Los Angeles Superior Court's criminal division saying that

> In talking to judges, I've found that it's clearly becoming an issue in almost every jury trial. . . . Defense lawyers will definitely raise Rampart no matter what the circumstances are. In some cases, where there does not seem to be any defense possible exempt Rampart, there have been acquittals.[94]

What we might call "the Rampart defense" was just one manifestation of growing mistrust of the police in the wake of early revelations in the scandal. Just months after the shooting and framing of Javier Ovando came to light, the *Los Angeles Times* conducted a poll that found that public approval of the LAPD was the lowest it had been since the videotape of the beating of Rodney King was first aired nine years earlier.[95] It took years of reform measures, and the lifting of the consent decree, before public approval of the LAPD began to rise significantly.[96]

Not surprisingly, understandings of the Rampart scandal appear to have varied according to race. The *Los Angeles Times* poll that I mention above showed that while 50 percent of respondents approved of the LAPD, only 18 percent of African Americans approved of the department, as opposed to 44 percent of whites, and 36 percent of Latinos. More tellingly, African Americans were far more likely than whites to think that the allegations in the Rampart scandal were "symptomatic of a larger problem rather than an isolated incident," while whites were nearly four times more likely to think that the allegations were "not representative of the police department as a whole." Even so, the systemic framing of the case seems to have influenced a good number of whites, given that 42 percent of white respondents did reject "bad apple" explanations for the scandal. Perhaps the most surprising finding was that, in contrast to whites, who tended to think that the scandal was damaging, African American respondents seemed pleased that the scandal was bringing problems that they were already aware of to light, as nearly a quarter of black respondents reported that "Rampart is having a positive effect on Los Angeles."[97]

Much of the critical coverage of Rampart can be understood by drawing upon Lawrence's analysis of "accidental events." Lawrence's work provides an important corrective to theoretical models that posit that news frames are generated by official sources who act as "primary definers" and set the agenda for debate. Lawrence observes that while it is true that "the news usually does present officially sanctioned realities," there are extraordinary circumstances that enable journalists to veer from standard routines of news gathering and reporting.[98] Lawrence's work helps to explain the conditions that would cause the media to turn to traditionally marginalized sources, including members of civil liberty groups, experts from liberal and left-wing think tanks, and members of grassroots organizations opposed to police brutality. It is important to note, however, that the notion of an "accidental event" suggests something that unfolds in a discrete moment of time. It is true that coverage of Rodney King focused not only on the beating, but also on both trials of the officers who beat him, and on the Los Angeles "riots," "uprising" or "rebellion,"[99] but it is important that the Rodney King beating involved the victimization of a single man on one particular night in 1991. There are clearly important lessons to be drawn from coverage of the beating of Rodney King, and important parallels between the King case and Rampart. Still, it is difficult to conceive of a scandal that unfolded over the course of several presidential administrations and that consisted of instances of misconduct, brutality and corruption involving dozens of officers and potentially thousands of victims, as an "accidental event."

Since the Rampart scandal lasted for more than a decade, there were numerous moments when media interest in the case, which might have died down a bit, was sparked anew by developments having to do with investigative findings, court decisions, reform measures, or related issues of police misconduct.[100] The longevity of Rampart-related coverage is especially noteworthy given that elected officials and the police generally do not want to focus on issues of police brutality, so any extensive coverage of police use of force can be read as a likely indication that "officials have lost control of the news."[101] Substantial coverage of police use of force is quite rare unless there is reason to think that there is a serious problem demanding both in-depth investigation and reliance upon non-traditional sources. Lawrence writes "the more coverage, the more critical coverage," explaining that "the more coverage an incident receives, the more likely it is to appear in articles that prominently feature critical nonofficial voices and systemic claims about police brutality."[102] Because even isolated "accidental events" can open doors to non-traditional sources including activists and police critics, it is worth asking what happens when these doors are forced open again and again over the course of many years.

The fleeting nature of most "accidental events" means that the challenges that they pose to standard journalistic practices are generally not sustained. Over time, as "bad cops" are convicted or otherwise punished, and as politicians and police departments agree to corrective measures, old routines are re-established, and officials are able to "regain control of the news."[103] Thus, at the very moment that the press starts to raise far-reaching questions about the nature of police misconduct, it "often simultaneously begins shutting down."[104] Lawrence sees this process as part of a "ritual of normalization,"[105] but it is not clear that such a ritual can occur when the doors opened by an "accidental event" never have the opportunity to close. I would suggest that a scandal as extensive and long-lived as Rampart has great potential to disrupt the journalistic status quo when it comes to coverage of police misconduct and the criminal justice system. When the press gets used to covering police brutality and misconduct by turning to sources such as the ACLU, academic experts on racism and police brutality, and grassroots activists, it is an open question whether control of the news will ever again be ceded to official sources, or whether basic journalistic conventions have changed. As of this writing, in August, 2010, any proposed answer would be premature, since we have only recently entered what might be called the "post-Rampart" era, marked by the lifting of the federal consent decree less than a year ago.

To the extent that the news media's treatment of the Rampart scandal exposed serious and far-reaching problems within and beyond the LAPD, and may have helped to change the very journalistic conventions by which police brutality and corruption are covered, the scandal may have played a crucial role in helping to combat the institutionalized racism and inequities that are embedded within the criminal justice system, since the "prison industrial complex" is in constant need of public support. Racist appeals to "tough on crime" measures might have considerably tougher sledding in a climate where police misconduct is not widely understood as aberrational. And yet, while there are strong indications that the doors to systemic critiques of the criminal justice system remain open,[106] the press is only one cultural force shaping public perceptions of race, crime, and police brutality. The value and importance of any possible shift in journalistic conventions of reporting on police misconduct must be weighed against the ways that these issues are represented in the wider culture. Most notably, I am concerned that whatever doors Rampart may have opened for far-ranging critiques of the criminal justice system may be shut by popular films and television shows, since there are still cultural producers who continue to resist systemic frames, and who are more comfortable with "bad apple" narratives. In Chapter 4, I discuss the ways that the entertainment industries have addressed the Rampart scandal, as I examine Hollywood's "reel bad cops."

4

REEL BAD COPS

Hollywood's Appropriation of the Rampart Scandal

"I'm the police, I run shit around here. You just live here. Yeah, that's right, you better walk away. Go on and walk away . . .'cause I'm gonna burn this motherfucker down. King Kong ain't got shit on me!"

Alonso Harris (Denzel Washington), *Training Day* (2001)

"Good cop and bad cop left for the day. I'm a different kind of cop."

Vic Mackey (Michael Chiklis), *The Shield* (2002)

In Chapter 3, I noted that the lack of any defining imagery meant that the Rampart scandal never really became a spectacle, at least in Debord's sense of the term as a "social relation among people, mediated by images."[1] Unlike the Rodney King case, there was no defining video footage that could easily define the nature of the scandal, or that could serve as a reference point or source of debate and contest. This helps to explain why, despite the fact that the scandal received quite a bit of press coverage and dominated headlines in Los Angeles area newspapers for several years, it never became a major national story on television news. Rampart did, however, reverberate beyond the press, and as it was picked up by Hollywood and translated into fictionalized films and television shows, imagery became central and scandal morphed into spectacle.

In order to assess the nature of this spectacle, this chapter first addresses the history and political importance of filmic and televisual representations of police corruption, arguing that such representations have played a key role in shaping public perceptions of the criminal justice system. As the chapter moves on to a discussion of *Training Day* and *The Shield*, the two highest profile pop cultural appropriations of the scandal, I consider the role that Hollywood plays in furthering or working to shut down the critical possibilities provided by news coverage of Rampart. In the previous chapter, I argued that it is possible that journalistic accounts of the scandal may have led to lasting changes in the conventions that news organizations use when reporting on police corruption and brutality, and consequently may have opened new doors for systemic critiques of institutionalized racism within the criminal justice system. However, in a case such as Rampart, which does not involve the kinds of dramatic video evidence that characterized the Rodney King case and other recent racial spectacles, Hollywood may be a more influential cultural force than the news media. When it comes to shaping the ways that substantial sectors of the population think about race and the criminal justice system, journalistic accounts may be less important than widely disseminated fictionalized versions of the scandal. The close readings of *Training Day* and *The Shield* that I offer in this chapter address the relationship between popular culture and the news media, as I consider the degree to which the kinds of systemic critique that were typical in news accounts of Rampart can be found in popular film and television representations of "bad cops."

Popular Culture and Understandings of the Criminal Justice System

As I argued earlier, it is not surprising that the Rampart scandal lacks defining imagery, since it is unlikely that police would do all of the work of framing innocent suspects in public, and because it is difficult to imagine compelling visual evidence that could capture such institutionalized problems as a code of silence that prevents police misconduct from coming to light, or a plea bargain system that encourages people to plead guilty to crimes they did not commit by imposing draconian prison terms upon poor defendants who demand their rights to a jury trial. Indeed, the lack of defining imagery in the Rampart scandal is far from unusual, and is in fact characteristic of a number of other high-profile recent and ongoing police scandals, including the Chicago police torture scandal of the 1970s through early 1990s, the federal corruption charges filed against members of the Philadelphia police department in the mid-1990s, and the investigations into unjustified killings and widespread brutality by members of the New Orleans police department in 2010.[2] The Justice Department has entered into consent decrees with sixteen police departments around the country, and none of the corruption or police misconduct that prompted these agreements has resulted in the production of visual evidence that was able to capture a fraction of the attention of the video of the beating of Rodney King.

The fact that so many of the most dramatic and extensive police scandals are so lacking in dramatic visual evidence points to the political potential of fictionalized appropriations of such scandals by Hollywood. If the kinds of systemic critiques of the criminal justice system characteristic of much of the news coverage of Rampart were presented in dramatized form within popular film and television, the resulting anti-racist spectacle could play a significant role in encouraging mass audiences to rethink common sense assumptions about race and crime. On the other hand, cinematic and televisual imagery that presents police corruption as aberrational can provide ideological support for "bad apple" narratives that deflect attention from institutionalized inequalities in the criminal justice system, and that consequently make it difficult to effectively challenge those inequalities. Whether Hollywood spectacles of police corruption proffer systemic or "bad apple" frames, the fact that these are some of the *only* spectacles of police corruption in American culture, and that they fill a visual void left by news coverage of police scandals, means that they have a great deal of power to shape popular understandings and collective memories of police corruption and misconduct, even when these spectacles are explicitly fictionalized.

Fictionalized representations of crime have played a major role in shaping public understandings of the criminal justice system for many years. Perhaps the clearest example has to do with popular perceptions of the *Miranda* warnings. The warnings, which stem from the Supreme Court's decision in *Miranda v. Arizona* (1966), are ubiquitous in crime films and television police shows. This ubiquity has ensured that the warnings have become one of the best-known parts of the American legal system, to the point that the phrase "You have the right to remain silent" is instantly recognizable to anyone with even a passing familiarity with popular culture. Television is widely credited with the fact that polls consistently show that the vast majority of the population is aware of the rights to have an attorney, and to remain silent, if arrested.[3] It is, in fact, arguably *because* the warnings are so firmly established in popular culture that they have survived as a constitutional requirement. In *Dickerson v. United States* (2000), the Supreme Court declined to overturn *Miranda* because the decision "has become embedded in routine police practice to the point where the warnings have become part of our national culture."[4] Naomi Mezey argues that several members of the Court who voted to uphold *Miranda* had previously voted to undercut the decision's constitutional rationale, but that they nevertheless decided to continue to require the warnings "not because the Constitution demanded them but because they had been popularized to the point that they were culturally understood as being constitutionally required."[5]

While it is clear that popular culture can influence public understandings of the criminal justice system, and that, as the *Dickerson* decision demonstrates, that influence can be powerful enough to in turn help shape the legal system itself, the kinds of understandings of the law that popular culture helps to generate are far from straightforward. Again, the *Miranda* warnings are a case in point. Television shows such as *NYPD Blue* and *Homicide* tend to depict the *Miranda* warnings as a procedural nuisance at best, and as a serious obstacle to justice that allows guilty suspects to go free at worst. Casual viewers of such shows would not be aware that the value of the *Miranda* warnings has been severely weakened by court decisions and police routines, or that the vast majority of suspects waive their *Miranda* rights. These shows would also, needless to say, not alert their viewers to the kinds of denials of due process that led to the *Miranda* decision in the first place. The value of the warnings as a method of securing constitutional rights is simply stripped away in most popular culture representations of *Miranda*, as are judicial and police efforts to undermine those rights. Such representations have likely taken a toll, as public anxiety about *Miranda* has forced numerous politicians to denounce the decision (alternatively, some politicians have gained political advantage by enthusiastically engaging in such denunciations), and in the process has helped to erode the value of the warnings.[6]

Police Corruption in Popular Film and Television

The political potency of televisual representations of the *Miranda* warnings is instructive when thinking about images of crime and policing within popular film and television more broadly, since it is precisely because these representations are so influential that they demand careful scrutiny. As Judith Grant says, "portrayals of police in popular culture contribute to public understandings of the police."[7] When thinking of the Rampart scandal, it is important to consider that popular understandings of police misconduct have been shaped by, and filtered through, crime films and cop shows that can be seen as a response to what Sasha Torres calls the "national fetishization of 'law and order' in post-1968 American culture."[8] The prevalence of cinematic and televisual images of police officers dutifully Mirandizing their suspects might suggest that the pop cultural landscape is one in which every potential criminal is accorded full due process. In fact, though, as Grant observes, crime movies and cop shows are littered with examples of police misconduct, and "the corrupt cop is a staple in popular culture."[9] Grant suggests that pop cultural images of police and crime help to foster a kind of collective amnesia, ensuring that mass audiences, who are exposed to new police scandals "every few years in every major city in America" can still be shocked by every new scandal.[10] The trope of the corrupt cop would appear to work against this suggestion, since "Far from allowing the public to forget about police corruption, [this figure] at first suggests the public is continually reminded of its presence."[11] It is not the case, then, that popular culture simply refuses to acknowledge police scandals. Instead, crime films and cop shows frequently draw upon widespread familiarity with such scandals in order to attract mass audiences. Grant suggests that the catch here is that the specific kinds of "reminders" of police corruption offered by popular film and television shows suggest that no more than a handful of rogue officers are responsible for such scandals. The entanglement of popular culture and collective memory here is quite striking, since popular culture draws upon collective memories of police scandals, but then works to reconfigure those memories in fictionalized forms that suggest that police misconduct is aberrational.

While there are countless examples of corrupt cops in television shows, until recently these characters have been minor figures: they lurked in the shadows, or showed up every now and then, only to be confronted by series regulars who rejected their cynicism and greed, valiantly standing up for the principles of law and order. Televisual representations of police corruption have generally been fleeting, and corruption stories have rarely been sustained for more than an episode or two. In contrast to the place of police corruption within popular television, there is a long history of Hollywood filmmaking that places corruption at the center of the narrative. The majority of films that deal with police corruption revolve around isolated rogue officers who are often brought to justice by their un-corruptible peers. Occasionally, the rogue officers travel in packs, leading to "the classic Hollywood scenario in which a few bad cops are balanced with a good one who upholds the 'true' meaning of being a law enforcement officer."[12] When Hollywood films do present problems within the criminal justice system as systemic, they tend to offer fairly muted critiques, at least when compared to the most challenging news coverage of scandals like Rampart. Some of the most celebrated filmic representations of police corruption come from film noir, or neo-noir, such as *The Big Heat* (1953) and *Chinatown* (1974). While these films often support the notion that "everybody is on the take and the whole system is corrupt,"[13] they generally ignore institutionalized racism and other structural inequalities that are at the heart of Rampart and many other police scandals. Hollywood appropriations of the Rampart scandal, then, follow on the heels of a decidedly unpromising trajectory. The cinematic and televisual template for narratives of police corruption provides little reason to think that pop cultural representations of Rampart would be likely to fulfill the potential for meaningful and far-reaching critiques hinted at by news coverage of the scandal. On the other hand, as I argued in Chapter 3, the longevity and extent of critical Rampart coverage appears to have been something new, and may well have changed the basic journalistic conventions involved in reporting on police corruption. In the discussion that follows, I suggest that the reverberations of Rampart in popular culture may have also led to far-reaching changes in genre expectations, even as the political nature of these changes is difficult to assess.

The cinematic potential of Rampart was hinted at in the earliest news coverage of the case, as reporters who were searching for ways to explain the nature of the scandal regularly looked to Hollywood films as precedent. It became commonplace to invoke film noir in order to emphasize that networks of corruption could no longer be seen as relics of the past, as in a *Los Angeles Times* story that quotes a public defender saying that "people who saw *L.A. Confidential* and said it could never happen now were wrong."[14] Because the similarities to the corruption narrative in *L.A. Confidential* seemed so clear, and because the film was set in Los Angeles, this film in particular became a regular reference point. The *New York Times* opined that "Here in the home of Hollywood, the case seems the stuff of noir fiction, of *L.A. Confidential*, come to lurid life."[15] References to the film were not confined to news coverage. In his campaign against Gil Garcetti for Los Angeles District Attorney, Steve Cooley regularly noted that "*L.A. Confidential* was a movie. Rampart is real."[16] Interestingly, when the press wanted to suggest that reality was more troubling than fiction, it often turned not to film but to television. For example, the world of law and order as depicted on prime time police procedurals was referenced as a point of contrast in an op-ed piece that sets the stage for a discussion of Rampart by noting "It's something you never see on TV: the victims of a police conspiracy pleading guilty to false charges."[17]

Hollywood's Turn: Pop Cultural Appropriations of the Rampart Scandal

It was perhaps inevitable that a story of police corruption on the scale of Rampart would eventually be thought of as something that would have the potential to capture a mass audience. There is, after all, inherent drama in a story that involves drug dealing cops who hold parties where officers are rewarded with plaques for shooting innocent suspects. Moreover, the appeal of such stories is long established. In fact, as early as 1951, Senator Estes Kefauver's hearings into organized crime created one of the first truly massive national televised spectacles, captivating the nation with tales of police corruption in a case involving a "sordid intermingling of crime and politics."[18] In an era in which only 1.5 percent of American homes used television sets during morning hours,[19] and when New York City had just become the first city in the world where more than half of the households had a television, thirty million people watched the testimony of a key witness in the hearings.[20] Twice as many people watched the hearings as had tuned in for the World Series the previous year, and stores complained that they could do no business while the hearings were on.[21] An editorial in *Life* magazine summed up the importance of the hearings thus:

> The week of March 12, 1951, will occupy a special place in history. . . . The U.S. and the world had never experienced anything like it. . . . For days on end and into the nights [people] watched with complete absorption . . . the first big television broadcast of an affair of their government, the broadcast from which all future uses of television in public affairs must date. . . . Never before had the attention of the nation been so completely riveted on a single matter.[22]

The hearings sought to establish not only that organized crime existed, but that it had strong links to police and politicians.[23] From the inception of the medium of television, then, it was clear that police corruption was fit for prime time.[24]

The entertainment potential of Rampart was quickly seized upon, and the scandal has had considerable impact in popular culture. Rampart provided a key plot point for *Grand Theft Auto: San Andreas*, a 2004 video game that was at the center of recent controversies over violence and gaming. The protagonist of the game is a man who was framed for murder by corrupt members of a CRASH unit. The officers are thought to have been patterned on Rafael Perez and Nino Durden.[25] A corrupt cop in the television show *Robbery Homicide Division* (2002) was also based on Officer Perez. Many corners of popular culture have been influenced by Rampart, but the scandal has proven to be particularly fertile ground for Hollywood directors and writers. A series of films that either revolved around police corruption or that had significant police corruption subplots are explicitly indebted to the scandal. *Rampart* (Richard Givens, 2005) and *Dirty* (Chris Fisher, 2005), were limited release films, intended primarily for a straight-to-DVD market, that borrowed heavily from the scandal. Several bigger-budget films, including *Cellular* (David Ellis, 2004), *Crash* (Paul Haggis, 2005), and *Dark Blue* (Ron Shelton, 2002) had subplots involving police corruption that mirror elements of the Rampart scandal. In order to provide context for the fictional corruption narrative in the film, the special features on the DVD of *Cellular* include a documentary called *Code of Silence: Inside the Rampart Scandal* (Chris Sikorowski, 2004). With the exception of *Crash*, these were all understood as fairly minor films with little depth, and only *Crash* lasted for more than a couple of weeks in the multiplexes.[26] *Crash* was a critical and commercial success, winning the 2006 Academy awards for best picture and best screenwriting, but the Rampart-related elements of the film received relatively little public commentary.[27] To date, the highest profile popular culture attempts to reckon with the legacy of Rampart are Antoine Fuqua's 2001 film *Training Day*, and *The Shield*, Shawn Ryan's television show that ran on the FX network from 2002–2008. Since these represent the two most serious popular culture engagements with Rampart, I discuss them in some detail below.

Training Day

To say that *Training Day* is an attempt to reckon with the legacy of Rampart is a bit tricky, since the original screenplay was written in 1995, years before the scandal came to light, and a full year before Rafael Perez and Nino Durden shot and framed Javier Ovando. But the film, which focuses on the events of one day in the lives of a corrupt Los Angeles police officer and his trainee, was shot in and around the Rampart district in 2001, as new revelations about the scandal were capturing headlines on a daily basis, and it is clear that the scandal influenced the making of the film in numerous ways. Most importantly, David Ayer, the film's screenwriter, has suggested that the film might not have been made if not for the scandal, since he'd been shopping the script around for years without luck, and only "when Perez got busted did the project gain momentum—it was now topical."[28] Antoine Fuqua told *Newsweek* that "when I was making [the film], I kept telling myself, 'Someone needs to tell this story – the riots in Cincinnati, the Abner Louima case in New York, the Rampart scandal,'"[29] and Denzel Washington is said to have patterned the appearance of his character, Alonso Harris, on Rafael Perez.[30] There are also numerous plot points that mirror or appear to

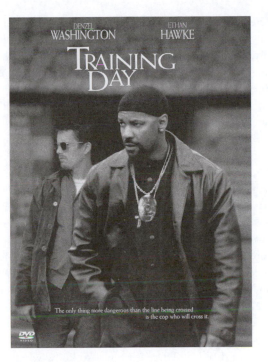

FIGURE 4.1 Training Day DVD Cover, 2001.

reference events in the Rampart scandal, but that do not appear in an early version of the script.[31] While Rampart was only one part of the inspiration for the film, the timing of the film's release, along with the fact that its corruption narrative paralleled the scandal in significant ways, meant that *Training Day* would inevitably be read as a "reel life" version of Rampart. Since the film capitalized upon collective memories of Rampart in order to attract a mass audience, and because it draws upon such memories in the form of borrowed plot points, it likely played a substantial role in shaping both the ways that Rampart itself would be remembered, and the ways that Rampart-era police corruption would be understood. In fact, as a big-budget, glossy Hollywood production seen by millions of people throughout the nation and the world, the cinematic spectacle of *Training Day* is quite likely to have played a *more* powerful role in shaping memories and understandings of Rampart and police corruption than did news coverage of the scandal, despite the fact that it is clearly presented as fiction.

In some respects, the plot of *Training Day* is strikingly similar to the real-life events of the Rampart scandal. The resemblance between Denzel Washington's Alonso Harris and Rafael Perez is not only physical, but extends to the circumstances that each officer finds himself in, starting with an ill-fated trip to Las Vegas.[32] Whereas Perez first attracted the attention of police investigators by celebrating in Vegas with Officer David Mack after Mack's robbery of a Bank of America branch in South Central Los Angeles, *Training Day* starts shortly after Harris has returned from a gambling trip to Vegas that went awry when Harris killed a Russian mobster. The plot of the film involves Harris's efforts to secure the $1,000,000 that the mob has demanded as payment for the death. Harris is the head of an elite and corrupt Rampart-like LAPD unit, though his unit investigates narcotics and not gangs. The members of Harris's group, like the members of Perez's CRASH unit, have matching menacing tattoos. (The CRASH members had a tattoo with a "grinning skull with demonic eyes . . . Atop the skull is a cowboy hat adorned with a police badge. Fanned out behind it are four playing cards—aces and eights—the so-called dead man's hand."[33] Harris and his men have a tattoo of a skull's head on angel wings, on top of crossed swords, with the motto "Death is certain. Life is not." The tattoos appear to have been inspired by the Rampart scandal, since they are not mentioned in the 1999 draft of the script.)[34] Perhaps the most telling analogue to the Rampart scandal involves a paraplegic drug dealer.

Towards the end of the film, Alonso Harris attempts to terrorize his partner, Jake Hoyt (played by Ethan Hawke), by casually boasting that he was responsible for a black drug dealer's paralysis. He references the dealer by asking: "That fool in the wheelchair? How you think he got there?" In the 1999 draft of the script, the drug dealer is not disabled. There is no way to know whether the screenplay was modified with Rampart in mind, but the resonance of Harris's boast, and its departure from what might be seen as the "original sin" of the Rampart scandal provides an important indication of the ways that the film wrestles with the legacies of the scandal. On the one hand, Alonso Harris's shooting of Blue (the drug dealer, played by Snoop Dogg) can be seen as roughly parallel to Rafael Perez's shooting of Javier Ovando, and the film might be seen as working to secure, or at least as acknowledging, a collective memory of the defining act of victimization of the Rampart scandal. On the other hand, Blue is not a character who inspires much sympathy. The first time we see him, he is trying to sell drugs to Jake, before quickly sensing that something is wrong. He flees, but only after confronting Jake: "Smells like bacon in this muthafucka. What I look like, a sucka to you, nigga? Fuck you, rookie." As he flees he curses at Jake and swats him aside before being knocked out of his wheelchair. When he is finally stopped he lies about being a dealer and falsely accuses Jake of having planted a gun on him.

If *Training Day* can be read, partly, as a cinematic reconstruction of collective memories of Rampart, then the differences between Javier Ovando and Blue are instructive for what they say about how we are to remember and understand the people who suffer because of police corruption. Because he was a gang member, Javier Ovando was probably not someone whose victimization at the hands of LAPD officers was likely to elicit much sympathy from the general public, and, for that reason, he might not appear to be all that different from Snoop Dogg's drug dealer. But Ovando was a fairly typical victim of the Rampart scandal, not only because he was an innocent victim of police brutality, but because he was young and Latino. It is true that, in general terms, African Americans and Latinos have both suffered at the hands of the LAPD, but Rampart was a scandal that involved the disproportionate targeting of a Latino population, and swapping Blue for Ovando is part of a process through which the film obscures the defining racial dimensions of the scandal.

The racial dimensions of police corruption are, in fact, muddled throughout the film. At one level, the film takes great pains to remove racial motivations as possible factors in Alonso Harris's crimes. Aside from Blue, Harris's victims include: several white college kids that he catches in a drug deal; a corrupt senior officer who is white; Jake Hoyt, Alonso's partner who may be biracial, part white and part Latino; two men, one white and one black, who attempt to rape a young Latina; and a black female drug dealer. Harris's brutality cuts across racial lines, and he appears to be an equal-opportunity crook, choosing his victims solely on the basis of convenience or necessity. Harris has a child with a Salvadoran woman (played by Eva Mendes) who lives in the community that he patrols—the apparently exclusively Latino and African American area referred to as "the jungle." While there is a clear sense that the residents of this community see Harris as a one-man occupying army who controls the population through fear, there is very little sense of their having suffered at his hands. Had the film depicted a white officer terrorizing a community of Latinos and African Americans, it would have been difficult to avoid focusing on possible racist motivations, but the decision to place an African American officer with a Latino lover and child at the center of a police corruption narrative helps to solidify the suggestion that race is irrelevant, since such an officer would presumably not be interested in targeting a Latino and black population because of racial animus.

Of course, there is also no reason to think that either Rafael Perez or Nino Durden (who were Puerto Rican and black, respectively) were driven by racist motivations, and, presumably, it would be possible to create a cinematic depiction of the racist victimization of a community that does not involve a corrupt officer driven by racist sentiment. This would require, however, conceptualizing racism in institutionalized rather than individualized terms. The most powerful kinds of systemic framing in news accounts of the Rampart scandal focused on racialized inequalities throughout the criminal justice and immigration systems, and painted a picture of suffering within the Rampart patrol district that had everything to do with institutionalized racism but nothing to do with personal prejudice. The key to this kind of frame involved journalistic decisions not to provide another monster story.

Training Day, on the other hand, is a monster story, and Alonso Harris is a monster through and through. He enjoys brutalizing street criminals, tracks down drug dealers only to steal their drugs and their money, conducts illegal searches with fake search warrants, bribes judges for illegitimate arrest warrants, murders the officer who was his first partner and mentor, and then shoots one of his teammates in order to help cover up the crime. Not only does he never exhibit a hint of regret for any of these actions; he is positively gleeful as he carries them out. And all of this is only the tip of the iceberg, since we eventually learn that Harris has spent a full week before the events depicted in the movie figuring out how to manipulate a partner that he has not yet met in order to set him up to take the blame for all of the crimes that are necessary to secure payment for the Russian mob. Harris's ultimate plan is not just to make Jake his fall guy, but eventually to have him killed in order to eliminate any possible trail of evidence.

While the film takes great pains to divorce police corruption and brutality from racism, it makes very little effort to separate corruption and brutality from race itself: Harris's blackness is central to his monstrosity. Robin Coleman and Jasmine Cobb argue that as an "innately savage, animalistic, hypersexual, destructive, and criminal" African American man, Harris is the perfect embodiment of the "buck" stereotype.[35] Indeed, Harris's hyper-sexuality and animalism are central to the ways that he understands his place in the world. His attempt to establish mastery over Jake begins with emasculating banter as he admonishes Jake for having spent a year working with a female partner without having had sex with her. When Jake objects that "I have a wife," Harris replies "you also have a dick." Later, Harris asserts his own hyper-masculinity by telling Jake "I have four kids. All boys. You need a son, you let me know, I hook your old lady up, you know? I can't miss."[36] When Jake tries to sum up Harris's attitudes about the residents of "the jungle" by asking "Let the animals wipe themselves out, right?" Harris responds by referencing his hierarchy in the animal kingdom: "If only they would . . . To protect the sheep you catch the wolves. And it takes a wolf to catch a wolf." If there was any doubt about his lupine status, Harris then issues a deep, throaty, howl. He coaxes Jake into joining him, but Jake's best efforts come across as nothing more than a pale imitation, as Harris urges "that's a rooster, give me a wolf!" Inadequate as man and as beast, Jake appears to be poor competition for Alonso. Eventually, though, Harris's schemes fall apart and, when he is forced to do battle with Jake, Jake emerges victorious. Before leaving him to face his fate at the hands of the Russian mob, Jake shoots Harris in the butt in an act that Jared Sexton reads as an emasculating symbolic anal rape, or "uninvited anal penetration."[37] Jake's actions render Harris powerless but they fail to challenge his sense of his place in the jungle's pecking order. The quote that I used to open this chapter, in which Harris declares that "King Kong ain't got shit on me!" comes as Jake has left the scene, and Harris is forced to confront the residents of the neighborhood. Harris's defiant exclamation may suggest that he is the king of the beasts, but the jungle was never really the issue for either Kong or Harris: both were brought down by white men invested with the power and authority of the state.

Harris's masculinity and animalism are linked to his corruption, as the film suggests that real men are not bound by the same rules that apply to the general population. Real cops need to be wild and unleashed, and cannot be bound by procedural rules and the constraints of due process. Whatever his problems, Harris is a deadly effective cop, and one who will not allow legal niceties to get in his way. When he suspects that a drug dealer has swallowed crack cocaine so as to avoid being caught with it, he simply jabs a pen down the dealer's throat, forcing him to vomit up the evidence. Rather than arrest two potential rapists and wait for a trial, he stabs one of them, threatens him with castration before kneeing him in the groin, steals both men's drugs and money, and leaves them to be killed by local gang members. But while Harris never appears to even consider playing by the rules, he is not alone in flouting them when need be. His interaction with the potential rapists comes only after Jake has seen the attempted rape and intervened, alone, to stop the act in progress. Jake is attacked by both of the suspects, and is nearly overwhelmed and killed. He survives only by putting one of the men in a choke-hold, a tactic that the film suggests has been banned. Alonso is pleased with Jake's actions, and as they're driving away, he tells Jake that he "did the right thing . . . That was some amazing shit back there." Harris does not appear to care at all about the attempted rape (he chided Jake for coming to the victim's rescue, and stood aside watching and smoking a cigarette while Jake fought the two men), and was annoyed that Jake wanted to waste time by taking the men into custody. Harris's approval, then, seems to be based solely upon Jake's willingness to employ force, and to buck procedure in doing so. After complimenting Jake, he smiles slyly, asking: "I noticed you applied that choke-hold, huh? I thought that was a no-no, procedure-boy?" When Jake responds that "I was gettin' my ass kicked," Harris affirms that Jake had no choice, saying "Yeah, and you did what you had to do, right? You did what you *had* to do." This is the one moment in the film where Jake accepts Harris's assessment of the necessity for "street justice," as he grins and nods in agreement.

This scene is pivotal in convincing Harris that his schemes might bear fruit, since they provide the first indication that Jake will be willing to go along with some unorthodox police tactics. This will be essential if Harris is to be successful in his attempt to frame Jake for crimes to be committed later in the day. Harris seizes upon Jake's willingness to break procedure as an opportunity to begin to instruct him about the ways of the street, and to start his "training day" in earnest. Harris's tutelage places him squarely within the tradition of popular culture representations of bad cops: one of the most common tropes of cinematic and televisual representations of police corruption involves grizzled veterans who socialize new officers into a culture of corruption. The officer who is undergoing this process of socialization is often meant to provide a point of identification for audience members, and part of the power, and danger, of these films is that the officer's growing acceptance of this culture is intended to mirror our own. While most cop corruption films reject the most egregious forms of corruption and brutality, to the extent that we are expected to accept some of the young officer's eventual transgressions as necessary, these films can constitute their own forms of socialization, encouraging mass audiences to see things such as evidence tampering, perjury, and excessive use of force as nothing more than somewhat regrettable parts of a job that needs to be done. Socialization narratives have been important for some of the most important and interesting police corruption films, including *Serpico* and *L.A. Confidential*. The very title of *Training Day* provides strong foreshadowing that such a narrative is centrally important for the film.

Because it helps constitute one of the central turning points of the film and is crucial for the film's implicit claim that procedural rules can create unnecessary and even life-threatening hurdles for police officers, the film's presentation of the choke-hold merits close interrogation. Jake defends his use of the tactic by suggesting that it was the only available method of self defense, but he sheepishly accepts the idea that he has knowingly violated department policy, and the film suggests that his actions put him on a continuum with Harris. Harris may have no regard for due process or accepted police procedures at all, while Jake may insist on their importance, but when push comes to shove, he too is willing to do what must be done to protect his own life and bring the bad guys to justice. He is willing to step outside of the law not because, like Harris, he is a monster, but because the rules that would prevent him from taking appropriate action are nonsensical and dangerous. The filmmakers have reinforced this understanding of curbs on police practices in interviews. Antoine Fuqua told the *Washington Post* that "Cops have one hand tied behind their backs a lot of the time. And they're dealing with people who don't have any hands tied behind their backs."[38] David Ayer has expressed sympathy for officers who are in positions like Jake's, claiming that "Any cops on the street for more than a week know there are these gray areas. You've gotta get messy, get your hands dirty."[39] Neither Fuqua nor Ayer approve of Harris's actions, but they do suggest that his behavior is dictated, at least in part, by having to deal with rules that were set up with excessive concern for due process and civil liberties. Fuqua refers to Harris as "One sick, depressed, far-gone guy. A victim of the system," while Ayer distinguishes between different kinds of police misconduct:

> There are cops who break the law to take out the lawbreakers. And there are cops who break the laws to enrich themselves. One I can justify. Others I can't . . . You can't survive in a place like this [the Rampart district] without having some edge, okay? It's okay with me if your intentions are to do the job. But if you're trying to get rich, if you're racist, it's not okay. Raping chicks—that's not okay.[40]

While it's good to see that Ayer can find ways to draw the line of unacceptable police conduct, the history of the choke-hold presents a particularly difficult fit for the kind of defense of rule violations that *Training Day* offers.

The use of choke-holds by members of the LAPD became controversial in the late 1970s and early 1980s, as sixteen people were killed by officers using the tactic over a seven year period. Black men, who constituted only nine percent of the population, accounted for seventy-five percent of the deaths.[41] In 1982, LAPD Chief Daryl Gates, who would later offer highly charged defenses of the officers who beat Rodney King, sought to explain these deaths by suggesting that it might be the case that African-Americans' "veins or arteries do not open up as fast as they do in normal people."[42] Lou Cannon, who argues that Gates mis-spoke here and did not believe in the racist sentiment that seems apparent, nevertheless acknowledges the racist use of the tactic, noting that "Choke holds were sometimes used to humiliate blacks by causing them to 'do the chicken'— flop around from a loss of oxygen."[43] The ban on the tactic that *Training Day* alludes to has its roots in a suit that was brought by Adolph Lyons, a twenty-four-year-old black man who had survived being placed in a choke-hold during a traffic stop. Lyons won the case at trial and a judge issued an injunction barring use of the practice "except in cases posing threats of death or serious bodily injury to the police."[44] The ruling survived an appeal to the Ninth Circuit, but was overturned by the Supreme Court, which ruled that Lyons was entitled to sue for damages, but not for injunctive relief, since, as Lisa Kloppenberg summarizes the Court's logic, "he could not prove that he would be injured *again* by an LAPD officer using a choke hold on *him*."[45] The department never did ban the practice, though it did eventually modify its policy so that the tactic would now be permitted only when "deadly force"[46] was required. In effect, the department had voluntarily accepted the trial judge's ruling.

Whether under the initial court ruling or the modified departmental policy, Jake would have been well within his rights to use a choke-hold in his battle with the attempted rapists, since he was clearly facing a threat of death or serious bodily injury. The film's suggestion that Jake had knowingly violated a problematic rule therefore represents a disingenuous engagement with the history of the tactic. When the choke-hold came under fire, members of the LAPD and other police departments and organizations objected to a possible ban in precisely the terms that are suggested in the film, arguing that the tactic was a necessary tool that could save lives. Harris's disdain for the ban taps into memories of law enforcement outrage while neglecting the kinds of suffering that the tactic caused and the racism that so frequently motivated its deployment. The film thus constructs a collective memory that justifies police lawlessness while positioning civil libertarians and critics of police violence as being on the side of criminals.

Jake's willingness to use the choke-hold and break procedural rules is important not so much for what it says about Jake, but because it sheds light upon the nature of Harris's monstrosity. While Harris is clearly positioned as a uniquely malevolent figure, Jake's actions suggest that Harris's monstrosity is not sui generis or disconnected from the duties of his job. Instead, it is possible to read Harris as an extreme case resulting from problems with the criminal justice system being taken to their logical conclusion. If even good cops are forced, as early as their training day, to begin to violate legally accepted procedures, and if it is clear that this is the only possible way to carry out their responsibilities as officers of the law, then lines begin to blur and the boundaries of the monstrous start to become unclear. In the director's commentary on the DVD of the film, Antoine Fuqua describes Alonso Harris by saying

> He's a guy that's probably done some good when he first started, and realized that, you know, if you just move this an inch this way, you can actually get a case to stick. And then you start moving it a foot, and a yard, and next thing you know, you're on the other side.

This sounds an awful lot like a potential trajectory for a character like Jake, and it raises the question of where good cops end and bad cops begin. The problem with monster stories is that they tend to isolate monsters and obscure the social production of monstrosity. Jake's decision to use a choke-hold and the film's presentation of this decision as a break with accepted procedures begins to disrupt any sense of Harris's isolation. This is only one of several moments in which *Training Day* becomes a somewhat atypical monster story.

It turns out that Harris could not function as a monster on his own, and that powerful players benefit from and contribute to his actions. The members of his elite narcotics unit are willing accomplices to many of Harris's crimes and, more importantly, the unit is supported by high-ranking members of the police force. Early in the film, Harris forces Jake to smoke PCP-laced marijuana. Once Jake sobers up, he becomes concerned that he will fail a routine drug test and that his career will be over. Harris reassures him that the standard rules don't apply for his unit: "Lieutenant's got our back. We know a week before we get pissed." Throughout the film, we get glimpses of the kinds of connections that Harris has formed with powerful players in the criminal justice infrastructure. He appears to be answerable to a group of high-ranking officers that he refers to as "the three wise men," including a corrupt police captain, the head of an agency that investigates officer-involved shootings, and an officer in charge of investigating particularly large thefts. The film suggests that each one of these men can direct the resources of their departments towards abetting, or curbing, Harris's exploits, and that their decisions are based solely on their own personal gain. The wise men sign off on Harris's decision to murder his first partner, and help him negotiate the price to bribe a judge for an illegitimate arrest warrant. The routine violations of police procedures and criminal laws that Harris engages in are thus revealed as firmly linked to a network of corruption. Tellingly, Harris is aware that it is not just the wise men, the judge, or the members of Harris's unit who benefit from his actions, but also the prison industrial complex as a whole, as he informs Jake that "They build jails 'cuz of me. Judges have handed out over 15,000 man-years of incarceration time based on my investigations." Hardly isolated in his monstrosity, Harris is an institution, and the film suggests that the criminal justice system as we know it is based on a foundation of corruption.

And yet, while the atypical aspects of *Training Day* are notable, in the final analysis the film *is* just another monster story. This becomes clear when considering the kinds of solutions that the film offers to the problems that it depicts. The DVD of the film includes an alternative ending in which Jake confronts the three wise men. In this version of the film, Jake manages to frustrate Harris's overseers and deny them their bounty from Harris's most recent crime spree. Still, as far as the wise men are concerned, Jake doesn't amount to much more than a nuisance. They walk away from him annoyed, but unbowed. If this had been the final scene of the movie, audiences would have left the theaters with a fresh reminder that Harris served at the pleasure of these corrupt officers, who would remain firmly entrenched as high-ranking power brokers even as the credits began to roll. To the extent that the film was intended to function as a commentary on real-life corruption, this ending would have directed attention to at least a mild systemic analysis. Instead, the film that made it into theaters ends after Harris has been killed by the Russian mob, with Jake returning home. Jake's weariness works against a reading of the ending as entirely triumphant, but as in any good monster story, the important thing is that the monster has been killed. Networks of corruption have dropped away as a point of concern and Jake prepares for another day on the job as a good cop without any lingering suggestion that he, or any other cop, might be indebted to Harris's legacy, or any sense that battles against it still need to be waged. Ultimately, the film does little to dispel the kinds of bad apple framing of police corruption typical of the genre.

The Shield

As important as *Training Day* might have been for constructing understandings of police corruption in the Rampart era, its availability to a mass audience was relatively ephemeral. It was a highly successful Hollywood film, but it was still out of the theaters within a few months of its 2001 release date. And while it garnered impressive DVD sales and rentals, once it left the multiplexes, it no longer occasioned much critical attention.

The Shield, on the other hand, lasted for seven years, attracting millions of viewers on a weekly basis and prompting numerous reviews and critical commentaries throughout its duration, especially in its first and final seasons. *The Shield* chronicles the exploits of a white detective named Vic Mackey (Michael Chiklis), and the corrupt Strike Team (a CRASH-like elite undercover unit) that he leads in the fictional Farmington district of Los Angeles. The show was directly inspired by the Rampart scandal ("Rampart" was, in fact, the title that was used in early advertisements for the show, but the producers abandoned this title when the LAPD objected to it), and represents the most sustained and extensive pop cultural engagement with police corruption in the Rampart era.

Like *Training Day*, *The Shield* almost never made it into production. While David Ayer was unable to sell the script to *Training Day* until the Rampart scandal

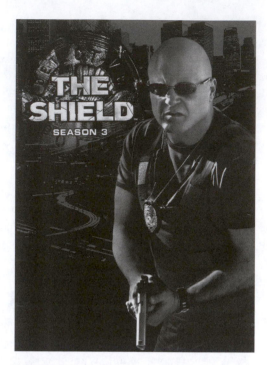

FIGURE 4.2 The Shield DVD Cover, 2002.

broke, Shawn Ryan was only able to convince the F/X network to take a chance on *The Shield* when it became clear that *Training Day* was a hit. Peter Liguoir, the chairman and chief executive of the network, told the *New York Times* that the positive reviews of *Training Day*, along with its opening weekend take of over twenty-two million dollars, convinced him that "there was an audience out there who wanted to see a fully dimensionalized representation of the police."[47] F/X's decision to buy the show bore immediate fruit: the pilot episode drew the largest audience for any series premier on cable television, and the show quickly became a signature hit for the network. The show won numerous awards, including a Golden Globe for best drama in 2003. Michael Chiklis won the Emmy for best actor in 2002, and the Golden Globe in 2003. In 2006, the series also won the first ever Peabody award for a cable drama. The show was instrumental in establishing a brand identity for the F/X network, which became known for edgy fare that could previously be found only on HBO and other pay cable stations.[48]

While David Ayer has referenced the Rampart scandal in order to highlight his own prescience in writing the script for *Training Day* (he told the *Ottawa Citizen* that "It was kind of spooky, really, because what I had written about four years before was now in the newspapers"),[49] Shawn Ryan has focused on the scandal as a way of highlighting the realism of *The Shield*. On the show's website,

Ryan explains that as he was wondering what kinds of characters should be in his new cop show, he

> opened the *Los Angeles Times* to find a story about a new scandal brewing—that of the CRASH unit of officers working in the Rampart district of Los Angeles. As I continued following the story over the next couple of weeks, two things became very clear—these guys were very bad. And they were very effective. And thus was born Vic Mackey and the Strike Team.[50]

The overriding lesson that Ryan appears to have taken from the Rampart scandal, and one that infuses every episode of *The Shield*, is that there is a strong link between "very bad" and "very effective" policing. The idea that the spirit of *The Shield* is based upon simply "following the story" suggests that the Rampart scandal is encoded in its DNA. While Ryan has claimed that the series did not borrow specific details from the scandal, his references to Rampart serve as a way to bolster the suggestion that this is not just another Hollywood cop show, but one shaped by the gritty reality of the street. The show's clear indebtedness to Rampart helps to ensure the scandal's status as a template or lens through which other instances of police corruption, and of "effective" policing, should be understood.

Like Alonso Harris, Vic Mackey is an extremely charismatic cop who regularly steals from drug dealers, enjoys beating up and even torturing suspects, and is willing to set up other cops to take the fall for his misdeeds. Perhaps it is only because the series lasted for so long, but Mackey actually commits far *more* crimes than does Harris. He and his team are responsible for no fewer than eight murders, along with numerous armed robberies and blackmail schemes. Not only do they bribe politicians and police officials, but they also accept payoffs from drug dealers and gang members, agreeing to look away as deals go down and rivals are killed. When troubles between rival rappers create problems on the street that threaten to cut into Mackey's profits, he locks the two men in a shipping container overnight, baits them into a fight to the death, and waits to see which one survives. If one were to formulate a checklist of "bad cop" behaviors (and it would not surprise me to learn that the writers at F/X did exactly this), Mackey would likely hit every mark, many of them on multiple occasions. Despite this, Mackey is a fully multi-dimensional character, and is consequently represented far more sympathetically than is Alonso Harris.

Mackey may be a lying, bribing and cheating murderer who puts his own well-being above everything else, but he is also a loving father struggling to meet the needs of his autistic children and legitimately concerned with the safety of the community that he polices, even if he may be willing to sacrifice that concern when put to the test. His corruption and misconduct are often motivated by nothing more complex than greed, but he is just as likely to channel his ill-gotten gains into admission fees for a special needs school for his kids as he is to use them for an extra-luxurious retirement fund. Similarly, his brutality might be prompted by the need to cover up one of his crimes, but will more frequently be employed to do things like forcing a kidnapper to reveal the location of his latest victim. Denzel Washington's performance in *Training Day* was absolutely magnetic, and it was impossible to turn away as he smiled, sneered, and howled his way through the film. But by the end of the film it was impossible to like Alonso Harris. In contrast, if fan blogs are any indication, devotees of *The Shield* love Vic Mackey. Shawn Ryan sums up Vic's appeal, setting aside some of his baser motivations in a way that is probably quite similar to what fans do:

> People root for Vic Mackey, even though he's a cop who does some very bad things. . . . He has a sense of humor. He has a family he likes. He lives by a code that justifies what he does. He feels he had the freedom to go after bad people, in any way, in order to make our lives safer.[51]

Unlike *Training Day*, *The Shield* is not a monster story, because Vic Mackey is not a monster.

For all of the problems with the monster-slaying narrative of *Training Day*, the film did have the virtue of at least representing extreme forms of police corruption as intolerable. I have suggested that the filmmakers' decision to shunt aside any kind of systemic critique by the end of the film and to instead find a measure of salvation in Alonso Harris's death represents a failure to grapple with the nature of the real problems that plague the criminal justice system. But the fact that the kinds of corruption that Harris stood for had to be excised from the community for there to be any semblance of a happy ending provides some indication that there are kinds of police misconduct that are beyond the pale. It is only possible to take any comfort in this message (which, after all, should be permitted to stand unspoken as a commonsensical assumption) when considered against the backdrop of *The Shield,* which offers no such assurance. In Farmington, Vic Mackey's corruption is not only tolerated, but seen as necessary—even, at times, by those who would hunt him down to bring him to justice.

It is the rule in virtually every cop show that police officers are represented sympathetically. In older cop shows in particular, officers "are intuitive and skilled, rather than raw and reckless. They all possess a victim-centered desire for justice. This quest for justice, at times in an unjust society where bad guys sometimes win, makes the traditional cop principled and dedicated, human, and notably humane."[52] From the inception of the genre the police have been positioned within frontier mythology as the people who would patrol the "moral boundary of society."[53] And it is not unusual for cop shows to excuse some forms of police misconduct. In shows like *Law and Order* and *NYPD Blue*, the complexities of due process are often represented as getting in the way of justice, and officers who violate the rights of the accused are generally seen as acting for the greater good. Sasha Torres argues that the show *Brooklyn South* takes this position to an extreme, going to great lengths to encourage its audience's identification with the police, to locate its viewers inside the "house" (the police station) and not as members of either "the community"—which the show depicts as violent, foolish, and irrational— or the Internal Affairs Bureau—which the show depicts as predatory and over-zealous.[54]

But, for the most part, the only way that this kind of identification is possible is if officers' misconduct is done in the name of a higher justice, or if the guilty officers take responsibility, and demonstrate contrition, for their actions. *The Shield* stands apart, since it manages to create a sympathetic portrayal even though only a portion of Vic's misconduct is in the service of the greater good and despite the fact that he rarely shows remorse for crimes that are far more serious than those committed by most of his televisual counterparts.

Vic Mackey is, as he says, a "different kind of cop." Part of what makes him different is his ability to commit monstrous crimes without ever coming across as a monster. In the pilot episode of *The Shield*, a police captain with higher ambitions decides that he can gain political traction by rooting out police corruption. To this end, he convinces a young officer to join Mackey's Strike Team and gather evidence to prove that Mackey is working with a high-level drug dealer. The episode ends with Mackey shooting the officer in the head at point blank range, and standing over his prone body, watching as he dies. Mackey's expression as the screen fades to black isn't one of guilt or even regret but of something akin to chagrin, as he seems mildly annoyed that the officer has forced his hand. In later episodes, Mackey *is* haunted by the murder, but he is never remorseful, since he remains convinced that he did what needed to be done. Cop killers are among the most reviled figures in American culture, and Mackey's actions in the pilot episode would appear to stack the deck so heavily against him that it would be impossible for an audience to ever again see him as a sympathetic figure. That he *does* come across as a sympathetic figure as the series progresses is all the more striking given that he continues to commit crimes of a similar magnitude.

If the pilot episode ends by setting Mackey up as a character who appears utterly beyond redemption, the key to the rehabilitation of his image has to do with the nature of the threats that he stands against. Cynthia Fuchs and Mike Chopra-Gant both note that "the protection of children is a key theme that runs throughout" *The Shield*.[55] Mackey is regularly confronted with children in peril, and he does everything within his power, with little regard for his own safety, to save, for example, a baby thrown off a balcony, or young girls forced into prostitution. Much of the punishment he metes out occurs either in the service of securing information needed to save children or is intended as a measure of vengeance for people who have harmed children.[56] Children are the only innocents in the world of *The Shield*, and Mackey is their only reliable guardian. More generally, the series consistently suggests that whatever degree of domestic comfort exists for most Angelenos and, by extension, for the rest of us, is as fragile as glass. The "thin blue line" of ordinary police officers is ill-equipped to provide the kind of security needed in this brave new world, and even the cleanest of cops eventually recognize the value of the services that Mackey provides.

The Shield is not just about a corrupt cop, but about police corruption itself. The show is concerned with the ways that fairly extreme forms of corruption and brutality fit in with the day-to-day workings of a major metropolitan police force. From the outset of the series, Vic Mackey shares screen time with a series of other officers and high-ranking officials who are, to varying degrees, concerned with his behavior. The pilot episode sets the stage: the Captain of Mackey's station, David Aceveda (Benito Martinez), launches a campaign to bring Mackey to justice. At one point in the episode, Aceveda attempts to convince another detective, Claudette Wyms (CCH Pounder), to join the campaign. Aceveda, who is Latino, and Wyms, who is black, have a frank discussion about public attitudes towards police corruption, race, and crime that provides a template for the ways that these issues are pursued throughout the series. Aceveda asks Wyms for her thoughts about Mackey, and she responds by assessing the ways that Mackey is thought of by higher powers in the department: "I hear things. But as long as Mackey's producing on the street, he's got friends. [Assistant Chief] Gilroy, even the Chief." From the outset of the series, then, the show resists a "bad apple" framing, suggesting that at least some of Mackey's corruption is understood and enabled by people at the highest level of the command structure. Aceveda is not content with this deflection, though, and instead presses the issue, resulting in the following exchange:

> Aceveda: "It doesn't bother you, the things he does?"
> Wyms: "I don't judge other cops."
> Aceveda: "Mackey's not a cop; he's Al Capone with a badge."
> Wyms: "Al Capone made money by giving people what they wanted. What people want these days is to make it to their cars without getting mugged. Come home from work, see their stereo still there. Hear about some murder in the Barrio, find out the next day the police caught the guy. If having those things means some cop roughs up some nigger, some spick in the ghetto, well as far as most people are concerned it's don't ask, don't tell. How you figure on changing that?"

Wyms presents a canny understanding not only of popular opinion about police corruption, but also of the kinds of audience reactions to Vic Mackey that allowed the series to continue for seven years. The murder of the police officer in the pilot episode aside, Vic's targets are frequently racialized others who are depicted in fairly straightforward stereotypical ways as mindless and/or brutal thugs. These characters are never fully realized or humanized, and the show never lingers upon their suffering. Wyms's understanding of Mackey's place in the department allows the show to simultaneously acknowledge ethical problems with allowing police corruption to continue unabated, while shunting aside those problems as simply the cost of effective policing. (Wyms's discussion of public opinion mirrors that of journalists who covered the Rampart scandal and claimed that there was a lack of public outrage because the victims were generally gang members, for whom the public had little sympathy. Missing in this analysis was not only the fact that this lack of sympathy was conditioned by long histories of media demonization of gang members, but also that the corrupt officers of the Rampart district did not target gang members only, but instead terrorized the community as a whole.) In subsequent episodes, Wyms becomes less reluctant to judge Mackey, but her assessment of the difficulty of dealing with the kind of misconduct that he represents proves to be perfectly on target, as virtually everyone who attempts to challenge Mackey turns out to be either ineffective or compromised.

Even as Aceveda starts to wage his campaign against Mackey, there are indications that he is not well-suited for the struggle. He is the person who decides to bring Mackey in to interrogate the kidnapper in the pilot episode, knowing full well that the only reason that Mackey is likely to be more effective than other detectives is that he will be willing to beat the suspect until he provides the required information. As Aceveda, Wyms, and another detective watch the interrogation on a closed circuit television monitor in another room, Mackey picks up a phonebook and starts slamming it against the suspect's head. Wyms and the other detective both appear disgusted, though neither speaks out or demands any intervention. Aceveda, recognizing that Mackey's tactics are the only way to save the life of the kidnapper's latest victim, simply turns off the video monitor. From the outset, then, it is clear that while Aceveda and other members of the department might find Mackey's policing strategies distasteful, they are willing to rely upon Mackey when necessary.

Over the course of the series, various characters make some kind of effort to bring Mackey to justice. While each of these characters succeeds in creating difficulties for Mackey and his Strike Team, they all stumble along the way. Early in the series, Aceveda is willing to do anything he can to find out exactly what Mackey is up to, and to either have him arrested or, at the very least, kicked out of the force, even if that means confronting the most powerful members of the department. When informed by Assistant Chief Gilroy (John Diehl) that "No one succeeds in this department by being anti-cop," Aceveda responds "I'm anti-criminal. Even if they're wearing a badge."[57] He soon comes to understand, though, that the biggest obstacle to the realization of his political ambitions is not police corruption itself, but the appearance of corruption, and that it is the appearance that needs to change. To this end, he abandons his crusade against Mackey and instead enlists him in an effort to ensure that the Strike Team cleans up its act, eliminating any outward signs of misconduct. Aceveda's alliance with Mackey is eventually strengthened when the Assistant Chief, caught up in his own murder and corruption scandal, targets both men in an effort to save his own career. Throughout the remainder of the series, Mackey and Aceveda's relationship switches back and forth between uneasy alliances and outright antagonism, but Aceveda is never in a position to seize the clear moral high ground from Mackey.

The character who is best-positioned to challenge Mackey in moral terms is Claudette Wyms. She is the most consistent voice of decency in the series, frequently acting as a moral compass for other characters, providing advice, and at times leading her own crusade to root out corruption. Wyms is so concerned with justice that when she finds out that hundreds of prisoners were convicted because of a public defender's negligence, she is willing to jeopardize her career in order to have the cases re-opened. When seventeen convictions are overturned and dozens more are appealed, she is denied promotion to captain, albeit temporarily.[58] (This plot line is an important inversion of the Rampart scandal, since responsibility for unjust convictions lies with the public defender's office, rather than with corrupt cops and a legal system that is frequently far too deferential to police officers and the District Attorney's office.) While Wyms's motivations are always beyond reproach, her silence during Vic's beating of the kidnapper highlights the fact that she too proves willing to accept a degree of brutality when other methods fail to secure justice. The kidnapping incident is admittedly an extreme case (the veritable "ticking time-bomb" scenario), where brutality is the only way to save a child's life, but Wyms's acceptance of Mackey's methods does not end here, and instead extends to support for some degree of vigilante justice. In the final episode of the first season, Mackey repeatedly stabs a cop killer with the pin from a police badge that the killer had stolen from the body of one of his victims. When Wyms comes onto the scene the suspect (who is writhing in pain and crying) tells Wyms what happened. She clearly believes him, but snarls "you look fine to me." [59] Wyms fills an interesting role in defining the politics of the series: the character works to provide a clear refutation of any possible bad apple framing, since her implicit support for some of Mackey's actions indicates that there is no corner of the department that is untouched by the kind of policing that he represents. At the same time, while some forms of brutality appear to be universally accepted within the culture of the LAPD as represented on the show, there is little evidence to suggest that the series finds this problematic in any way. Certainly, the show presents Mackey's more egregious actions as unacceptable, but it provides no basis for objecting to apparently mild forms of brutality and torture. Wyms's acceptance of Mackey's actions does nothing to compromise the depiction of her integrity.

If Wyms provides the moral center of the series, institutionalized assurances of department integrity are meant to come from elsewhere. After all, as Vic's colleague, Wyms has little power or authority to challenge him head-on. Even when she is eventually promoted to Captain, Wyms's need to keep crime rates down and to have a smoothly-running precinct hinder her ability to confront

Mackey. No such hurdles are in the way, however, of the Internal Affairs Department (IAD). Season five introduces the character of IAD Lieutenant John Kavanaugh (Forrest Whittaker), who is brought in to investigate the Strike Team when a new assistant police Chief decides that he, too, can make a name for himself by going after police corruption. Kavanaugh soon becomes Mackey's most dogged and resourceful adversary. As an outsider, Kavanaugh is the only person who can deal with Mackey without having to be concerned with such things as political perceptions of crime. He has no other charge but to root out corruption, and no incentive to ignore the kinds of tactics that make Mackey so effective. As he starts to find out about Mackey's misdeeds, Kavanaugh becomes more and more outraged, and more and more determined to uncover the full scope of the problem that Mackey represents. At first, Kavanaugh's motivations seem unassailable. Eventually, though, as he comes up against a series of roadblocks in his investigation, and as it becomes increasingly clear that Mackey has high-powered allies, and that conventional IAD methods will not suffice in bringing him to justice, Kavanaugh's frustrations mount and his motives become less pure. When Mackey takes Kavanaugh's investigation personally and decides to send him a message by sleeping with his mentally ill wife, Kavanaugh goes over the edge, and begins to enact his own form of vigilante justice, working with an imprisoned drug lord to have members of the Strike Team killed. Eventually, Kavanaugh is brought down when one of the detectives in Mackey's precinct house discovers that he has planted evidence in Mackey's home. Kavanaugh's transformation (from the one high-ranking official who had no need to rely upon Mackey's brutality and corruption, to a lost soul who decides to do his own dirty work, becoming a mirror image of Mackey in the process) speaks to the appeal and persuasiveness of the kinds of tactics Mackey employs. Eventually, the series suggests, everyone in law enforcement who needs to get difficult tasks done will succumb to their call.

By the time that Kavanaugh is imprisoned, *The Shield* has painted a picture of ubiquitous police misconduct and corruption. It's not that every cop is a Vic Mackey, but that virtually no one can exist within the structure of the LAPD without being touched by or indebted to the kinds of actions that Mackey engages in. In order to explain the overwhelming acceptance of, or reliance upon, brutal policing, *The Shield* follows very much in the mold of earlier pop cultural representations of bad cops, including *Training Day*, as socialization into corruption is a recurring theme of the series. The most direct forms of socialization involve Mackey's relationships with his Strike Team members, since he is regularly scheming with these younger and less experienced officers, and instructing them in ways to avoid getting caught for their crimes. The Strike Team, however, is meant to be understood as exceptional: this is a group of elite officers, answerable directly to Mackey, who work from their own "clubhouse" set aside from the rest of the station. With Mackey as their leader, it would be shocking to discover that these officers did *not* become corrupt, and, indeed, the crimes that they commit independently of Mackey rival the crimes that they commit as his accomplices. Each one of these officers is what Jake Hoyt might have become had he spent a few more days training with Alonso Harris. But the Vic Mackeys and Alonso Harrises of the world are, even in the Los Angeles of *Training Day* and *The Shield*, few and far between, and not many officers get to serve so closely with mentors like them. To explain the ubiquitous tolerance of corruption within the LAPD, the show turns to other forms of socialization.

The most serious corruption problems facing major metropolitan police forces arguably involve not the kinds of extreme crimes committed by real-life officers like Rafael Perez and Nino Durden or their fictional counterparts, but more mundane acceptance of minor acts of brutality, evidence tampering, and perjury. This kind of acceptance is fostered by the "code of silence" that has been documented in virtually every serious report on police corruption in Los Angeles and beyond. *The Shield* devotes quite a bit of time towards demonstrating how this code is taught and enforced at the earliest stages of an officer's career, and most of the demonstrations revolve around rookie Julien Lowe (Michael Jace). Lowe is a complicated character. As an African American, devout Christian, and closeted gay man, he is particularly badly suited for life within the racist, corrupt and homophobic climate of the Farmington police department. Julien's religion fuels his sense of morality, and initially ensures that he will speak up against corruption wherever he sees it. The conflict between his religious beliefs and his sexuality, however, creates emotional turmoil and vulnerability, which Mackey is soon able to exploit. When Mackey discovers that Julien is gay, he threatens to out him unless he helps in covering up some of Mackey's exploits. Julien goes along with Mackey, but becomes erratic in his behavior on the job, teaming up with other cops to brutalize a drag queen one moment, and trying to convince an armed suspect to kill him the next. While Julien's initial entry into corruption can be traced to the very specific kinds of suffering he is dealing with because of heterosexist oppression (and, of course, because of Vic Mackey), his acclimation into the department also involves more routine kinds of pressures.

When Julien attempts to report having witnessed Mackey and other members of the Strike Team stealing cocaine from a crime scene, the audience is treated to a multi-faceted portrait of the forces that prevent officers from coming forward with information about crimes committed by other officers. Chief Aceveda, who at this point in the series is still intent on rooting out corruption, nevertheless tries to talk Julien out of reporting the theft to IAD, warning him that "Most cops here will treat you like a traitor. You're going to take more shit than you've ever taken before."[60] When his partner, Danny Sofer (Catherine Dent), learns that Julien is planning to turn Mackey in, she tells him that "You don't testify against a fellow officer without first looking them in the eye and hearing their side of the story."[61] When Julien ignores Danny's advice and goes to IAD, she chides him, noting that "This is a brotherhood. Everyone knows that but you."[62] (Officer Sofer's comments are driven partly by self-interest, since Mackey has informed her that, as Julien's training officer, she will be held accountable for his actions: "I just don't want any of that mud sticking to you."[63]) Even Detective Wyms suggests that Julien tread cautiously. When asked for advice, she wants to make sure that he is aware of the consequences, letting him know that "You're talking about jeopardizing two careers here, his and yours. . . . Nobody likes a rat. Especially one who hasn't proven himself." While she doesn't tell him to remain silent about what he has witnessed, she does tell him that "You gotta ask yourself if it's something bad enough that's worth risking that kind of heat. Is it something you can't live with holding?"[64] This might seem like somewhat innocuous advice, especially since Wyms does eventually usher Julien into Aceveda's office to file a report, but the calculation that she urges arguably provides the greatest insight into the ordinary workings of a police culture that allows for the code of silence, since her clear suggestion is that it is only the most extreme forms of corruption that need to be challenged.

As a basically good cop who remains silent in the face of Mackey's crimes, Julien provides one strong indication of the intractable nature of police corruption.[65] Mackey's longevity on the force serves as an even starker argument that the LAPD and the rest of the city power structure simply have no effective method of addressing police corruption. In this respect, *The Shield* is very different from other cop shows. Sasha Torres's point about *Brooklyn South*, that "Mistakes are made; highly charged situations sometimes get out of hand, but the disciplinary systems internal to the department are entirely adequate to correct those mistakes, to ease those situations" is true for any number of other cop shows, ranging from *NYPD Blue* to the *Law and Order* and *CSI* franchises.[66] That this is not the case for *The Shield* is best demonstrated by considering Kavanaugh's IAD investigation of Vic Mackey. Not only are the department's internal disciplinary systems wholly inadequate to the challenge Mackey represents, but the person most closely identified with those systems resorts to precisely those methods that he is meant to police. By the end of the series, two of the Strike Team members are dead and another is in prison, but this has little to do with effective internal disciplinary measures and can instead be traced to the clashing personalities within the Team and retribution from various crime lords that Team members have worked with and betrayed. A federal agency, Immigration and Customs Enforcement (ICE), appears to have had some success in targeting Mackey, since it is able to get him to retire and to testify against the sole surviving Strike Team member, but the price they pay for Mackey's cooperation is to guarantee him immunity for his crimes. There is no semblance of justice here.

The series ends where the Rampart scandal began: a corrupt officer has just provided endless hours of testimony admitting to horrendous crimes that he will not be held accountable for. As the credits roll at the end of the final episode of the series, Mackey has lost everything he cares about. His Strike Team is no more, his best friend has committed suicide, he has betrayed the trust of officers that he thinks of as brothers, and his wife, having cooperated with an investigation into his misconduct, has taken their children and entered a federal witness relocation program to avoid his wrath. Perhaps more important than any of this is the fact that he is no longer a police officer. The terms of his immunity agreement require him to work a new job, as a desk jockey for ICE, forced to turn in daily ten page memos analyzing gang activity, not permitted to change the thermostat in his office, much less fight street thugs and drug dealers. And yet, in the final sequence of the show, he appears to realize that as confining as his job might appear, a cubicle is not a prison cell. With no bars to cage him, there is nothing to prevent him from resuming some of the routines of his previous life. He smiles, puts his gun in his waistband, grabs his jacket, and enters the dark night of the city. Vic Mackey, and all he represents, is still very much with us.

Concluding Remarks: From Scandal to Spectacle

The Rampart scandal may have been one of the most notable police scandals in recent American history, but its importance and foundation have more to do with the routine workings of the criminal justice system than with exceptional acts of corruption and brutality. News coverage of the scandal was most promising precisely when it refused to treat the issues at hand as "scandalous," as reporters veered away from the crimes of people like Rafael Perez and instead focused on the institutionalized inequities that make the prison industrial complex one of the primary engines of racial stratification in the United States. It is still too early to know whether Rampart has led to lasting changes in journalistic conventions about how to cover police corruption, but it is at least clear that news reports of the scandal shed light upon aspects of race, crime, and justice that are all too often obscured. As powerful as many of these reports were, their ability to challenge common-sense understandings of race and crime and impact national processes of racial formation was limited by a lack of dramatic imagery that prevented the scandal from ever becoming a national issue on the scale of events like the Rodney King beating. Because the producers of Hollywood films and television shows are not limited by existing imagery, but are instead free to create their own, popular culture appropriations of Rampart had the potential to shape understandings of police corruption in ways that the news media never could.

As the two highest profile and most seriously engaged pop cultural attempts to reckon with the nature of Rampart-era police corruption, *Training Day* and *The Shield* had tremendous potential to help define the meaning of the spectacle, and of police misconduct more broadly, for mass audiences. Together they mark the emergence of new generic conventions in filmic and televisual representations of police corruption, moving police misconduct and brutality to center stage by featuring "bad cops" as protagonists.[67] The popularity of *Training Day* and *The Shield* highlights what may be a growing cultural preoccupation with police corruption, fed by Rampart and other real-life police scandals. To varying degrees, both of these productions resist bad apple framings of police corruption. To the extent that they address corruption as part of a systemic problem, they stand as an implicit challenge to dominant understandings of police misconduct, and as a rebuke to many earlier representations of dirty cops in popular culture.

If *Training Day* and *The Shield* join news coverage of the Rampart scandal in helping to popularize systemic critiques of police corruption, they also share the unfortunate tendency of the news media to minimize the toll that police corruption takes on the communities that are policed by "bad cops." Just as most news coverage of Rampart said very little about the suffering of the largely Latino community that officers Perez and Durden terrorized, so too do *Training Day* and *The Shield* gloss over the lives of the people targeted, tried, and imprisoned on the basis of racist policing strategies, fabricated evidence, and perjury. The only "victims" dwelled upon at any length in *Training Day* are other dirty cops, betrayed by Alonso Harris. By virtue of its longevity, *The Shield* has a broader canvass and depicts a wider range of victims, but the residents of Farmington are almost unfailingly depicted as one-dimensional stick figures, and the crimes committed by Mackey and his Strike Team primarily affect the lives of their fellow officers and family members.

The lack of a meaningful depiction of the suffering caused by police brutality and corruption in *Training Day* and *The Shield* speaks to the limitations of the kinds of systemic critiques that this film and television series offer. On the one hand, both productions seek to explain police corruption by focusing, to some extent, on cultures of corruption that enable the crimes of fairly low-level officers. On the other hand, neither production looks very far beyond the LAPD itself when examining the root causes of these crimes. As "bad cop" productions, *Training Day* and *The Shield* are most interested in the street. They neglect the courtroom, the prison, and the campaign trail. They start with poverty, street crime, and violence as a given—the natural conditions of the communities represented on screen. These productions pay no attention to deindustrialization, three-strikes legislation, draconian cuts in government spending on social programs and education, or other socio-economic forces that have so thoroughly decimated poor communities of color in Los Angeles and beyond. They are thus unable to provide a meaningful assessment of the ways that police corruption fits in with and is enabled by the structural inequalities that are characteristic of the criminal justice system as a whole. As spectacles of police corruption, *Training Day* and *The Shield* happily move beyond a "bad apple" framing, at the same time that they justify routine forms of police corruption and brutality and obscure the costs and nature of the contaminated orchards that they point to.

5

RACIAL SPECTACLES UNDER AN ANTI-RACIST GAZE

New Media and Abu Ghraib

Prologue: Camcorders, Cell-phone Video, and Visions of Racist Brutality

It has been nearly twenty years since George Holliday aimed his video camera out of his Lake View Terrace apartment window in Los Angeles and recorded members of the Los Angeles Police Department brutally beating Rodney King. Much has been said in this time about the potential for harnessing the power of portable video and new media technologies in order to subject the abuses of power to national scrutiny. Social movements have sought to take advantage of new media, as organizations like Copwatch have worked to decrease police brutality by observing and documenting police behavior, and by circulating video images of police violence on the internet.[1] In recent years, activists have regularly relied upon digital video taken by ordinary people in order to press the mainstream media to provide more extensive and more responsible coverage of racist violence, at the same time that they have relied upon the web for alternative methods of distribution. New digital recording technologies including relatively inexpensive digital cameras and camera-equipped mobile phones have played important roles in generating racial spectacles and scandals that, at least momentarily, appeared to provide opportunities for activist interventions into troubling state policies.[2] While a variety of spectacles of police violence have hinted at the ability of new media technologies to disrupt the ordinary brutality of the state, perhaps the most dramatic example of a new media–generated racial spectacle occurred in May of 2004, when digital photographs of the 2003 torture of Iraqi prisoners at the Abu Ghraib prison circulated around the world, prompting international condemnation of an increasingly unpopular war.

Anti–racist activists have long worked to draw attention to violence directed against people of color. Antilynching activists in the late nineteenth and early twentieth centuries circulated photographs of lynchings in an effort to highlight the barbarism of the mob and to condemn the violence needed to shore up white supremacy. Decades later, Martin Luther King Jr. and the Southern Christian Leadership Conference were quite conscious of the impact that the mass media could have on national political processes, and some of the most important successes of the Civil Rights Movement can be traced to the outrage generated during the 1963 Birmingham campaign, when television cameras documented firemen dousing unarmed protestors with fire hoses powerful enough to strip bark from trees, while police unleashed their dogs and made full use of their clubs. A key task facing anti-racist activists in these movements involved crafting new kinds of vision. Whereas dominant discourse has frequently put forward images of people of color as criminally violent threats, anti-racist activists have long struggled to re-focus a national gaze. At times, activists have asked national audiences to look at exactly the same images that they were already seeing, but to see them in new ways.

When examining photographs of lynchings or news footage of African Americans being arrested, anti-racist movements have instructed us to look at these images as spectacles of whiteness rather than blackness. It is only with the intervention of the antilynching movement that national audiences would no longer see the Black Rapist that southern editors had long claimed could be found at the end of the mob's rope, but would instead gaze upon the members of the mob itself, seeing them not as chivalrous defenders of white womanhood but as barbaric threats to the very civilization that they claimed to protect. For generations, anti-racist activists have sought to render whiteness and State power visible as sources of racist brutality. The question emerging from the circulation of the Abu Ghraib photos is: what role do new media technologies play in facilitating this sort of struggle?

In order to address this question, I first consider the kinds of claims that have been made about the power of new media in coverage of the Iraq war, and I address the importance of digital photography for members of the American military. I argue that much of the power of the photographs stems from increasingly powerful links between personal and collective identities and digital photography. In assessing the ideological messages of the Abu Ghraib photos, I discuss the connections that some commentators have drawn to lynching photography. While there are clear and important parallels, I caution against too simple a comparison. Finally, because I argue that the meaning of the Abu Ghraib photographs is open and contingent upon political struggle, I examine a number of critical readings and artistic responses to the photographs. If struggles over the meanings of racial spectacles are also, at least in part, struggles over what we are meant to see, and over how we are to understand visual evidence, then it is imperative for cultural critics to come to terms with the racialized production of the visible in a digital age. This chapter is a step in that process.

Introduction: Immediacy, New Media and Identity in the Iraq War

From the outset of the Iraq war, dramatic claims were made about the ability of new media technologies to provide a "more intimate and multifaceted view" of war than had ever before been possible.[3] The ready availability of powerful satellite phones and relatively cheap and portable digital video cameras enabled "embedded" reporters to file reports directly from the battlefield in real time, and to leave overseas audiences with the impression that they were being presented with an unfiltered view of the war as it was being fought. Military personnel were able to rely upon digital cameras and the internet to document their experiences, and to disseminate that documentation quite widely, not only to friends and families, but also to a variety of websites that aimed to provide more comprehensive coverage than what could be found in traditional journalistic outlets. The extent of the American public's access to the perspectives of ordinary soldiers was unprecedented. While there were some rumbles of discontent (there was a good deal of punning on what it meant for reporters to be "in bed" with the very soldiers upon whom they were dependent for survival), it was difficult to deny the sense of immediacy that new media was capable of providing. And yet, the kinds of claims made for new media were, in some ways, not really all that new.

The histories of warfare and visual recording technologies are inextricably linked, and news coverage of every war in recent memory has been discussed as more immediate than that of its predecessor. The Vietnam war has been talked about as the first truly televised war,[4] and the fact that it was referred to as a "living room war" provides a sense of the perceived intimacy of the coverage: this was a war that American audiences could experience directly, in their own homes, despite the fact that the images flickering across TV screens around the country were always at least a day old, since the cameras recording the war used film, which required processing time.[5] By the time of the first Gulf War, satellite and video technology made it possible to provide instantaneous coverage of events halfway around the world. The sense of the immediacy of the coverage is captured most tellingly in stories about Americans learning from CNN that SCUD missiles had been launched at Israel, and phoning relatives in Tel Aviv to warn them before local air raid sirens had sounded,[6] or in reports that soldiers in Iraq were calling family members in the United States to find out how the war was proceeding.[7] Thus, the claim that audiences watching initial coverage of the 2003 invasion of Iraq would have even more immediate access to the war meant that the media had an awful lot to live up to.

David Bolter and Richard Grusin have argued that while there is a cultural desire for ever-increasing levels of immediacy in media the very promise of transparent access to unmediated reality inevitably calls attention to the limitations of emerging media technologies, since such transparency is never achievable.[8]

When it comes to coverage of war, claims of immediacy are particularly problematic, since in working to convince audiences that they have full knowledge of the events on the ground, such claims can help to deflect from the question of what is left out of the camera's frame. Thus, numerous critics have pointed out that the Gulf War that was presented to American audiences was almost entirely bloodless; sanitized to the point that it became commonplace to refer to it as a "Nintendo war," or a war whose dominant images (including night-vision footage of missiles still in flight, and missile-eye views transmitted from "smart bombs" as they approached their always-legitimate targets) were those of a video game. Marita Sturken makes the point that it was *because* of the technological ability to transmit images of the war as it was occurring that the government instituted some of the most stringent measures of censorship in U.S. military history.[9] Early estimates of the numbers of Iraqi dead were in the hundreds of thousands, yet few of these bodies were ever shown on American television broadcasts. And few American television audience members were ever made aware of the systematic destruction of the Iraqi infrastructure, including the intentional bombing of sewage systems, electrical plants, and transportation networks.[10] Similarly, much of the contemporary critique of embedded reporting during the Iraq war centers not only on the kinds of biases that the soldiers who inevitably become primary sources can be expected to hold, but also on the kinds of sources that are never heard from, and the kinds of information and images that are never presented.

The most dramatic development in the sense of immediacy offered by new media technologies in the Iraq war has to do with soldiers' access to digital cameras and the internet. Soldiers have carried cameras on the battlefield for a very long time, but they were never ubiquitous during wartime until the current wars in Afghanistan and Iraq. Because they are easy to use, portable, relatively inexpensive, and capable of producing photographic images without a lag in development time, digital cameras and camera-equipped mobile phones have had a dramatic impact upon cultural ideas about photography. In the very recent past, few people were likely to carry cameras with them on a daily basis. Now, it is not at all uncommon for people to have cameras with them all the time. And as cameras have become part of everyday life, photography has moved beyond "the realm of the occasional, or even the exceptional, that gave it its traditional function."[11] Digital cameras are used to record all of the pitfalls and pleasures of daily life, and because the images they produce are available for immediate viewing, they can be easily shared, and can facilitate new forms of social interaction, becoming intrinsic parts of the events that they are documenting. Baraba Scifo's comments about cell-phone photography are applicable to all portable digital cameras:

> the camera-phone is not only an increasingly personal technology (being deeply set within the subject, his or her universe and relationships) but also a collective technology, a resource for "face-to-face" sociality,

> entertainment and communicative exchanges within contexts of local
> interaction and principally within a group of peers.[12]

Photography has always been a technology of memory, but the ease with which
digital images can be reproduced and transmitted has led to a new visual culture
in which the sharing of photographs plays an ever stronger role in creating group
or collective memories for their recipients, while helping to reinforce a sense of
group cohesion and collective identity.

If digital photography is increasingly linked to identity in American society
in general, it makes sense to think that this would be even more true for military
personnel overseas who can make use of the technology not only to forge new
friendships, but also to stay in touch, and maintain bonds, with friends and family.
One of the soldiers sentenced in the Abu Ghraib case has estimated that seventy
percent of her company had digital cameras,[13] and JoAnn Wypijewski has sought
to answer the question about why soldiers would photograph the Abu Ghraib
atrocities by noting that

> Soldiers in Iraq take pictures like crazy. . . . They take pictures because
> they're bored or want souvenirs. They take pictures of people they arrest
> (an abrogation of the Geneva Conventions), of fighters they kill (ditto), of
> bodies they desecrate (a war crime). They email them home or send them
> with photos of their wives to a porno website or string them together and
> add sound to make commemorative videos.[14]

Wypijewski is discussing extreme and troubling forms of documentation, but her
examples get to one of the key reasons that the Abu Ghraib photos were so
startling. These photographs mark a moment, I think, when many of us have
come up against the limits for the desire for immediacy in media. It's not just
that new media technologies offer us access to parts of the war that we'd never
otherwise have. Instead, because digital photography is so closely linked to
personal and collective identity, we appear to have been provided with direct
access to the minds of torturers, as we are not only exposed to, but also exposed
by, ideas and thought processes that might be more comfortably understood from
a distance. Jean Baudrillard suggests that the Abu Ghraib photos render the notion
of transparency and immediacy in representation obsolete, claiming that

> There is no longer the need for "embedded" journalists because soldiers
> themselves are immersed in the image—thanks to digital technology, the
> images are definitively integrated into the war. They don't represent it
> anymore; they involve neither distance, nor perception, nor judgment. They
> no longer belong to the order of representation, nor of information in a
> strict sense. And, suddenly, the question whether it is necessary to produce,
> reproduce, broadcast, or prohibit them, or even the "essential" question

of how to know if they are true or false, is "irrelevant." For the images to become a source of true information, they would have to be different from the war.[15]

Baudrillard is likely too dismissive of the "need" for embedded journalists, who still provide a substantial amount of the coverage coming out of Iraq, but the idea that the photos do not represent the war because they help to constitute it is intriguing. In this formulation, the media's promise of immediacy has been more than fulfilled, since distance is collapsed to the point where when we gaze upon the images of Abu Ghraib, we are presented with, and in a sense, enlisted in, the war itself. Baudrillard does not address the sense of complicity on the part of the viewer of the Abu Ghraib images directly, but much of what is so disturbing about the photos for American audiences surely has to do with the question of our stance in relation to the imagery. (In what sense are *we* the subject of the photographs? What responsibility do we have for the crimes depicted in the images?) To come to terms with that stance, however, I'd like to take a step back from Baudrillard's position, and note that while I would agree that the photographs should be understood as part of the war, they are *also* part of the representation of the war, in that the photographs have been read in many different ways and contexts precisely to provide information and insight into the nature of the war. The danger, I would suggest, in accepting that the photographs *are* the war is the same danger in accepting that the media can ever provide us with a transparent or unmediated window into war; namely, that we can be lulled into ignoring everything outside the frame.

Festivals of Violence: Lynching Photography and Abu Ghraib

When the first set of Abu Ghraib torture photographs was broadcast on CBS's *60 Minutes II,* and published on the *New Yorker*'s website in April, 2004, many observers were sickened by what appeared to be clear and straightforward evidence of atrocities committed by U.S. military personnel. As horrendous as the photographs were, however, for some commentators, there was something all too recognizable about them. The photos that have become arguably the most iconic images of the Iraq war, in which Iraqi citizens, most of whom had been stripped naked save for hoods that obscured their vision and enhanced their terror, were made to pose in humiliating sexualized positions, were forced to stand in what are euphemistically called "stress positions" (excruciatingly painful positions that can eventually cause ankles to swell, skin to blister, and kidneys to shut down), or were made to suffer in any number of other ways, generally while soldiers stood by, laughing, pointing, or posing with a "thumbs up" sign, were uncanny, in the Freudian sense that they belonged to "that class of the terrifying which leads back to something long known to us, once very familiar."[16] When seeking to explain the Abu Ghraib photos, numerous critics have drawn comparisons to lynching photography.[17]

The starkest similarity between the Abu Ghraib and lynching photos has to do with the sense of impunity on the part of the perpetrators of violence. In neither set of photos is there even a hint that the people responsible for the violence are concerned that anyone might judge them for their actions, much less that the photographs that they are posing for could conceivably be used as evidence against them in a court of law. Instead, the members of the lynch mobs and the soldiers at Abu Ghraib who are pictured proudly posing with their victims as though they were trophies appear buoyed by a sense that their actions will have unquestioned community support. Clearly, there is a continuity between these images, in terms of what they say about understandings of American identity and racial superiority. And yet, too close a focus on the similarities between the images runs the risk of obscuring very consequential differences.

In her discussion of World War II atrocity photographs, Barbie Zelizer argues that Holocaust photos have played such a powerful role in shaping our understandings and collective memories of atrocity that they have altered the ways that we approach, evaluate, and make sense of contemporary acts of brutality. She notes that Holocaust photographs have been "recycled" in news coverage of atrocities in Bosnia and Rwanda, with newspapers often running two sets of images next to each other to draw implicit comparisons. Zelizer is concerned that such comparisons have the potential to blunt "the immediacy and depth of our response to contemporary instances of brutality, discounting them as somehow already known to us."[18] This concern is worth considering when thinking about lynching and Abu Ghraib.

Lynching photography, largely forgotten for decades, had been very much in the public mind when the Abu Ghraib photographs were leaked to the media. A touring exhibition of lynching postcards, titled *Without Sanctuary*, debuted in New York in 2000, and had occasioned hundreds of articles, editorials and op-ed pieces over the following several years. The exhibition and photographs were consistent reference points in coverage of the 2005 decision by the United States Senate to apologize for its failure to enact federal antilynching legislation. While comparisons between lynching imagery and the Abu Ghraib photos can be instructive, I am concerned that the widespread circulation of, and discourse about, lynching photography might have created the same kind of problem that Zelizer warns about. If we are lulled into thinking about the Abu Ghraib photographs as overly familiar, or "already known," then there is a danger of missing features that make them distinctive. Moreover, if we see lynching photos as the template for Abu Ghraib, we run the risk of distorting our understandings of lynching itself.

One of the most troubling aspects of the Abu Ghraib photographs is the apparent glee on the part of the torturers. Several of the most widely circulated images show soldiers with broad grins as they are pointing to the genitals of male prisoners, standing over the bodies of naked prisoners posed in a "human pyramid," or posing with a "thumbs up sign" over the corpse of an Iraqi prisoner in a body bag packed with ice. Some of the most influential critiques of the photographs discussed this glee as reminiscent of lynching photography. Most famously, Susan Sontag wrote in the *New York Times Magazine* that

> If there is something comparable to what these pictures show it would be some of the photographs of black victims of lynching taken between the 1880's and 1930's, which show Americans grinning beneath the naked mutilated body of a black man or woman hanging behind them from a tree.[19]

Allen Feldman has written that the first set of Abu Ghraib photos "had the celebratory and horrific carnivalesque atmosphere of the postcards sold as mementos of the lynching and mutilation of African Americans in the 1920s,"[20] while Luc Sante's op-ed piece on Abu Ghraib in the *New York Times* observes that, in lynching photos,

> black men are shown hanging from trees or light fixtures or maybe being burned alive, while below them white people are laughing and pointing for the benefit of the camera. . . . Often the spectators at lynchings of African-Americans are so effusive in their mugging that they all seem to be vying for credit. Before seeing such pictures you might expect the faces in them to express some kind of collective rage; instead the mood is giddy, often verging on hysterical, with a distinct sexual undercurrent.[21]

The problem with these comparisons to lynching photography is that, while there are many journalistic accounts that suggest that the festival-like attitudes referenced in these passages were very much a part of the ritual of spectacle lynchings, this is generally *not* evident in lynching photography. Of the ninety-eight reproductions of lynching photographs gathered in the companion book to the *Without Sanctuary* photo exhibition, I count no more than four in which *any* of the spectator/participants are clearly smiling, and in none of those photos is a majority of the participants doing so.[22] (It is not always possible to know with certainty whether mob members are smiling, since the long shutter speeds that were required in early photography often led to photographs with somewhat blurred facial expressions.) The *Without Sanctuary* collection is not exhaustive, but it does include most of the best-known lynching photographs, and it is not clear what other lynching photographs these commentators might be invoking.

That lynching photographs generally did not capture members of the mob laughing, grinning, or smiling is not incidental. Amy Louise Wood has argued that there was a set of photographic conventions specific to spectacle lynchings which "assured that members of the mob were visually represented as stalwart and controlled." She notes that these characteristics were partly due to the nature of posing itself, but that they were "likewise characteristics that reproduced and reinforced the ideological role of the lynch mob as determined and heroic."[23] Lynching photographs worked to support a variety of white supremacist myths in the post–Reconstruction South, not least among them the notion that lynching was a necessary method of defending a civilization threatened by the recent extension of rights to an African American population that was incapable of exercising those rights responsibly. In order for lynching photography to support this ideological purpose, the members of the mob needed to be pictured as engaged in a serious pursuit, and, by convention, lynching photos provided "images of orderly, respectable mobs."[24] Part of the difficulty in seeing lynching photography as providing a template for Abu Ghraib is that this understanding makes it difficult to see that the glee expressed in the latter set of images suggests that the Abu Ghraib photos are the result of very different kinds of cultural conditions and serve very different ideological purposes.

The lynching and Abu Ghraib photos both provide evidence of severe levels of racist dehumanization, but the kinds of dehumanization, and the reasons for it, are qualitatively different. Lynching photography worked to consolidate a sense of white identity among a population that thought of its way of life as threatened. The photographic depiction of solemnity on the part of mob members was necessary if the images were to convey a sense of purpose, and to let allies and enemies know that white supremacy was a power to be reckoned with. The kinds of sadistic violence evident in lynching photographs (in the images of scarred and charred African American bodies) leave little doubt that mob members thought of their victims as somehow less than human. And yet, the specific forms of punishment that were meted out, including not only hanging and, frequently, castration, but also shooting, beating, and myriad other forms of torture that, combined, could amount to virtually the complete destruction of a human body, suggest that the targets of such violence were thought of as serious threats; lynch mobs and lynching photos sent the message that a southern caste system would be defended at all costs, with a kind of violence that can best be characterized not only as thorough and extreme, but also as deliberate. In contrast, the gleeful poses on the part of the torturers at Abu Ghraib betray nothing so much as casual degradation.

Rush Limbaugh has been rightly criticized for likening the Abu Ghraib atrocities to fraternity pranks, and excusing the torture as just the product of the need to "blow some steam off,"[25] but the sense that these were people *just* having fun seems to me chillingly accurate. The soldiers at Abu Ghraib were literally under siege (Abu Ghraib was shelled on a daily basis in the fall and winter of 2003), but unlike white southerners in the post–Reconstruction South, they were the representatives of a government and military power whose might and destructive capacities were without peer. Unlike the victims in lynching photographs, most of the victims in the Abu Ghraib photos survived their ordeals, and none of the reports about the torture at Abu Ghraib suggest that the violence perpetrated by American military personnel (and independently contracted interrogators) comes close to that delivered by lynch mobs. On the other hand, lynching photos rarely convey the sense that members of the mob were *playful* in their violence. They surely took pleasure in the destruction of their victims, but those victims were not reduced to the status of toys. (And, really, whatever logic was in play when determining that Arab men should be subjected to "culturally specific" forms of torture, how better to explain the process of forcing hooded and naked men to pose in human pyramids than to recognize that these men were thought of as nothing more than clay, or human playdough, to be molded as their captors saw fit.) Lynching photographs were intended partly as an intervention into, and refutation of, emerging understandings of American national identity, but as such, they were essentially defensive in nature. Part of what is lost in the conflation of the photos of lynching and Abu Ghraib torture is a specifically twenty-first century sense of American arrogance that made the latter set of photos and practices conceivable.

This arrogance is linked to a virulent form of post-9/11 Orientalist discourse that is itself a central component in the dehumanization of Iraqis. In Edward Said's conceptualization of the term, "Orientalism" is a way of talking about "the Orient" (or "the east"), or of dividing the world in two, but it is also a "Western style of dominating, restructuring, and having authority over the Orient."[26] This formulation is explicitly indebted to Michel Foucault in its insistence upon seeing discourse as inseparable from, and constitutive of, power. For Said, ways of talking and producing knowledge about Arabs and Muslims mattered materially, and were inseparable from broader political practices including imperialist ventures. The raw power of Orientalism could be felt in full force in the wake of the September 11th attacks, as American airwaves were flooded with hate speech directed against Arabs and Islam, and as the rate of hate crimes directed against Arabs, Muslims, and anyone mistaken for an Arab or a Muslim, skyrocketed. Public support for the invasion of Iraq arguably had less to do with the credence given to apocryphal claims about weapons of mass destruction than with an inability (encouraged by the Bush administration) to distinguish between Osama Bin Laden, members of the Taliban, Saddam Hussein, and Iraqi citizens. The rhetoric behind the increasing popularity of Samuel Huntington's "clash of civilizations" thesis relied upon neat binary divisions between "east" and "west" in which not only were "they" everything that "we" were not, but, more specifically, "they" were an unrelenting terrorist threat that "we" were honor-bound to meet head on. Orientalist discourse was mobilized in numerous ways throughout the early stages of the Iraq war, most notably in the media's ready acceptance of Pentagon claims about the Iraqi treatment of Jessica Lynch (which have since been almost entirely discredited), and in the Bush administration's open lack of concern with the number of Iraqi civilian deaths. Most pertinent to the topic at hand, Orientalist discourse played a direct role in the torture policies at Abu Ghraib, and in public discussions once those policies were revealed.

Bruce Tucker and Sia Traintafyllos call the mainstream media to task for its failure to address the racial dynamics of the torture at Abu Ghraib, and they contextualize the treatment of the detainees by referencing histories of similar kinds of violence perpetrated by such colonial powers as the French in Algeria and Belgium in the Congo. They write that, had this context been brought to bear in news coverage, it would have been impossible to treat Abu Ghraib as exceptional, since it would have been more readily understood as a standard method of imperial rule. Comparisons to other forms of "racialized imperialism"[27] can, however, obscure the specifically Orientalist elements of the torture and methods of abuse employed at Abu Ghraib. Seymour Hersh (one of the first journalists to break the Abu Ghraib story, in the *New Yorker*) has explained the nudity, forced masturbation, and simulated sex acts in the Abu Ghraib photographs by reporting that the

> notion that Arabs are particularly vulnerable to sexual humiliation became a talking point among pro-war Washington conservatives in the months before the March, 2003, invasion of Iraq. One book that was frequently cited was *The Arab Mind*, a study of Arab culture and psychology. . . . The book includes a twenty-five page chapter on Arabs and sex, depicting sex as a taboo vested with shame and repression. . . . [In neoconservative circles] two themes emerged—one, that Arabs only understand force, and, two, that the biggest weakness of Arabs is shame and humiliation.[28]

The notion that sexual humiliation was a particularly valuable tool to use when treating Iraqi prisoners was at the center of the strategy used by the defense teams in the various courts-martial stemming from the Abu Ghraib photographs, since, rather than deny that specific instances of "abuse" had occurred, the soldiers' legal teams argued that such things as "subjecting a naked Arab man to the authority of a small American woman" constituted "legitimate exploitation[s] of culture" and, thus, "an approved element of U.S. military psychological-operations doctrine."[29]

Even some of the most important critics of Abu Ghraib, including Seymour Hersh and Mark Danner, have accepted the premise that there was something about Arab culture that made sexualized humiliation a "culturally specific interrogation method."[30] Sherene Razack sums up the problem with this acceptance by noting that

> Few in the media questioned the Orientalist underpinnings of this claim. . . . Unlike us, they are sexually repressed, homophobic, and misogynist and are likely to crack in sexualized situations, particularly those involving women dominating men or those involving sex between men. . . . Through the idea of cultural difference, sexualized torture became something more

generic—torture for the purpose of obtaining information. . . . Through the idea of culturally specific interrogation techniques, Americans were marked as modern people who did not subscribe to puritanical notions of sex or to patriarchal notions of women's role in it. The Iraqis, of course, remained forever confined to the pre-modern.[31]

The fact that Orientalist assumptions were central not only to the torture that occurred at Abu Ghraib, but also to the critiques of that torture, is important to consider when assessing the role of the Abu Ghraib photos in American political discourse.

An Anti-Racist Spectacle? The Abu Ghraib photos as critique of U.S. policy

When the photos were first broadcast and published, there was a sense on the part of many commentators that, as horrific as they were, their publication would mean that the policies that had allowed for the practices depicted in the photos would be brought to an end, and that the people responsible would be brought to justice. Neither of these things has come to pass, at least not in a way that satisfies most critics of Abu Ghraib. Despite numerous government reports acknowledging widespread abuse and reports by international human rights organizations documenting systematic violations of the Geneva conventions both within and beyond Abu Ghraib, the government took the position that only low-ranking soldiers would be prosecuted, and that only the atrocities that were photographed would be addressed in military courts martial. As of this writing, only twelve defendants have been tried for the atrocities. Only one of these defendants was an officer, convicted only of disobeying an order not to talk about the investigation.[32] More troubling, the "bad apple" explanation for Abu Ghraib served to deflect responsibility from Bush administration policies and statements that weakened the protection provided by the Geneva conventions, and that "made legally possible the adoption of the various 'enhanced interrogation techniques'" used at CIA secret prisons, Guantánamo Bay, and Abu Ghraib.[33]

While the Senate Armed Services Committee has concluded that "The abuse of detainees in U.S. custody cannot simply be attributed to the actions of 'a few bad apples' acting on their own,"[34] and that "interrogation policies and plans approved by senior military and civilian officials conveyed the message that physical pressures and degradation were appropriate treatment for detainees in U.S. military custody,"[35] it is not yet clear that the reforms that are necessary to ensure that the kinds of atrocities committed at Abu Ghraib are not repeated have been enacted. Instead, as the *New York Times* notes,

[T]he Military Commissions Act of 2006 did not provide adequate protection to military prisoners, and it gave the Central Intelligence Agency carte blanche to run overseas prisons to which anonymous men are sent for indefinite detention and abuse. In July [2007] Mr. Bush issued an executive order reaffirming his policy of ignoring the Geneva Conventions when he chooses, and approving abusive interrogations at C.I.A. prisons.[36]

The Bush administration re-defined torture so as to exclude such things as forced nudity, "simulated drownings, extreme ranges of heat and cold, prolonged stress positions and isolation,"[37] all of which have been recognized as torture within the guidelines of the Geneva conventions for decades, and some of which were evident in the Abu Ghraib photos. In February, 2005, only two months after publicly declaring torture "abhorrent," the Justice Department issued a secret opinion providing an "expansive endorsement of the harshest interrogation techniques ever used by the Central Intelligence Agency."[38] In October of 2007, then-president Bush declared that "This government does not torture people," but he never renounced the Justice Department opinion.[39] It was not until the first days of the Obama administration that the United States government would again insist upon only non-coercive interrogation methods, as outlined in the Army Field Manual, but even now, the practice of "extraordinary rendition" in which the United States sends suspects to foreign countries where they will likely be tortured, has not been firmly repudiated. The Abu Ghraib photographs may well have played a crucial role in shaping public opinion about the Iraq war, but the question of whether they will continue to play a role in helping to generate more meaningful institutional change remains open.

Commentators who expected more immediate and more meaningful change as a result of the exposure of the photos might have made an error in assessing the meaning of the images. Rather, they might have made an error in assessing the ways in which the images could be made to mean. Writing about the shock that people around the country felt when the officers who beat Rodney King were acquitted in their first criminal trial, Robert Gooding-Williams says that

> Having seen the videotape of King being beaten, we allowed ourselves to indulge the . . . positivist fantasy . . . that the facts . . . were enough, because *brute* (and brutal) facts, plain and unembellished, speak for themselves. If ever there were brute facts, we thought, then surely this fact— that Rodney King had been unjustly beaten and unforgivably abused—was one of them.[40]

Gooding-Williams goes on to argue that, of course, facts don't speak for themselves; images never have inherent meaning, and always require interpretation. I think that the horror of the Abu Ghraib atrocities may have been stark enough to encourage many of us to engage in a similar kind of fantasy. It was just so clear that the photos were evidence of a kind of brutality that had to be systemic, that the notion that it could be dismissed as inconsequential, or that it could all be successfully blamed on just a few "rotten apples" didn't need to be seriously considered.

One of the most important similarities between the Abu Ghraib and lynching photographs is that while both sets of images were apparently intended to circulate primarily among like-minded audiences (among people who could be expected to share the assumptions of the photographers and of the perpetrators of violence), the meaning of the photographs has been thought to have changed dramatically once they migrated to new contexts. The NAACP's magazine *The Crisis* started publishing lynching photographs as early as 1912, not to celebrate the power of white supremacy, but to condemn it. When circulated by antilynching activists in black-owned newspapers and in antilynching pamphlets and fundraising flyers, lynching photographs worked to expose the brutality and the hypocrisy of the mob. Accompanying texts frequently argued that lynching was a terrorist tactic justified by racist stereotypes, used to maintain white power. The photographs became major weapons in the antilynching struggle, and played a key role in securing support for federal and state antilynching legislation, and in weakening public support for mob justice. Similarly, many commentators have argued that once the Abu Ghraib photos were taken out of their original context they began to function as a site "of resistance against the very acts they represent."[41] I am not convinced that this is, at least automatically, true.

Lynching photographs did not become antilynching photographs the second they were taken out of their original contexts. Instead, they became a valuable anti-racist tool only when actively yoked to an organized anti-racist movement, and, even then, their anti-racist effectiveness was dependent upon numerous factors including not only broader antilynching strategizing, but also economic and political factors that helped to erode the foundation of public support for lynching. Without black northern migration (which lessened the effectiveness of lynching as a terroristic method of securing a black labor force), and without the eventual mechanization of southern agriculture (which lessened the need for black labor), it is unclear whether southern or national audiences would have been receptive to the critique of lynching that antilynching activists argued should be seen in the photos of the mobs.

Similar points can be raised about other kinds of atrocity photos. Before the Abu Ghraib photos were made public, the best-known photographs of atrocities committed by the American military or its allies came from the Vietnam War. Atrocity photographs, including those of the My Lai massacre; of the point-blank shooting and execution of a Vietcong suspect by Vietnamese General Nguyen Ngoc Loan; and of children, including the naked and burned Kim Phuc, fleeing after a napalm strike on Trang Bang Village, have become the iconic images of that war. All of these photos were mobilized for anti-war purposes, and, eventually, they were all almost universally recognized *as* atrocity photos. But it is far from clear that this recognition was inevitable. These photographs were all taken fairly late in the war, and the dwindling support for the war clearly influenced the reception of the photographs. The first two photos were taken in 1968, as the Tet offensive was starting to convince large segments of the American public that the war was unwinnable, and as an elite policy-making consensus in favor of the war was starting to break down. By the time that the 1972 photograph of Kim Phuc was taken, this consensus had been shattered, and American public opinion was decisively anti-war by large margins.

The fact that the most lasting visual images of the Vietnam War were atrocity photos that emerged only as public support for the war was winding down is not coincidental. There was no shortage of atrocities committed by American troops and the South Vietnamese military well before the Tet offensive, and there is every reason to believe that some of these atrocities were documented photographically (indeed, in 1962 a freelance photographer had taken a photograph similar to that of General Loan, but could not interest the press in the image), yet it was not until there was massive opposition to the war that such images had extensive circulation.[42] Even then, the photographs of My Lai and of General Loan were not immediately or universally seen as providing evidence of atrocity. Instead, initial coverage in the *New York Times* encouraged a reading of General Loan's execution of his prisoner as "a tough but necessary measure at the height of an all-out offensive by the enemy."[43] Early coverage of the My Lai massacre, meanwhile, presented the killings as "a bewildering story, alien to Americans," and as "an isolated incident, unexplainable, and wholly out of character with US military activities."[44] It was not until the anti-war movement actively mobilized around these photographs (for example, by circulating 50,000 copies of a poster of the most famous My Lai photograph with the text "Q: And Babies? A: And Babies" superimposed in "blood-red lettering", for use by activists in demonstrations and publicity campaigns) that they began to attain their stature as anti-war photographs. (See Figure 5.1.)[45]

The histories of lynching photography and Vietnam-era atrocity photos provide some sense of the range of factors that are necessary for atrocity photographs to play a role in anti-racist or anti-war struggles. If the Abu Ghraib photographs do function as a site of resistance to the Abu Ghraib torture then it is important to ask to what degree this is the case, and what cultural forces make this possible. One factor to consider when thinking of the changing political meanings of the Abu Ghraib photos is the impact of new media. If the migration of the photos is critical for them to acquire a resistant meaning, then the easy transferability of JPEG photos taken with digital cameras, and the ready access to the variety of forms of distribution possible through the internet and satellite technology are of critical importance, since, unlike lynching photographs, the Abu Ghraib photos could move to new contexts incredibly rapidly. Once taken out of their original contexts, the photos could be put to new uses. In the pages of the *New Yorker*, they were presented as evidence of systematic policies of torture that existed well beyond Abu Ghraib, and that were instead central tactics that helped to define the Bush administration's approach to the "war on terror." For

FIGURE 5.1 **"Q: And Babies? A: And Babies."** Artists Poster Committee of Art Workers Coalition: Frazier Dougherty, Jon Hendricks and Irving Petlin. Photographer: R. L. Haeberle. Offset, 1970.

Source: Courtesy of the Center for the Study of Political Graphics.

the International Center of Photography in New York, and the Warhol museum in Pittsburgh, the photos became the raw material for museum exhibitions, in which it was claimed that

> the images from Abu Ghraib contradict the studied heroics of twentieth-century war photography that have been updated to the current conflict. Away from the photojournalistic flourishes designed to make war palatable—the heroic flag-raisings, the dogged foot soldiers close to the action, the sense of shared humanity among combatants, and the search for visual evidence that war is universal and inevitable—the often-banal JPEGs from Iraq proffer a very different picture: war is systematic cruelty enforced at the level of everyday torture.[46]

I would like to believe that this is the case, but I am concerned that it is instead a version of Gooding-Williams's "positivist fantasy." To think that the photos, on their own and automatically, offer this kind of assessment of war is to neglect the fact that an awful lot of people have had a vested interest in providing different kinds of readings, and that those readings have had tremendous amounts of institutional backing.[47] As noted above, for the Bush administration, the photos captured only the aberrational actions of a few "rotten apples." I see no reason that putting them on display in a museum exhibition would cause any viewer sympathetic to such readings to change their understandings of the atrocities.

If some commentators have been overly optimistic in assuming that the Abu Ghraib photos automatically provide far-reaching critiques of U.S. foreign policy once removed from their original contexts, others have taken an entirely less hopeful approach. Mark Danner, for example, has provided some of the most persuasive arguments and evidence that the Abu Ghraib atrocities *are* examples of systematic policies of torture, but has suggested that the photos actually work to *prevent* this understanding from coming to light. Danner argues that the photos

> having helped force open the door to broader questions of how the Bush administration has treated prisoners in the War on Terror, are now helping to block that door; for the images, by virtue of their inherent grotesque power, strongly encourage the view that "acts of brutality and sadism," which clearly did occur, lay at the heart of Abu Ghraib. Even public officials charged with investigating the scandal . . . at the same time seek to contain it by promoting the view that Abu Ghraib in its essence was about individual misbehavior and sadism.[48]

Even more troubling, Liz Philipose has argued that the photos are so thoroughly integrated into Orientalist processes of "othering" Arabs and Muslims by constructing them as terrorists, that, no matter the context, the "torture photos implicate the detainees in practices that produced their detention."[49] For Philipose, "the photos are part of a technology that produces the racialized Muslim terrorist. . . . The photos teach us to see a Muslim terrorist in custody."[50] The idea that, even in their new contexts, the Abu Ghraib photos further consolidate Orientalist understandings of terrorism, provides an important note of caution for anyone who would suggest that their circulation in the American and international media is automatically a good thing.[51] If Said saw Orientalism as a style of domination, it might also be understood as a "style of remembrance," or as a fully rationalized way of grouping images of Arabs and understandings of Islam and providing an ideological foundation for linking every new image to those that have gone before and that have been stockpiled in a "storehouse" of racial imagery.[52] If Philipose is correct in her assessment, then long histories of stereotyping Arabs and Muslims as terrorists may have blinded mass audiences to the possibility of being able to see or recognize Arab or Muslim victimization. Such audiences may be able to see only what they have seen before.

Philipose is the only critic that I am aware of who has suggested that, no matter their contexts, the Abu Ghraib photos continue to function in ways that are very similar to the original functions of lynching photography: as a method of celebrating and reinforcing racist domination.[53] The history of lynching photography suggests that too pat a dismissal of this claim might be a mistake, since, as I've noted above, context alone was not enough to turn lynching photographs into antilynching tools. I would be more convinced of the antiracist (or anti-Iraq war) value of the Abu Ghraib photos if they were more clearly linked to a vibrant anti-racist or anti-war movement. Still, what Philipose and Danner have in common with critics who argue that the Abu Ghraib photos are automatically oppositional is the assumption that the photographs have inherent meaning, or at least that their meaning is inherent once the photos exist in a particular context.

If it is a mistake to assume that the Abu Ghraib photos carry anything approaching an inherent meaning, or to think that we can know in advance how they will be interpreted within a given context, then it is important to consider the variety of ways in which the photos have been read, and the consequences of those readings. In her analysis of the Rodney King beating, Judith Butler has argued that when dealing with imagery of racist victimization,

> there is no simple recourse to the visible, to visual evidence, that it still and always calls to be read, that it is already a reading, and that in order to establish the injury on the basis of the visual evidence, an aggressive reading of the evidence is necessary.[54]

Evidence does not speak for itself, and Butler argues that there are good reasons to think that relevant audiences may not automatically understand evidence of racist victimization *as* evidence of racist victimization. To extend her analysis to the case of Abu Ghraib, I would suggest that anyone who would like for the photographs to serve as a broad indictment of U.S. foreign policy has quite a bit of interpretative work to do.[55] The difficulty of the task is compounded when powerful state actors have an investment in presenting readings that minimize the extent and nature of the torture, attempting to limit responsibility to a few "bad apples."

Kari Andén-Papadopoulos has argued that the Abu Ghraib photos were initially presented to American audiences in journalistic reports that framed the story in one of two ways. On the one hand, the photos were first broadcast on CBS's *60 Minutes II*, in a story that generally accepted Bush administration rhetoric, presenting the case as a story of the relatively isolated actions of a few low-ranked soldiers. In stark contrast, Seymour Hersh's first article about the case in the *New Yorker* provided a more systematic critique of U.S. decision elites, and saw the case as representative of U.S. "war on terror" policies broadly defined. Andén-Papadopoulos writes that these two reports provided the "competing 'master narratives'" that would shape much of the subsequent coverage of the scandal, but notes that the bulk of journalistic accounts of the case in the mainstream media accepted the CBS frame.[56] Indeed, claims for the democratic potential of new media notwithstanding, it turns out that the photos were not able to migrate all that quickly or freely, and were not able to escape Bush administration efforts at control, since it took five months for the photographs to make their way to CBS News, which agreed to a Pentagon request to refrain from broadcasting them for two weeks. This reprieve gave the administration plenty of time to ensure that a damage control campaign was in place by the time that the photos hit the air, and it is thus no accident that the dominant way of framing the photos within the mass media was as evidence of isolated "abuse" rather than systematic torture.[57] However, if mainstream journalists were reluctant to deviate from this frame, a number of activists and artists have been unwilling to allow Bush administration interpretations of the events at Abu Ghraib to go uncontested, and have instead provided extremely aggressive and politically provocative readings of the Abu Ghraib photographs. Each of these readings endeavors to help us see the photos in a new light.

Critical Responses to Abu Ghraib: "Aggressive Readings" of the Evidence

Errol Morris and the Bad Apples: Standard Operating Procedure

Perhaps the most dogged and prominent critic of the "bad apples" framing of the case has been Errol Morris. Morris's film about the Abu Ghraib photographs, *Standard Operating Procedure* (Sony Pictures, 2007), and the book of the same title, written by Philip Gourevitch in collaboration with Morris, based upon transcripts of interviews that Morris conducted for his film,[58] have both received a great deal of media attention. Lengthy interviews with Morris about the film have been published in most major American newspapers and have been conducted for several National Public Radio programs. Morris has also written about the case for his *New York Times* blog and has participated in a website devoted to activism surrounding the film.[59] The film and book created opportunities for reassessing the photographs at a moment in which they had largely receded from public discourse, and were intended to construct and secure a new kind of collective memory of the scandal.

Morris shares Mark Danner's sense that the Abu Ghraib photographs have worked to obscure the extent of the scandal and the role of policy-makers. In a letter addressed "Dear Activist" on the TakePart.com website, he writes that the photographs

> serve as both an exposé and a cover-up. An exposé because the photographs offer us a glimpse of the horror of Abu Ghraib; a cover-up because they convinced journalists and readers they had seen *everything*, that there was no need to look beyond the photographs and the seven so-called "Bad Apples."[60]

While Morris would generally agree that photographs have no inherent meaning, here he accepts Danner's position that the photographs automatically draw attention to the handful of soldiers who were tried for their actions at Abu Ghraib, and away from the people who gave them their orders or who instituted the policies that they were carrying out. The goal of both versions of *Standard Operating*

Procedure is to delve deeper into the conditions at Abu Ghraib and to look beyond the camera's (and the Bush administration's) frame. Together, the film and book attempt to turn the spectacle of Abu Ghraib on its ear, resisting Bush administration efforts to isolate responsibility for the crimes committed in the prison, at the same time as they engage in a problematic effort to exonerate the low-level soldiers who became the public face of the scandal.

Morris's central concern is with what he sees as "a terrible miscarriage of justice,"[61] which is that the "Bad Apples" were forced into the roles of "scapegoats" as the role played by "the real perpetrators" went unexplored.[62] Morris has said that he does not mean to imply that the soldiers who were convicted of the Abu Ghraib crimes were innocent (for example, he told Andrew O'Hehir of *Salon* magazine that "I do not see these people as lily-white, blameless, as devoid of responsibility or choice"),[63] but at times, he does rail against the prosecutions. An interview in GQ magazine is typical: Morris says that

> The soldiers got blamed because they took pictures of things that embarrassed the U.S. Army and the administration. They were punished for being photographers. The crime is photography. I don't see it as a crime. Under another set of circumstances, Sabrina Harman would have gotten the Pulitzer Prize. What did she give us? She gave us evidence of a murder that we would not have otherwise.[64]

Morris is referring to one of the most famous of the incidents captured in the Abu Ghraib photographs—the murder of Manadel al-Jamadi. Manadel al-Jamadi's name is not well-known, but the picture of Specialist Sabrina Harman bent down over his dead body, staring up at the camera with a wide smile, and displaying a "thumbs up" sign, was one of the photographs that forced an American president "to apologize to the world."[65] (See Figure 5.2.)

Along with a similar photograph featuring Corporal Charles Graner, also grinning and posing with a thumbs up sign over al-Jamadi's corpse, this is one of the images that has been most frequently compared to lynching photography and seen as a "trophy" shot, since Harman's smile has been interpreted as gloating over her kill. Morris has taken great pains to dispel this understanding.

The first thing that must be said here is that Harman is certainly *not* gloating over her kill. She was not responsible for al-Jamadi's death, and was never charged with any offense related to his death. Instead, al-Jamadi's death resulted from injuries sustained during a C.I.A. interrogation, and the photographs of Harman and Graner with al-Jamadi's body were taken after they had discovered his body in a shower room more than sixteen hours after his death.[66] When Morris says that Harman provided us with evidence of a murder, he is not just referring to the photographs of Harman and Graner posing with the body, but also to a series of photographs that Harman took later on, which reveal that there was an attempt to cover up the cause of al-Jamadi's death. Harman had been told that al-Jamadi died of a

FIGURE 5.2 Sabrina Harman Standing Over the Body of Manadel al-Jamadi.
I have cropped Manadel al-Jamadi's body out of the photograph.

heart attack, but she knew that wasn't true, since she saw injuries all over his body, and blood coming out of his nose. Her photographs "provide unmistakable evidence of the gruesome treatment al-Jamadi received: broken teeth, a mangled lip, contusions, bruises, the cartilage of his nose crushed, a gash under his right eye."[67] Harman's photography required her to remove bandages that were apparently affixed post-mortem, and she has said that she took the photos "to prove to pretty much anybody who looked at this guy, Hey, I was just lied to. This guy did not die of a heart attack. Look at all these other existing injuries that they tried to cover up."[68] For Morris, this latter set of photographs begins to tell the real story of Abu Ghraib, while the more commonly circulated photos of Harman grinning over the corpse are mere distractions.[69]

The notion that Specialist Sabrina Harman was guilty only of documenting atrocities was first publicized by Stjepan Mestrovic, a sociologist and an expert witness for the defense in the 2005 trials of several of the soldiers who were charged with crimes at Abu Ghraib. In his book on the trials, Mestrovic quotes from a letter home that Harman wrote to her partner soon after arriving at Abu Ghraib. In it, Harman discusses her reaction to the kinds of treatment that had become routine in the prison:

> Ok. I don't like that anymore. At first it was funny but these people are going too far. . . it went too far even I can't handle what's going on. I can't get it out of my head. I walk down stairs after blowing the whistle and beating on the cells with an asp to find "the taxi cab driver" handcuffed backwards to his window naked with his underwear over his head and face. He looked like Jesus Christ. At first I had to laugh so I went on and grabbed the camera and took a picture. One of the guys took my asp and started "poking" at his dick. Again I thought, ok that's funny then it hit me. That's a form of molestation. You can't do that. I took more pictures now to "record" what is going on. . . . Not many people know this shit goes on. The only reason I want to be there is to take the pictures to prove that the U.S. is not what they think.[70]

For Mestrovic, this letter offers clear evidence of the bankruptcy of the prosecution's case. Harman was simply in an untenable situation in which any action she took would be perceived as actionable: "She writes to her partner that she will take photos to document the abuse—but her photos were used against her at her court-martial."[71] In Mestrovic's account, Harman's apparent documentary intent becomes emblematic of the plight of all of the court-martialed soldiers. These were people caught up in a system they did not understand, forced to carry out actions they did not approve of, "trapped," along with their victims, "in what seemed to be an endless cycle of abuse."[72] Mestrovic expands upon and rejects the "bad apple" metaphor, claiming that "the orchard is contaminated, and the orchard keepers have escaped the sort of scrutiny that was leveled at low-ranking soldiers."[73] He is not content, however, in merely attempting to shift the focus to the "contaminated orchard." Instead, he endeavors to exonerate the "bad apples."

Like Morris, Mestrovic argues that the soldiers who were tried for crimes at Abu Ghraib were scapegoats convicted of crimes that they sought only to report. While Morris argues that the soldiers who took pictures of the Abu Ghraib atrocities did so with some sort of documentary intent, Mestrovic goes further in his insistence that these soldiers should be seen as "whistle-blowers."[74] Harman's letter home is seen as providing insight into the motivations of *all* of the court-martialed soldiers, who were facing a Catch-22, since "testimony revealed—and it was unanimous—that these soldiers were taking the photographs to document the abuse. So the very photographs that they were taking to document were now used against them."[75] Morris has similarly said that "One thing people don't understand is that the pictures, in part, were an act of disobedience, and soldiers took the pictures because they believed it would provide evidence."[76] There are important problems with this argument.

Morris and Mestrovic both place Sabrina Harman at the center of their narratives, highlighting her letters home, and, in Morris's case, the responses that she gave while being interviewed for *Standard Operating Procedure*.[77] In the film version of *Standard Operating Procedure*, Morris has Harman read from her letters while the camera alternates between focusing on re-enactments of the scenes, or nightmares, that Harman is describing, and lingering on close up shots of Harman's words as written in what appears to be Harman's own handwriting in the original letters. We are thus encouraged to see the world through Harman's eyes, as we are forced to pay attention to her every word. Harman's voice is contemplative, and quite possibly regretful. Morris has written that one of the goals of *Standard Operating Procedure* was to humanize the "bad apples," and Harman certainly comes across as a full human being here.[78] There is, however, scant evidence that she ever intended to act as a whistle-blower, and there is no evidence at all that any of the other convicted soldiers had any whistle-blowing intent.

Harman never actually claims to have been planning to turn her photographs in to her superior officers, and she has been quite clear that she never wanted the photographs to be used as evidence against any of the soldiers who were involved in the Abu Ghraib atrocities.[79] She told Errol Morris that "I wasn't trying to expose actual individuals . . . I was trying to expose what was being allowed . . . what the military was allowing to happen to other people."[80] Gourevitch sums up Harman's position by writing that "she wanted to expose a policy . . . by assuming the role of a journalist she had found a way to ride out her time at Abu Ghraib without having to regard herself as an instrument of that policy."[81] Gourevitch's assessment of Harman's intent parallels Morris's suggestion that, under other circumstances, Harman might have received a Pulitzer prize, and, along with Morris, he glosses over the fact that journalists must not only document, but also report. While Harman would eventually tell Morris that she had wanted to turn the photographs over to CNN, there is nothing in her original letters to indicate this intent. Moreover, while Mestrovic suggests that the photographs exist only because of a documentary intent, Harman's letter and interviews present clear evidence that at least some of the photos were taken for other reasons.

The first letter home that is cited by Morris and Mestrovic, which is excerpted above, suggests quite clearly that any possible documentary intent came only after Harman had already taken at least one photograph because she was amused that a prisoner had been handcuffed in a stress position with women's underwear over his head. This treatment initially elicited not revulsion, but laughter. In an earlier letter, Harman notes that "Until Redcross came we had prisoners the MI put in womens panties trying to get them to talk. Pretty funny but they say it was 'cruel', I don't think so. No physical harm was done."[82] The following day, she wrote another letter to her partner that suggests, at best, a degree of ambivalence about the conditions the prisoners were facing:

They've been stripping "the fucked up" prisoners and handcuffing them to the bars. Its pretty sad. I get to laugh at them and throw corn at them. I kind of feel bad for these guys even if they are accused of killing US soldiers. We degrade them but don't hit and that's a plus even though Im sure they wish we'd kill them. They sleep one hour then we yell and wake them—make them stay up for one hour, then sleep one hour—then up etc. This goes on for 72 hours while we fuck with them. Most have been so scared they piss on themselves. Its sad. It's a little worst than Basic training ie: being naked and handcuffed. . . . But pictures were taken, you have to see them! A sandbag was put over their heads while it was soaked in hot sauce. Ok, that's bad but these guys have info, we are trying to get them to talk, that's all, we don't do this to all prisoners, just the few we have which is about 30–40 not many.

Harman certainly seems to have at least a bit of compassion here, but she is also writing about torture as a form of amusement ("I get to laugh at them"), and while there is a sense that she sees photography as playing a role in documenting this treatment, the point of the documentation doesn't appear to have anything to do with whistle-blowing, but is instead geared towards convincing her partner of the outlandishness of the situation.[83] Harman might see the torture as regretful, or "sad," but she also excuses it by minimizing its severity ("a little worst than basic training") and extent ("we don't do this to all prisoners"), and by arguing that there is a legitimate military purpose behind it. Harman implicates herself in the degradation without providing any indication that she believes that any of the soldiers' actions are illegitimate, or that they should be brought to the attention of any higher authorities.

The notion that Harman had intended to act as a whistle-blower is further belied by her sense that, as upsetting as some of the prisoners' suffering might have been, none of the soldiers had done anything illegal. She explains her reaction to learning that she was under investigation by telling Morris that

> I didn't think I was going to be in trouble at all. . . . I didn't think I did anything wrong. Like, I took photos, and I was in a photo. But I didn't really think I was really a part of what went on, and it really didn't matter, because it was allowed.[84]

Shortly before leaving Abu Ghraib, Harman had stopped taking photos. She told Morris that

> What was going on wasn't right, which of course you know from the beginning. But I didn't want to take any more photos. I don't think that taking photos helped me cope. It didn't relieve any stress. I had had enough.[85]

Harman's assessment that the continuing abusive treatment of the prisoners "wasn't right" doesn't appear to have affected her decision to discontinue taking photographs. This might seem odd had her photography been intended as part of a whistle-blowing endeavor, but that's not how she casts her efforts here. Instead, the only potential value of the photographs that Harman references is for personal comfort. Since the photography did not fulfill this potential, Harman abandoned it.

While claims that Harman should be seen as a reporter or whistle-blower are inflated, there is at least some evidence that she wanted other people to know about what was going on at Abu Ghraib because she thought that the prisoners were being treated unjustly. There is no such evidence for any of the other soldiers who were tried for crimes at Abu Ghraib. Only one other soldier, Corporal Graner, appears to have had any interest in documentation, but, while Graner took photos constantly, his efforts at documentation were never intended for whistle-blowing purposes. Lynndie England explains Graner's documentary impulse by noting that he had had difficulty documenting a post-traumatic stress claim with the Veterans Administration after the first Gulf War, since they didn't believe that he had been in a combat zone. England told Morris that

> This time around he [Graner] said that he was going to have proof of whatever he saw and went through. He wanted to take pictures of everything, because then there would be evidence that it happened. So I was like, OK, makes sense to me. And whenever he wanted me to grab his camera to take a picture when he couldn't I did it.[86]

Graner's interest in documentation was, at best, entirely self-serving. No one has presented any evidence that he believed that his actions or the actions of any other officer or interrogator at Abu Ghraib were problematic in any way. While Graner did eventually show some of his photographs to superior officers, including images of naked prisoners being forced into a pyramid, there is no reason to believe that he did this to alert them to any possible crimes. The fact that he also turned one of the naked pyramid shots into a screensaver on his laptop and displayed it in a way that ensured that "anyone that entered the Tier 1A office could see it" suggests instead that he wanted full acknowledgement of his exploits. Gourevitch writes that

> The extent to which Graner's exhibition of the photographs was showing off, and the extent to which it was his way of saying that it was no big deal, was anybody's guess. In either case, he said, "It wasn't a secret, but nothing was done about it."[87]

Graner might have had some sense that it was important to be able to indicate that his actions were implicitly sanctioned by higher authorities, but there is simply no indication of whistle-blowing intent in his actions, nor of disobedience.

While Morris's efforts to reconstruct and challenge dominant collective memories of Abu Ghraib are problematic in that he is far too credulous in accepting exculpatory claims on the part of the low-level soldiers who were convicted in Abu Ghraib related crimes, both versions of *Standard Operating Procedure* play an important role in resisting the "bad apple" narrative put forward by CBS news and the Bush administration. Still, Morris's film does little to support the position he frequently takes in interviews, which is that what you see when you look at the photos is "American foreign policy,"[88] and I suspect that the reason for this is that his use of the photos and reenactments constrains his focus: Morris might want to look outside of the frame, but his decision to stick so closely to the events depicted in the photographs keeps bringing us back to the low-level soldiers, "bad apples" or not, and prevents him from providing the kinds of information and context that would allow for a fuller consideration of larger issues of U.S. policy-making and national identity.[89]

The history of antilynching activism is helpful in considering the difficulty of Morris's position. While photographs of lynching eventually became important tools for antilynching organizing, the antilynching movement used these photos sparingly, and with great consideration. Spectacle lynchings were not only spectacles of punishment but also of complete dehumanization, entailing the reduction of human beings to lifeless, often mangled and charred, flesh, captured on film as nothing more than trophies. Because the production of lynching photographs was part of this spectacle of dehumanization, antilynching activists wrestled with the question of how to reproduce the photos without reproducing or enhancing the spectacle. When the NAACP decided to mount an exhibition of antilynching artwork in 1935, the organizers debated whether to include lynching photographs. There is no clear evidence about why they decided not to, but James Polchin suggests that lynching photography posed challenges that could be more easily overcome through antilynching art:

> The art transformed and countered the objectifying views of the photographs. Indeed, whereas photographs document through the eyes of the complicit spectator, art can testify and criticize, fostering different ways of humanizing what the camera objectifies. . . . the organisers in the 1930s found that the art better represented the truth of lynching.[90]

While I would argue that the antilynching movement was at times able to make use of lynching photographs in ways that minimized further dehumanization of the victims of the mob, shedding light instead on the lack of humanity not only of mob members, but of a society that allowed lynching to define southern racial dynamics, it was never a simple matter to display or circulate these photos while preventing them from fulfilling at least part of their original purpose. Visual artists, on the other hand, could respond to lynching while more easily avoiding some of the potential pitfalls involved in displaying lynching photographs. And just as artistic responses to lynching photography provided some of the most visceral and far-reaching critiques of lynching, some of the most powerful "aggressive readings" of the Abu Ghraib scandal can be found in the work of visual artists.

Portraits of Torture and the Men Beneath the Hoods: Art and Abu Ghraib

In the years since the Abu Ghraib photographs first came to light, numerous artists have seized upon the iconic potential of the photos in order to present scathing indictments of U.S. foreign policy.[91] As the photographs themselves have faded from public view ("consigned to the realm of the unimaginable and unspeakable," as J.T. Mitchell says), numerous artists have worked to keep Abu Ghraib alive in public discourse.[92] Some of the most striking pieces of oppositional Abu Ghraib related artwork seek to link the photos that have become icons of torture to more traditionally recognized icons of American national identity. One example that has received a lot of attention is a mural in a Baghdad suburb by the Iraqi artist Salaheddin Sallat, featuring the infamous hooded man on a box.[93] (See Figure 5.3.)

The hooded man has become an immediately recognizable symbol of Abu Ghraib around the world, but Sallat is not content to merely invoke memories of the torture. Instead, he actively indicts American foreign policy by including

FIGURE 5.3 Salaheddin Sallat's Abu Ghraib Mural in the al-Sadr District of Baghdad. May 27, 2004. Photographer: Ali Jasim.

Source: Courtesy Corbis Images.

a portrait of the Statue of Liberty to the left of the Hooded Man. Lady Liberty's right arm is stretched out above her head in familiar fashion, but instead of using that arm to hold her torch of liberty, welcoming immigrants to the new world, her hand grasps the switch of an electrical box, with wires connected to the hooded man's fingers. Like the man on the box, the statue's head is hooded, but whereas the Abu Ghraib prisoner's hood is black, the Statue of Liberty is wearing the white mask of a Klansman. The doubling of hooded figures presents the notion of Liberty itself as a mask, obscuring the true nature of an American national identity based upon long histories of torture and racist violence.[94] Lest there be any doubt as to where responsibility for the Abu Ghraib torture lies, "That Free dom For Bush" is written next to the mural. The notion that the events at Abu Ghraib can be laid at the feet of a "few bad apples" is never entertained here.

The London-based artist Giuseppe Di Bella also actively connects Abu Ghraib imagery to American (and British) national identity, but instead of drawing upon well-known American icons, Di Bella's critique is expressed most forcefully in the medium that he has chosen for his artwork. Di Bella has converted Abu Ghraib photos into sheets of postage stamps, and has affixed some of these stamps to postcards that have been circulated through the British and U.S. mail systems. (See Figures 5.4, 5.5 and 5.6.)

He has thus taken advantage of a vehicle through which the nation has traditionally chosen to celebrate its past, in order to redefine the very meaning of the nation.[95] Di Bella emphasizes that the mechanical reproduction of the images is intended to draw attention to the dehumanization of the Abu Ghraib victims, and to the ways in which the continued circulation of the images works to foster a collective amnesia of the experiences of the individual prisoners:

> The repetitions of images on the stamp sheets are also a reflection of the depersonalization that happens to victims of such abuse. The intimate and personal details of each account, and the consequences for the abused/ tortured is hidden and forgotten as the images are multiplied, repeated, and "consumed" by society.[96]

Just as Andy Warhol used repetition to attest to the costs of a media culture that reduces not only celebrities but also traumatic national events to a few essential characteristics by relegating them to the status of icons, Di Bella's work suggests that much is lost in the public circulation of the Abu Ghraib imagery.

Di Bella's critique of the public consumption of the photographs is literalized in his choice of medium, as he notes that

> the mechanical act of licking and stamping a postage stamp could be linked to a notion of humiliation and abuse/torture as revealed in the photographs. I was conscious that this process could turn the viewer into an active consumer and make the user aware of the consumption and treatment of public images in circulation.[97]

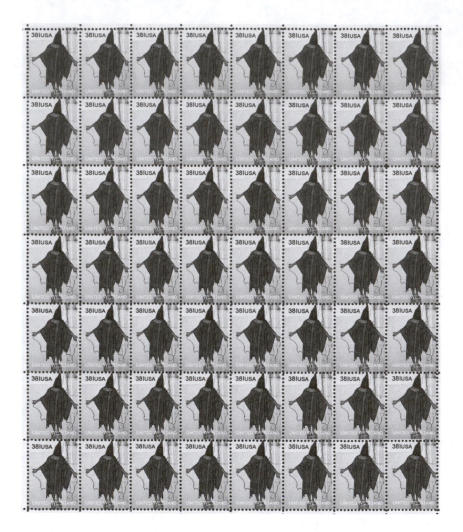

FIGURE 5.4 Giuseppe Di Bella, from the series Abu Ghraib 2004/2006. "USA Stamp Sheet."

Source: Courtesy of the Artist.

The decision to affix the stamps to postcards and send them through the mail adds to the sense that the images have been reduced to the level of commodity, since postcards have historically been associated with the rise of consumer culture. Indeed, much of the power of Di Bella's work is that it resonates so closely, albeit ironically, with lynching postcards, which have been understood as a method of commodifying and disseminating the spectacle of lynching.[98] And, just as lynching postcards would eventually make their way into museum exhibits intended to transform them into antilynching postcards, Di Bella has exhibited some of the

FIGURE 5.5 Giuseppe Di Bella, from the series Abu Ghraib 2004/2006. "Postcard."

Source: Courtesy of the Artist.

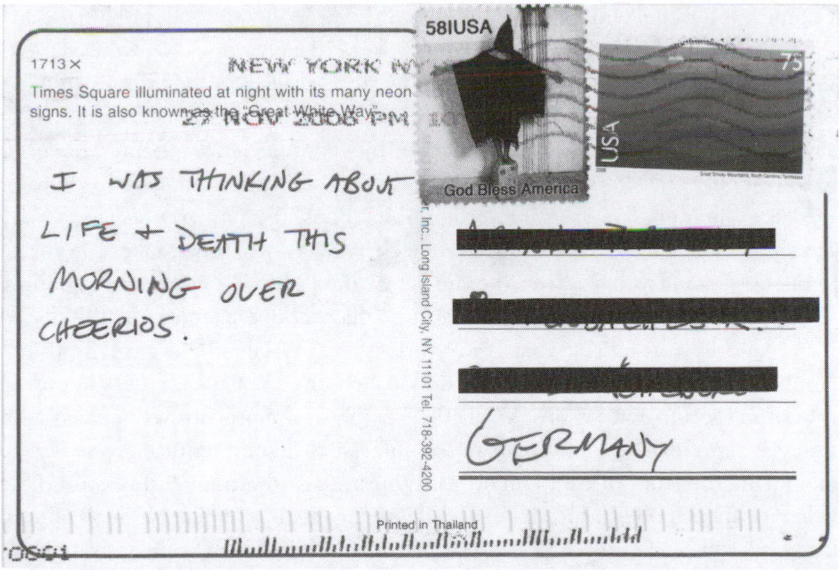

FIGURE 5.6 Giuseppe Di Bella, from the series Abu Ghraib 2004/2006. "Postcard Back."

Source: Courtesy of the Artist.

Abu Ghraib-stamped postcards that have successfully travelled through the mail, noting that his intent was to present the postcards as "trophies" that draw attention "to the contemporary society's appetite to consume violent and gruesome imagery."[99] In 1934, the NAACP responded to the lynching of Claude Neal in a town near Greenwood Florida by releasing a pamphlet about the murder that included a collage of press clippings from around the country. The original articles were printed days before the lynching, and, like so many earlier stories in the white press, they served not to condemn the violence, but to alert potential members of the mob to the upcoming event, in effect advertising the killing. The collage was headlined "All of America Knew of Lynching in Advance," as the NAACP charged the general population of the nation with silent complicity that allowed lynching to continue.[100] More than seventy years later, Di Bella's work suggests that contemporary audiences remain passive consumers, rather than active opponents, of spectacles of racist torture.

If Di Bella is interested in drawing attention to the dehumanization that is central to the spectacle of Abu Ghraib, other artists and activists have endeavored, instead, to move past the icons and humanize the Abu Ghraib victims. Much of the power of the photograph of the hooded man has to do with a lack of specificity: the fact that we don't see the victim's face enables us to think that the victim could be anyone, and it then becomes possible for the image to become iconic— a symbol whose meaning is open to contest and subject to the kinds of readings that I have been discussing. The process of turning a photograph of one man's victimization into a symbol of something much larger has obvious potential value for people across the political spectrum, but the details not only of the victim's suffering, but also of his life, are inevitably lost in this process of translation.[101] As a figure of pure and iconic victimization, "Hooded Man" stands stripped of all identity and, ultimately, of all humanity. Indeed, the victim's identity has been so thoroughly effaced that it became possible for the American press to think of the Abu Ghraib prisoners as interchangeable. Thus, the *New York Times*, *Vanity Fair*, and *PBS* felt little need to fact check what turned out to be one man's erroneous claims to have been the subject of the "Hooded Man" photograph.

Ali Shalal Qaissi is the man that early media accounts identified as "Hooded Man," and he was indeed a victim of torture at Abu Ghraib, and the head of a group of former Abu Ghraib prisoners called the Association of Victims of American Occupation Prisons. While the group was not primarily concerned with issues of representation, it did share the interest that some critical artists had in mobilizing the icons of Abu Ghraib, as its business card prominently featured the image of the Hooded Man. It turns out, however, that, while Ali Shalal Qaissi may well have been placed on a box with a hood, he was apparently not the person captured in the photograph that has been circulated around the world. According to military records, the "real" Hooded Man turns out to have been a man named Abdou Hussain Saad Faleh, and the *New York Times* and other media outlets were ultimately forced to retract their initial stories when questions about the man's identity were raised by *Salon*.[102] There is no evidence that Ali Shalal Qaissi was intentionally misleading the press when he claimed to be "Hooded Man." Instead, it is quite possible that his ordeal was close enough to that of Abdou Hussain Saad Faleh that he actually believed that he was the person in the photograph.[103] Whatever his intent may have been, however, his organization's business card serves an important purpose, as it redeploys the imagery of Abu Ghraib and encourages people to look beyond the icons to the real people whose identities had been masked by the hoods that are so prominently featured in most of the well-known Abu Ghraib photographs.

The American artist Daniel Heyman shares a similar goal. When Heyman decided to do work on Abu Ghraib, his initial impulse was to engage the same iconic images that had captured the attention of so many other artists, and of people around the world. Once he began working with the image of the hooded man, however, he realized that he was at a loss: "I tried to use that image as a shorthand to comment on torture. . . . But it started to become ubiquitous, and I think it lost its ability to have much impact."[104] Heyman quickly became convinced that he could not base his artwork upon the iconic imagery of Abu Ghraib if he wanted to avoid contributing to the very dehumanization that he wanted to critique. He notes that, by the time he was considering how to approach Abu Ghraib artwork, the victims'

> human identities had already been removed twice: first as wrongly accused and brutally tortured prisoners, second in the photos their captors took of them, hooded and faceless, where they became global icons but lost their individuality. I wanted the Iraqis to regain their humanity, to regain their faces and their voices.[105]

In the Spring and Summer of 2006, Heyman was accorded a unique opportunity to learn about the lives of Abu Ghraib victims, and to try to bring the fact of their humanity to larger audiences.

Several months after the first batch of Abu Ghraib photographs came to light, the law firm of Burke O'Neil launched the first of a series of lawsuits seeking to hold to account the private contractors that were involved in the torture. The lead attorneys in the case, Susan Burke and Shereef Akeel, travelled to Baghdad, Amman, and Istanbul to gather victims' testimony against the Titan and CACI Corporations, since the companies had provided employees who were responsible for translation and interrogation at Abu Ghraib. The suit charged the firms with "conspiring with the American military and civilian personnel to commit torture."[106] They invited Heyman and filmmaker Rory Kennedy (who would go on to direct *Ghosts of Abu Ghraib*, 2007, the first feature-length documentary about Abu Ghraib) to join them in Amman and Istanbul. As the former prisoners described their treatment at Abu Ghraib, Heyman sketched their portraits (using copper plates for some of the sessions, and watercolors and drypoint for others), and then transcribed portions of their testimony in the blank space around the portraits as they spoke. (See Figures 5.7 and 5.8.)

The resulting artwork avoids the sense of mechanical reproduction and dehumanization captured in Di Bella's stamps and in most other artistic renderings of Abu Ghraib, as it highlights intimate details and represents the victims in their regular clothing rather than in uniforms or masks. Even the lettering, which is written in un-even block characters, often swirling around the victims' heads and bodies, seems to suggest that each prisoner's experiences were unique.

At first glance, Heyman's work may not be as arresting as Di Bella's, since we are presented with only ordinary-looking people, and not with the icons that captured the attention of the world. But while Di Bella's stamps are undeniably powerful, I would suggest that theirs is the power of shock and recognition, and that Heyman's portraits likely have a different kind of capacity to move audiences. Wendy Hesford, commenting on the number of anti-war artists who have incorporated the iconic Abu Ghraib images into their work has raised the question of whether it is possible to "have critique without spectacle."[107] Heyman's portraits suggest that one particularly effective way of subverting the spectacle of Abu Ghraib is to probe beneath the superficial politics of imagery and anchor the icons to the real-life human beings whose stories have seldom been told.

Concluding Remarks: Critical Readings and Cultural Climate

In the end, it is impossible to fully assess the significance of any of the representations of Abu Ghraib, since their power is not intrinsic to the representations, but is instead a product of the interactions between the images and their audiences. One reason to suspect that some of the most interesting artistic responses to Abu Ghraib might have a good deal of political resonance has to do with the role of new media: like the Abu Ghraib photographs themselves, much of the work of artists like Daniel Heyman and Giuseppe Di Bella has been reproduced digitally and can be easily accessed through the internet. And, yet, I would argue that no matter how striking any particular rendering of the Abu Ghraib atrocities may appear to any particular person, in order for representations of Abu Ghraib to gain significant political heft, "aggressive readings" aren't enough, since there is no guarantee that those readings will be shared among broad sectors of the population, even if new media technologies aid in their dissemination. As a case study in the reception of atrocity photos, it is important to consider the factors that separate the Abu Ghraib images from such things as lynching photographs and photos of Vietnam-era atrocities, and a central issue to pay attention to is surely the role of new media. But it is possible to overstate the significance of new media. It is certainly true that the Abu Ghraib photographs were able to migrate to new contexts far more rapidly than could photographs of My Lai, to say nothing of lynching, but it is also true that the capacity for rapid circulation alone was not enough to ensure that the photographs would be read in a politically useful manner.

FIGURE 5.7 Daniel Heyman, from the Amman Watercolor Series, 2006: Edition 30. "When I Saw My Sons Dead."

Source: Courtesy of the Artist.

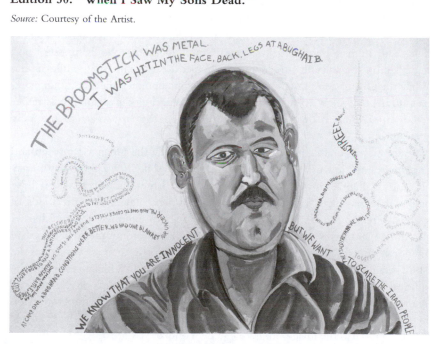

FIGURE 5.8 Daniel Heyman, Istanbul: August 2008. "The Broomstick Was Metal," Gouache on Nishinoushi Paper.

Source: Courtesy of the Artist.

In order for politically consequential audiences to share the aggressive readings put forward by various critics and artists, powerful sponsorship is essential.

The potential for critically engaged readings of the Abu Ghraib photos to gain popular currency was likely greatest when the photos were first released, not only because that is when they were "freshest" and thus most newsworthy, but also because their release coincided with a still-strong international anti-war movement that was well equipped to popularize such readings.[108] While the movement had peaked in February 2003, when the BBC estimated that between 10 and 13 million protestors rallied across the world in hundreds of cities around the world,[109] the release of the photos coincided with a CBS/*New York Times* poll indicating that, for the first time, a majority of Americans disapproved of the conduct of the war.[110] Social movements are, however, only one potential source of sponsorship that might extend the resonance of critical responses to Abu Ghraib. Powerful state actors can play a role too, and the cultural landscape shaping understandings of Abu Ghraib may have shifted during the 2008 presidential campaign and in the early days of the Obama presidency. One of Barack Obama's first official acts as president (only days after then-attorney general nominee Eric Holder flatly declared, during his confirmation hearings, that waterboarding is a form of torture) was to sign an executive order banning coercive interrogation methods, signaling that public perceptions of the United States' relationship to torture were of central concern to the new administration. Such concerns provided new opportunities for some of Obama's most important constituencies, including civil rights and human rights organizations, which worked to apply pressure and capitalize on the ways that their support helped to usher in a new political era. While the Obama administration has repeatedly disappointed these constituencies, the pressure that they have applied has helped to keep a spotlight (admittedly rather a dim one) focused on issues of torture during the first years of the new administration.

In a new cultural climate engendered, in part, by the Obama campaign and presidency, artistic work that critically engages the Abu Ghraib photographs may become intelligible in new ways, and may reach larger audiences who will be prepared to see racist violence through a new lens. Then, too, the kinds of aggressive readings that I've discussed are also open to interpretation and debate, and not all audiences will, for example, see the kinds of critiques that Heyman intended when gazing upon his portraits. Abu Ghraib-related artwork, like the Abu Ghraib photographs themselves, demands to be read. When considering the political impact not only of the Abu Ghraib photographs, but of any atrocity images, it is important to interrogate the technologies that enable the production and distribution of the imagery, and to assess the kinds of readings of the evidence that are offered as the images migrate to new contexts. Context, technology, and aggressive readings alone, however, tell only part of the story, as the meaning and political impact of representations of atrocity will always be dependent upon broader social struggles.

CONCLUSION

Lessons from a Campus Movement

In February and March, 2010, the campus of the University of California, San Diego was rocked by a series of racist incidents. First, students discovered a Facebook invitation to a "Compton Cookout" that was sponsored by members of a campus fraternity. The advertisement claimed that the ghetto-themed party was intended to celebrate Black History Month, and included a description of the desired dress code, filled with racist and misogynistic stereotypes. Female guests were encouraged to emulate "Ghetto chicks" who "have short, nappy hair . . . speak very loudly . . . have a very limited vocabulary [that they] attempt to make up for . . . by forming new words, such as 'constipulated,' or simply cursing persistently." Male guests were expected to comply with the stereotypical fashion of hip hop culture, complete with "stunner shades" and "Tats." The invitation promised that "coolade," malt liquor, watermelon, and fried chicken would be served.[1] The following week, a campus magazine long known for racist, misogynistic, and homophobic content broadcast a television program on a student-run station defending the party, ridiculing Black History Month, and using racist epithets to disparage African American students. Members of the Black Student Union (BSU) searched the television station's office and discovered a piece of cardboard with the words "Compton Lynching" scrawled upon it.

Racist incidents continued as students and other members of the campus community began to organize anti-racist protests. On February 24th, students walked out of an official university-sponsored teach-in on racism in order to hold their own rally on the steps of the student center. Two thousand students, faculty, staff, and their supporters protested against racism, classism, sexism and homophobia within the UC system and the state of California, as well as against a campus climate that had allowed for the emergence of the "Compton Cookout" and related events. The next evening, a noose was found hanging from a bookshelf in the main university library, and a group of African American students, who had every reason to believe that they might be targeted by violent racist hate crimes, felt the need to seek safe harbor and slept in the campus Cross Cultural Center. Several days later, a pillow case that had been crudely fashioned to resemble a Ku Klux Klan hood was found covering the head of a statue of Theodore Geisel (better known as Dr. Seuss) near the same library.[2]

This spate of racist incidents came against a backdrop of growing concerns about the lack of racial diversity on UC campuses, and fears about the increasing privatization of the university.[3] Earlier in the academic year, the BSU had started working within a statewide coalition to increase the enrollment of African American students throughout the UC system. (African Americans made up only 1.3 percent of the student population at UCSD, and had historically never been higher than 3 percent of the student population.[4]) The "Do UC us?" campaign was concerned not only with admission but also retention of African American students. Well before the "Compton Cookout," members of the coalition were therefore already struggling to change a campus climate that had alienated students of color for many years. At the same time, students across the UC, California State University, and Community College systems had spent months gearing up for a March 4th statewide day of action to protest massive budget cuts to every sector of California public education. The fact that so many members of the UCSD community had spent so much time thinking about and organizing against racism and inequality within the UC system might have helped to foster a climate in which UC and UCSD administrators and most public commentators were compelled to acknowledge that there were serious problems on campus that needed to be addressed with real urgency.

The BSU and their supporters chose to respond to the racist incidents as part of a broader series of problems. The BSU declared a "State of Emergency" and issued a series of demands that focused on access to education, and on improving the racial climate on campus. Their demands included, for example, funding for the Black Student Union, changes in the ways that the 2011 applicant pool would be evaluated, money for research-based scholarships to help retain African American students, and an increase in the number of African American students, PhD candidates, faculty, staff, and administrators. The BSU linked its demands to the March 4th day of action and joined forces with the campus chapter of Movimiento Estudiantil Chicano de Aztlán (MECHA) and other social justice organizations. The BSU called for or supported a series of additional protests and organizing sessions, all of which were well-attended. The protests were covered extensively in the local and national press, and the BSU and its supporters maintained a significant web presence, so anyone interested in following ongoing events, learning about new protests, or reading analyses of the movement, could do so quite easily. Many of the protesters took digital photographs and video of the demonstrations, and uploaded these images to their own blogs or social networking accounts, becoming citizen-journalists who were able to supplement the accounts provided by professional news organizations. Faculty and staff members who had been working at the university for decades agreed that this was the largest campus movement since the Vietnam era. In this atmosphere, the administration quickly indicated that it was open to negotiation with the BSU, and by March 4th had entered into an agreement with the student organization, promising to meet many of its demands.

The UCSD anti-racist movement of 2010 follows in the tradition of other struggles discussed in this book, and presents a useful opportunity to reconsider the political possibilities of racial spectacles. Like lynching photography and the Abu Ghraib photographs, the "Compton Cookout" advertisement was apparently intended to circulate only among like-minded people who could be counted upon to share the racist sentiments expressed in the invitation. The intent behind the display of the noose and Klan's hood may not be clear,[5] but there is no indication that the people who created them thought that they would become part of a larger media spectacle: Neither object would have been seen by many people if not for efforts of anti-racist activists to publicize them.[6] Regardless of what their makers had in mind, the noose and the Klan's hood served the purposes that such objects were originally intended for—there was a palpable sense of fear, exclusion, and sadness on campus in late February. However, members of the BSU and other anti-racist activists were not content to allow these objects to serve only as instruments of terror and intimidation. Instead, they made use of every form of communication technology at their disposal to "spectacularize" them. Once displayed in new contexts, the invitation, noose and hood were invested with new meanings and used for new purposes, as speakers at rallies and members of the movement who were invited to comment about the protests in the press regularly linked these objects to histories and memories of minstrelsy and racist terrorism. The resulting anti-racist spectacle provided the BSU and its allies with tools that they could use to mobilize an anti-racist movement capable of eliciting significant concessions from an administration that had turned a deaf ear to complaints about institutionalized racism for many years.[7]

The contested nature of racial spectacles has been a central concern throughout this book. From spectacle lynchings to Abu Ghraib, the meanings of racial spectacles have been hotly debated, and questions of how they should be interpreted have been linked to broader struggles over matters as weighty as southern race relations and American foreign policy. At first glance, there appears to have been little contest over the UCSD racist incidents. After all, the University agreed not only that these *were* in fact racist incidents, but also that they pointed to larger problems, and that the administration had an obligation to work to address those problems. The racist campus magazine did issue a public defense of the "Compton Cookout," but the magazine itself had no prominent public defenders, and was generally understood as voicing extremist viewpoints. There were also an unsettling number of overtly racist comments about the incidents in the readers' response sections of many websites that reported on the events, but these too can probably be thought of as fairly marginalized voices.[8]

The more significant way that the meanings of the incidents were contested can be detected in comments by various officials who were in agreement that an anti-racist stance was necessary, but who nevertheless worked to limit the scope of the inquiry. Governor Arnold Schwarzenegger, for example, condemned the "intolerable acts of racism and incivility" in the UC system, and declared that "The acts of racism and intolerance that we have witnessed are completely unacceptable," but he focused only on the handful of isolated racist incidents, and not on broader patterns and histories of institutionalized racism and exclusion.[9] The president of the University of California, Mark Yudof, issued a joint statement with Russell Gould, the chair of the UC Board of Regents, in which they similarly denounced the display of the noose as "a despicable expression of racial hatred," expressed "sympathy" for "the UCSD students and all others who have been confronted with this ugliness," and pledged to "root out racism whenever and wherever it arises on our campuses." They seemed to suggest, however, that the problems could be dealt with through enforcement of campus conduct codes, rather than through a more thorough reckoning with the structure of the UC system.[10] An early statement about the "Compton Cookout" from UCSD Chancellor Mary Anne Fox and Vice Chancellor of Student Affairs Penny Rue framed the case as highlighting the importance of "mutual respect and civility."[11]

Members of the administration soon began to define the scope of the problem in broader terms, but the fact that this was contrary to their initial impulses suggests that the campus anti-racist movement was able to exert sufficient pressure to change the terms of debate. Still, even as the protests grew in strength and frequency, there continued to be a significant gulf between the kinds of systemic critiques offered by members and allies of the BSU and members of the University administration. The administration agreed to a number of measures intended to increase campus diversity and provide resources for research and curriculum development having to do with issues of race and ethnicity, but it continued to define the problems as having to do with "hurtful incidents" and the campus climate, as it promised to work to "create a campus that respects differences and ensures diversity."[12]

The administration rarely, if ever, focused on institutionalized inequalities or spending priorities within the UC system or the state budget. It was left to members and supporters of the BSU to draw attention to the fact that students of color have always been severely underrepresented in the UC system, and to address the structural barriers that place low income students, who are disproportionately students of color, at a tremendous disadvantage. UCSD Ethnic Studies professor Sara Clarke Kaplan, for example, used her appearance on a public radio talk show to explain that many low income schools are generally unable to offer Advanced Placement courses that can raise high school students' grade point averages, and are frequently incapable of offering even the basic courses that are required for admission to either the University of California or the California State University.[13] The administration's statements about the ways that the university intends to improve the campus climate say nothing about efforts that might address the impact of this kind of systemic inequality on the UC system and its student population.

In many ways, the UCSD anti-racist movement of 2010 was a dramatic success. The anti-racist spectacle that the movement created out of the noose, hood, and "Compton Cookout" enabled it to draw attention to deeply-rooted problems within the UC system, and, consequently, to extract significant concessions from an otherwise intractable administration. It is not at all clear, however, that those concessions will result in higher enrollment of students of color. And it is, sadly, all too clear that the concessions will do nothing to address larger patterns and structures of racist inequality within California public education. The anti-racist movement is ongoing, and it is possible that there are more challenges and changes yet to come. But it is also the case that it became difficult to sustain momentum once the administration signed its agreement with the BSU, and once the flurry of racist incidents had begun to recede into memory. As the urgency of the moment began to fade, so did the anti-racist spectacle that the movement had generated. It faded so thoroughly that, when a second noose was discovered in the stairwell of a campus theater in July, 2010, there was almost no press coverage, no protests (or at least none that were publicized in any notable way), and no perceived need for a public response from the administration.[14] The absence of widespread and vocal outrage surely owes something to the fact that the UCSD campus is only sparsely populated in the summer months. But I think that the lack of organized resistance to this more recent display of racist hatred also says something about the limitations inherent in social struggles that are centered around racial spectacles.

The power of the anti-racist spectacle that the BSU and its allies were able to create out of the invitation, noose, and hood lay in the movement's ability to publicly explore the meanings of those objects, and to link those meanings to systemic inequalities and a hostile campus environment. The initial creation and semi-public display of these objects was only a starting point for activism and critical inquiry. The anti-racist movement that was generated by drawing attention to them drew its strength by quickly moving beyond them. When attempting to deal with the systematic underrepresentation of students of color within the Californian public university systems, the invitation, noose, and hood are best understood as nothing more than symptoms of a much more severe malady. And yet, the fact that they were so central to the spectacle that was at the heart of the campus movement meant that the movement was inextricably tied to them. Speakers and public commentators may have focused on other issues, but the invitation, noose, and hood were constant reference points in almost every public discussion of the problems on campus, even when they served only as a point of entry to conversations that addressed more far-reaching issues. Over time, however, as it appeared that the university was doing what it could to deal with the invitation, noose, and hood, it became more difficult to use them as examples of the failures of the administration, the UC system, or the government of the state of California. The fact that none of these objects had any prominent and credible public defenders meant that they could effectively serve as sites of protest for only a limited time. Once the initial acts of racist aggression that allowed for the creation of the anti-racist spectacle had been so thoroughly and consensually repudiated, the spectacle itself could not last, and, consequently, could no longer serve as a vehicle for social protest.

The Politics of Racial Spectacles: Limitations and Potential as Sites of Anti-Racist Struggle

The ephemeral nature of racial spectacles presents a serious quandary for anti-racist activists. On the one hand, racial spectacles are frequently prompted by extraordinary events that can be used to mobilize members of aggrieved communities. This kind of mobilization, in turn, can provide opportunities for critiquing and resisting not only extraordinary racist incidents, but also the routine workings of a racist society.

The chance to create anti-racist spectacles out of extraordinary incidents can offer possibilities for meaningful changes that anti-racist organizers can ill-afford to pass up. On the other hand, a movement that is closely tied to isolated racist events may appear to lose urgency once those events have been effectively dealt with, even if the goals of the movement were always defined in broader terms. In this regard, the UCSD anti-racist movement follows a similar trajectory to that of the movement to free the Scottsboro defendants in the 1930s. The Communist Party and much of the larger Scottsboro defense movement never wavered in their determination to present the Scottsboro case as just one especially noteworthy example of an exploitative, racist, and corrupt system. Yet, once four of the defendants were freed and the state had dropped its pursuit of the death penalty for the remaining defendants, it became difficult to continue to organize on behalf of "The Scottsboro Boys," and the Scottsboro defense movement, which had never been solely about Scottsboro, could no longer mount an effective struggle against wider injustice.

More generally, the fact that racial spectacles revolve around extraordinary events means that the opportunities that they provide for anti-racist organizing and critiques can be undercut once those extraordinary events have faded or been effectively managed. For example, when they were first published and broadcast, the Abu Ghraib photographs provided anti-war activists with important tools that could be used to indict American foreign policy, but once the Abu Ghraib trials and investigations had run their course, it became difficult for the anti-war movement to continue to shine a spotlight upon the costs of war. Years later, the Abu Ghraib photographs remain the only set of images of Iraqi suffering that has been seen by much of the American public. Similarly, the Kobe Bryant case and the Rampart scandal (along with its popular culture iterations) helped to foster a climate in which the mass media was willing to open its doors to systemic critiques of racism and, in the Bryant case, sexism, within the criminal justice system. It is not clear, however, that those doors could remain open once the criminal charges were dropped and the civil suit was settled in the Bryant case, and once the justice department's consent decree was lifted in Los Angeles.

It would be a mistake, however, to think that the fact that racial spectacles eventually fade away means that they do not have lasting consequences. The efforts of the Scottsboro defense movement to create an anti-racist spectacle out of the trials of the Scottsboro defendants helped to debunk the myth of the black rapist and to change public perceptions of lynching. The movement therefore helped to pave the way for national outrage over the lynching of Emmett Till, and for the emergence of the modern civil rights movement, two decades later. The Rampart scandal led to meaningful reforms of the LAPD and may have also led to new ways of representing and understanding police violence and corruption. It is still possible that these new understandings will result in diminished public support for draconian "tough on crime" legislative measures, and add fuel to growing movements for prison reform or abolition. It is too early to tell how the months-long public debates about racist stereotypes and rape mythology that were central to the Kobe Bryant case will impact popular understandings of racism and sexism within the criminal justice system, but it is a safe bet that the case will at least provide an important reference point for the next racial spectacle involving interracial sexuality and allegations of violence. The Obama administration may be unwilling to fully come to terms with the Abu Ghraib scandal (and unwilling to appropriately allocate responsibility in the case), but the controversy over the photographs may have helped to change public opinion about United States foreign policy, contributed to Obama's election, and led to changes in the ways that the wars in Afghanistan and Iraq could be prosecuted. As spectacles fade, the opportunities to mobilize around them as sites of anti-racist struggle become scarce, but this does not diminish the importance of such struggles. As these examples demonstrate, the effects of racial spectacles are unpredictable. I would argue, though, that it is precisely because racial spectacles can reverberate throughout popular culture and social discourse in unpredictable ways that they merit close analytic scrutiny and have so much potential political potency.

The events at UCSD in the winter of 2010 are instructive not only for thinking about the limitations and anti-racist potential of racial spectacles, but also for a consideration of the range of factors necessary for racial spectacles to emerge as valuable sites of social struggle. The racist incidents on campus would have been likely to generate widespread outrage and condemnation regardless of when they occurred (so long as they occurred during the regular academic year), but it is not clear that they could have been used to spark a larger anti-racist movement if the UC system had not already been buffeted by waves of budget cuts and fee hikes that had alerted members of the campus community to the costs of the increasing privatization of the system, and if the BSU had not already been working to combat the underrepresentation of African American students on campus. Already-existing anger and frustration at the state of the UC system and with the UCSD campus climate certainly helps to explain the rapidity with which the movement emerged. The fact that the incidents came just as so many students were gearing up for the March 4th statewide protests against the budget cuts and fee hikes is also significant, since it suggests that there was fertile ground for a social movement to take root.

The idea that racial spectacles and their political potential are not self-contained, but can be assessed only by looking to wider social conditions, is important when seeking to explain the variety of political responses to such spectacles. The lynching of Emmett Till provides an important example. The killing was particularly grisly, and the fact that Till was such a young boy certainly played into the public anger at his death, but it is unlikely that Mamie Till Bradley's decision to display Emmett's corpse would have created the same kind of anti-racist spectacle that it did had Till been lynched thirty years earlier. By 1955, demographic changes and changes in southern agriculture, coupled with a half-century of antilynching activism that had battered away at racist lynching mythology, had led to a dramatic decline in lynching rates. It was only in this new climate that each new lynching could become a source of national outrage, and that the lynching of a fourteen-year-old boy could help spark a national movement for civil rights.

Similarly, a variety of factors must also be considered for any explanation of public reactions to the Abu Ghraib photographs. Hundreds of thousands of Iraqi children, and nearly a million Iraqi civilians in total, are estimated to have died of malnutrition and disease due to a combination of a severely damaged infrastructure, a harsh sanctions regime, and the Iraqi government's disruption of oil-for-food programs in the years immediately following the first Gulf War.[15] Conservative estimates are that an additional 100,000 Iraqi civilians had died in the Iraq War by September, 2010.[16] By the time that the Abu Ghraib photographs were circulated, images of Iraqi suffering had been readily available to the press for well over a decade, yet these were the first such images to be widely broadcast and published within the United States. The photographs were released not long after the largest anti-war movement in American history had reached its peak, and at a moment where anti-war sentiment was still quite high. Had they been released before this sentiment had developed, it is not clear that they would have generated the kind of spectacle that they did. On the other hand, had similar photographs been released a year earlier, as millions of people were protesting against the war around the world, it is possible that their impact would have been considerably more dramatic. As discussed in Chapter 5, critics who thought that the Abu Ghraib photographs would result in immediate changes to U.S. foreign policy and in high-level members of the Bush administration being held accountable for systematic violations of human rights laws likely made the mistake of thinking that they could assess spectacular imagery on its own terms, without a fuller consideration of a wide variety of social factors.

Attention to the broader cultural climate is important not only for assessing the ways that particular racial spectacles are likely to play out, but also for considering why some events that might appear likely to generate racial spectacles never do. I have argued, in Chapter 3, that one of the reasons that the Rampart scandal did not become a full-fledged racial spectacle is that the kinds of systemic problems that were at the heart of the scandal (including racist policing strategies and sentencing guidelines, a plea bargain system that uses the threat of incredibly harsh prison terms to coerce even innocent defendants into accepting guilty pleas, and a code of silence that pressures officers into ignoring the crimes of their colleagues) are not easily photographed, and consequently do not easily lend themselves to the politics of spectacle. But the fact that the primary victims in the case were the residents of a poor Latino community with a large immigrant population also played a role. Many of the members of this community had long been demonized as "illegals" and "gangbangers," and had few resources that they might use to draw attention to their plight. Long histories of racist stereotyping had an impact on public opinion, as there was little organized opposition to LAPD "gang profiling" policies that had been responsible for the wholesale violation of the civil liberties of Rampart district residents (the vast majority of whom were not gang members) for years before Javier Ovando was shot by Rafael Perez and Nino Durden. Under these circumstances, it is difficult to imagine what kind of anti-racist activism might have been required to successfully turn the shooting and framing of Javier Ovando into the kind of anti-racist spectacle that could be used to mobilize significant resistance to the institutionalized racism of the criminal justice system within and beyond Los Angeles. That the corruption and brutality in the Rampart district *did* eventually become a source of constant media attention is testament to the enormity of the scandal, but the fact that the largest police corruption scandal in the history of Los Angeles never became a full-blown racial spectacle, and never provided the spark for an anti-racist mass movement, can best be explained by looking to the structural disempowerment of community residents.

As racial spectacles (or scandals that had the potential to become racial spectacles), the case studies discussed in this book are, by definition, exceptional. Most poor African Americans who are unjustly convicted of rape serve their sentences in relative isolation and do not have the benefit of an international mass movement working to secure their freedom. Nor can most black men charged with rape afford the kind of legal defense available to Kobe Bryant. Few such defendants have the opportunity to instruct national audiences about the intertwined histories of lynching and allegations of interracial rape, just as few media inquiries into rape allegations entail wide-ranging investigations of sexist rape mythology. Brutality and corruption may well be endemic to many American police forces, but no more than a handful of corruption scandals can begin to approach the scale of Rampart. Iraq has lost as much as seven percent of its population to violence, disease, and malnutrition in the past two decades, so evidence of Iraqi suffering is all too plentiful. However, the particular kind of Iraqi suffering depicted in the Abu Ghraib photographs had never before been published in glossy news magazines or broadcast on American television stations.

These exceptional events have provided exceptional opportunities for social struggle, and yet, the victors in these struggles are seldom clear. The State of Alabama eventually renounced its claim to the lives of the Scottsboro defendants, but not before those lives were irrevocably damaged. It is difficult to say who benefited from the Kobe Bryant case, as media coverage of the case worked to simultaneously reinforce and challenge a host of racist and sexist stereotypes. The Rampart scandal led to a series of reforms of the LAPD, but the "prison industrial complex" continues to thrive, and institutionalized racism within the criminal justice system continues apace. The impact and importance of the Abu Ghraib photographs is still hotly contested, even as official U.S. combat operations in Iraq have come to a close (and as tens of thousands of American troops remain in other roles), and even as the war in Afghanistan shifts to center stage in American political discourse.

The internet and new media technologies have provided oppressed groups and anti-racist social movements with methods of communication that were impossible to imagine not very long ago, and there are more avenues available for resisting dominant representations of race than has ever before been the case. Still, it should not be surprising that there are few straightforward victories for activists who attempt to mobilize around racial spectacles when seeking to challenge structures of power and privilege. Debord's original conception of the "society of the spectacle" highlighted the oppressive nature of spectacles, figuring them as instruments of capitalist ideology. In an environment defined by ever-increasing concentration of corporate ownership of the media, Debord's warnings are as important as they ever were, and activists and social movements face daunting odds when they seek to subvert the hegemonic messages inherent in so many racial spectacles. My case studies suggest, however, that while the glare of racial spectacles may indeed frequently blind people to real social needs, such spectacles can also bring deeply entrenched social problems to light. As so many activists whose struggles have never garnered any kind of meaningful media attention would attest, it is much more difficult to fight systemic inequalities when they remain shrouded in shadow.

WORKS CITED

Acham, Christine. *Revolution Televised: Prime Time and the Struggle for Black Power.* Minneapolis: University of Minnesota Press, 2004.

Alexander, Elizabeth, "'Can You be Black and Look at This?': Reading the Rodney King Video(s)." In *Black Male: Representations of Masculinity in Contemporary American Art*, edited by Thelma Golden, 91–110. New York: Whitney Museum of American Art, 1994.

Alexander, Nikol G., and Drucilla Cornell. "Dismissed or Banished? A Testament to the Reasonableness of the Simpson Jury." In *Birth of a Nation'hood: Gaze, Script, and Spectacle in the O.J. Simpson Case*, edited by Toni Morrison and Claudia Brodsky Lacour, 57–96. New York: Pantheon Books, 1997.

Allen, James, ed. *Without Sanctuary: Lynching Photography in America.* Santa Fe: Twin Palms Publishers, 2000.

Alvarez, Luis, Roberto Alvarez, Cutler Edwards, Stevie Ruiz, Elizabeth Sine, Maki Smith, and Daniel Widener. *Another University is Possible.* San Diego: University Readers, 2010.

Ames, Jessie Daniel. "Southern Women and Lynching," Atlanta: Association of Southern Women for the Prevention of Lynching. From *Association of Southern Women for the Prevention of Lynching* papers, 1936.

Ames, Jessie Daniel. "Editorial Treatment of Lynchings." *Public Opinion Quarterly*, January (1938): 77–85.

Amnesty International. "United States of America: Death by Discrimination – the Continuing Role of Race in Capital Cases." 2003. http://www.amnesty.org/en/library/info/AMR51/046/2003 (accessed October 20, 2009).

Andén-Papadopoulos, "The Abu Ghraib Torture Photographs: News Frames, Visual Culture, and the Power of Images." *Journalism*, 9 (2008): 5–30.

Anderson, Benedict. *Imagined Communities.* New York: Verso, 1991.

Apel, Dora. *Imagery of Lynching: Black Men, White Women, and the Mob.* New Brunswick, NJ: Rutgers University Press, 2004.

Arendt, Hannah. *Eichmann in Jerusalem: A Report on the Banality of Evil.* New York: The Viking Press, 1963.

Arnold, Carrie. "Racial Profiling in Immigration Enforcement: State and Local Agreements to Enforce Federal Immigration Law." *Arizona Law Review*, 49 (2007): 113–142.

Association of Southern Women for the Prevention of Lynching (ASWPL). *Association of Southern Women for the Prevention of Lynching papers, 1930–1942*. Ann Arbor, Michigan: University Microfilms International, 1983.

—— "Torture Culture: Lynching Photographs and the Images of Abu Ghraib." *Art Journal*, Summer (2005): 89–100.

Baker, Aaron. "Beyond the Thin Line of Black and Blue: Movies and Police Misconduct in Los Angeles." In *Bad: Infamy, Darkness, Evil, and Slime on Screen*, edited by Murray Pomerance, 55–64. Albany: State University of New York Press, 2004.

Bandes, Susan and Jack Beermann. "Lawyering Up." *Green Bag 2D*, 2, Autumn (1998). http://tarlton.law.utexas.edu/lpop/etext/bandes.htm (accessed July 15, 2007).

Banet-Weiser, Sarah. "Hoop Dreams: Professional Basketball and the Politics of Race and Gender." *Journal of Sport & Social Issues*, 23 (1999): 403–420.

Barnhart, Tracy. "Risk Indicators for Misconduct." *Corrections.com*, August 10 (2009). http://www.corrections.com/new/article/22079 (accessed July 15, 2007).

Baroody, Judith. *Media Access and the Military*. Maryland: University Press of America, 1998.

Baudrillard, Jean. "War Porn." *International Journal of Baudrillard Studies*, 2 (1), January 2005, translated by Paul Taylor, from Jean Baudrillard, "Pornographie de la guerre." In *Liberation*, May 19, 2004. http://www.ubishops.ca/baudrillardstudies/vol2_1/taylor.htm (accessed July 15, 2007).

—— "Simulacra and Simulations." In *Jean Baudrillard: Selected Writings*, edited by Mark Poster, trans. Raul Foss, Paul Patton and Philip Beitchman. Stanford: Stanford University Press, 1988.

Benedict, Helen. *Virgin or Vamp: How the Press Covers Sex Crimes*. New York: Oxford University Press, 2004.

Bennett, W. Lance., Christian Breunig and Terri Givens. "Communication and Political Mobilization: Digital Media and the Organization of Anti-Iraq War Demonstrations in the U.S." *Political Communication*, 25 (2008): 269–289.

Bennett, W. Lance., Regina Lawrence and Steve Livingston. "None Dare Call it Torture." *Journal of Communication*, 56 (2006): 467–85.

Bennett, W. Lance., Regina Lawrence, and Steve Livingston. *When the Press Fails: Political Power and the News Media from Iraq to Katrina*. Chicago: University of Chicago Press, 2007.

Bernhard, Nancy. *U.S. Television News and Cold War Propaganda, 1947–1960*. Cambridge: Cambridge University Press, 2003.

Bolter, Jay David and Richard Grusin. *Remediation: Understanding New Media*. Cambridge: MIT Press, 1999.

Bonczar, Thomas and Allen Beck. "Lifetime Likelihood of Going to State or Federal Prison." Washington, D.C.: U.S. Dept. of Justice, Office of Justice Programs, Bureau of Justice Statistics, 1997. http://www.drugpolicy.org/docUploads/Lifetime_Risk_of_Incarceration.pdf (accessed July 15, 2007).

Bourdieu, Pierre. *Language and Symbolic Power*, trans. Gino Raymond. Cambridge: Harvard University Press, 1999.

Boyd, Todd and Shopshire, Kenneth. "Introduction: Basketball Jones: A new world order?" In *Basketball Jones: America Above the Rim*, edited by Todd Boyd and Kenneth Shopshire, 1–12. New York: New York University Press, 2000.

Breyer, Stephen. Supreme Court of the United States, No. 04A73 Associated Press, et al. *v.* District Court for the Fifth Judicial District of Colorado, On application for stay, July 26, 2004. https://web.lexis-nexis.com/universe (accessed August 30, 2004).

Brown, Mary Jane. *Eradicating this Evil: Women in the American Anti-Lynching Movement, 1892–1940.* New York: Garland Publishing, 2004.

Brownmiller, Susan. *Against Our Will: Men, Women and Rape.* New York: Bantam Books, 1975.

Brundage, W. Fitzhugh. *Lynching in the New South: Georgia and Virginia, 1880–1930.* Chicago: University of Illinois Press, 1993.

Butler, Judith. "Endangered/Endangering: Schematic Racism and White Paranoia." In *Reading Rodney King, Reading Urban Uprising,* edited by Robert Gooding-Williams. New York: Routledge, 1993, 15–22, 17.

Butler, Judith. "Photography, War, Outrage." *PMLA,* 120 (2005): 822–827.

—— "Torture and the Ethics of Photography." *Environment and Planning D: Society and Space,* 25 (2007): 951–966.

Cafferty, Pastora San Juan and David Wells Engstrom. *Hispanics in the United States: An Agenda for the Twenty-first Century.* Rutgers: Transaction Publishers, 2002.

Cannon, Lou. *Official Negligence: How Rodney King and the Riots Changed Los Angeles and the LAPD.* New York: Times Books, 1997.

Carby, Hazel. "A Strange and Bitter Crop: The Spectacle of Torture." *Open Democracy,* October 11, 2004. www.opendemocracy.net (accessed June 10, 2005).

Carrigan, William D. *The Making of a Lynching Culture: Violence and Vigilantism in Central Texas, 1836–1916.* Champaign: University of Illinois Press, 2004.

Carrigan, William. D. and Clive Webb. "The Lynching of Persons of Mexican Origin or Descent in the United States, 1848 to 1928." *Journal of Social History,* 37 (2003): 411–438.

Carter, Dan. *Scottsboro: A Tragedy of the American South.* Baton Rouge: Louisiana State University Press, 1969, revised edition 1979.

Chemerinsky, Erwin. "The Rampart Scandal and the Criminal Justice System in Los Angeles County." *Guild Practitioner,* 57 (2000): 121–133.

—— "An Independent Analysis of the Los Angeles Police Department's Board of Inquiry Report on the Rampart Scandal." *Loyola of Los Angeles Law Review,* 34 (2001a): 545–657.

—— "The Role of Prosecutors in Dealing with Police Abuse: The Lessons of Los Angeles." *Virginia Journal of Social Policy & The Law,* Winter (2001b): 1–17.

Chopra-Gant, Mike. "The Law of the Father, the Law of the Land: Power, Gender and Race in *The Shield.*" *Journal of American Studies* 41 (2007): 659–673.

Circuit Court of Morgan County. 1933. *Transcript of trial of Clarence Norris, appellant, vs. State of Alabama, appellee, in the Circuit Court of Morgan County, held in December, 1933,* Montgomery, Alabama, certified 5/8/1934.

Cole, David. *No Equal Justice: Race and Class in the American Criminal Justice System.* New York: The New Press, 1999.

Coleman, Robin R. Means and Jasmine Nicole Cobb, "*Training Day* and *The Shield*: Evil Cops and the Taint of Blackness." In *The Changing Face of Evil in Film and Television,* edited by Martin Norden, 101–123. Amsterdam: Rodopi, 2007.

Colorado v. Richard Thomas McKenna, No. 27681, Supreme Court of Colorado. 196 Colo. 367; 585 P.2d 27; (Colo. 1978). https://web.lexis-nexis.com/universe (accessed November 15, 2003).

Colorado v. Kobe Bean Bryant, Case No. 04SA200, Supreme Court of Colorado. 94 P.3d 624 Colo. (2004, July 19). https://web.lexis-nexis.com/universe (accessed November 15, 2003).

Colo. Rev. Stat. § 18-3-407 (1977). https://web.lexis-nexis.com/universe (accessed November 15, 2003).

Commission on Interracial Cooperation (CIC). *Commission on Interracial Cooperation papers, 1919–1944*. New York: NYT Microfilming Corporation of America, 1983.

Crary, Jonathan. "Spectacle, Attention, Counter-Memory." *October*, 50 (1989): 96–107.

Crenshaw, Kimberlé. "Mapping the Margins: Intersectionality, Identity Politics, and Violence Against Women of Color." In *Critical Race Theory: The Key Writings that Formed the Movement*, edited by Kimberlé Crenshaw, Neil Gotanda, Garry Peller, and Kendall Thomas, 357–383. New York: The New Press, 1995.

—— "Color-Blind Dramas and Racial Nightmares: Reconfiguring Racism in the Post-Civil Rights Era." In *Birth of a Nation'hood: Gaze, Script, and Spectacle in the O.J. Simpson Case*, edited by Toni Morrison and Claudia Lacour, 97–168. New York: Pantheon Books, 1997.

Crenshaw, Kimberlé, Neil Gotanda, Garry Peller, and Kendall Thomas. "Introduction." In *Critical Race Theory: The Key Writings that Formed the Movement*, edited by Kimberlé Crenshaw, Neil Gotanda, Garry Peller, and Kendall Thomas, xiii–xxxii. New York: The New Press, 1995.

Croce, Fernando F. "Nonstandard Operating Procedure: An Interview with Errol Morris." *Slant Magazine*, May 3, 2008. http://www.slantmagazine.com/film/features/errol morris.asp (accessed May 10, 2008).

Danner, Mark. *Torture and Truth: America, Abu Ghraib, and the War on Terror*. New York: New York Review of Books, 2004.

Davis, Angela. *Women, Race, and Class*. New York: Vintage Books, 1981.

—— "Race and Criminalization: Black Americans and the Punishment Industry." In *The House that Race Built*, edited by Wahneema Lubiano, 264–279. New York: Vintage, 1997.

—— *Are Prisons Obsolete?* New York: Open Media, 2003.

Debord, Guy. *Society of the Spectacle*. Detroit: Black and Red, 1967.

—— *Comments on the Society of the Spectacle*. London: Verso, 1990.

Department of Justice Office of Justice Programs. "Growth in Prison and Jail Populations Slowing." Washington, D.C.: Bureau of Justice Statistics, 2009. http://www.ojp.usdoj.gov/newsroom/pressreleases/2009/BJS090331.htm (accessed May 10, 2008).

Di Bella, Giuseppe. "The Story Behind the Abu Ghraib Series." *The Democratic Image* (April 25, 2007). http://thedemocraticimage.opendemocracy.net/2007/04/25/the-story-behind-the-abu-ghraib-series (accessed November 12, 2007).

Di Bella, Giuseppe and Norman Wilcox. "Defiant Exclamations." *Stimulus Respond*, 19 (Aug–Sept. 2007). http://www.stimulusrespond.com (accessed November 12, 2007).

Ducey, Mitchell F. "The Commission on Interracial Cooperation Papers, 1919–1944 and The Association of Southern Women for the Prevention of Lynching Papers, 1930–1942: A Guide to the Microfilm Editions." Ann Arbor, MI: University Microfilms International, 1984.

Ebb, Fred. *Fred Ebb Papers*. 1927–2004. The New York Public Library for the Performing Arts.

Edy, Jill. "Journalistic Uses of Collective Memory." *Journal of Communication*, Spring, 1999: 71–85.

Entman, Robert M. *Democracy Without Citizens: Media and the Decay of American Politics*. New York: Oxford University Press, 1989.

Eyerman, Ron. *Cultural Trauma: Slavery and the Formation of African American Identity*. Cambridge: Cambridge University Press, 2001.

Faulkner, William. *Requiem for a Nun*. New York: Random House, 1951.

Feagin, Joe and Hernán Vera. *White Racism: The Basics*. New York: Routledge, 1995.

Feffer, John. "Interview with Daniel Heyman." Washington, DC: Foreign Policy In Focus, October 17, 2008.

Feldman, Allen. "Abu Ghraib: Ceremonies of Nostalgia," *Open Democracy*, October 18, 2004. www.opendemocracy.net (accessed November 12, 2007).

Foucault, Michel. *Discipline and Punish: The Birth of the Prison*. Translated by Alan Sheridan. New York: Vintage Books, 1979.

Fraser, Rhone. "The Black Panthers, A Photo Journey: Interview With Bobby Seale." *WBAI Arts Magazine*, 2006. http://wbai.org/index.php?option=com_content&task=view&id=9458&Itemid=2 (accessed July 20, 2007).

Freud, Sigmund. *On Creativity and the Unconscious: Papers on the Psychology of Art, Literature, Love, Religion*, edited by Benjamin Nelson. New York: Harper Colophon Books, 1958.

Fuchs, Cynthia. "Terrordome." *Flow*, 2 (2005). http://flowtv.org/2005/04/the-shield-kojak-police-drama (accessed September 12, 2009).

Gaines, Jane. *Fire and Desire: Mixed Race Movies in the Silent Era*. Chicago: University of Chicago Press, 2001.

Gilmore, Ruth Wilson. *Golden Gulag: Prisons, Surplus, Crisis and Opposition in Globalizing California*. Berkeley: University of California Press, 2007.

Giroux, Henry. *Beyond the Spectacle of Terrorism: Global Uncertainty and the Challenge of the New Media*. Boulder: Paradigm Publishers, 2006.

Giroux, Susan Searls and Henry Giroux. "On Seeing and Not Seeing Race: *Crash* and the Politics of Bad Faith." In *Popular Culture*, 5th edition, edited by Murray Pomerance and John Sakeris, 163–178. New York: Pearson Education, 2006.

Goldman, Eric. *The Crucial Decade – And After*. New York: Vintage Books, 1960.

Goldsby, Jacqueline. *A Spectacular Secret: Lynching in American Life and Literature*. Chicago: University of Chicago Press, 2006.

Gonzales-Day, Ken. *Lynching in the West: 1850–1935*. Durham: Duke University Press, 2006.

Gooding-Williams, Robert. "Look, A Negro!" In *Reading Rodney King, Reading Urban Uprising*, edited by Robert Gooding-Williams, 157–177. New York: Routledge, 1993.

Goodman, James. *Stories of Scottsboro*. New York: Vintage Books, 1995.

Gourevitch, Philip and Errol Morris. *Standard Operating Procedure*. New York: Penguin Press, 2008.

Grant, Judith. "Assault Under Color of Authority: Police Corruption as Norm in the LAPD Rampart Scandal and in Popular Film." *New Political Science*, 25 (2003): 385–405.

Gray, Herman. *Watching Race: Television and the Struggle for "Blackness."* Minneapolis: University of Minnesota Press, 1995.

Gunthert, André. "Digital Imaging Goes to War: The Abu Ghraib Photographs." *Photographies*, 1 (2008): 103–112.

Halberstam, David. *The Fifties*. New York: Villard Books, 1993.

Halbwachs, Maurice. *On Collective Memory*, trans./edited by Lewis Coser. Chicago: University of Chicago Press, 1992.

Hale, Grace Elizabeth. *Making Whiteness: The Culture of Segregation in the South, 1890–1940*. New York: Vintage Books, 1998.

Halkias, Alexandra. "From Social Butterfly to Modern-Day Medea: Elizabeth Broderick's Portrayal in the Press." *Critical Studies in Mass Communication*, 16 (1999): 289–307.

Hall, Jacquelyn Dowd. "'The Mind That Burns in Each Body': Women, Rape, and Racial Violence." In *Powers of Desire: The Politics of Sexuality*, edited by Ann Snitow, Christine Stansell and Sharon Thompson, 328–49. New York: Monthly Review Press, 1983.

——— *Revolt Against Chivalry: Jessie Daniel Ames and the Women's Campaign Against Lynching.* New York: Columbia University Press, 1993.

Hamilton, Robert. "Image and Context: The Production and Reproduction of *The Execution of a VC Suspect* by Eddie Adams." In *Vietnam Images*, edited by Jeffrey Walsh and James Aulich. London: MacMillan Press, 1989.

Hancock, Lynnell. "Wolf Pack: The Press and the Central Park Jogger." *Columbia Journalism Review*, January/February, 2003. https://web.lexis-nexis.com/universe (accessed November 19, 2005).

Harris, Angela. "Race and Essentialism in Feminist Legal Theory." *Stanford Law Review*, 42 (1990): 581–616.

Hayden, Tom. "LAPD: Law and Disorder." *The Nation*, March 22, 2002.

Heath, Chris. "The Great Interrogator." *GQ Magazine*, October 15, 2008. http://men.style.com/gq/features/landing?id=content_6768 (accessed December 27, 2008).

Heller, Dana. "Anatomies of Rape." *American Literary History*, 16 (2004): 329–349.

Herndon, Angelo. "The Scottsboro Boys: Four Freed! Five to Go!" New York: Workers Library Publishers, 1937.

Hersh, Seymour. *Chain of Command: The Road from 9/11 to Abu Ghraib.* New York: Harper Collins, 2004.

——— "The Gray Zone." *New Yorker*, May 24, 2004.

Hesford, Wendy S. "Staging Terror." *TDR: Drama Review*, 50 (2006): 29–41.

Horne, Gerald. *Powell v. Alabama: The Scottsboro Boys and American Justice.* New York: Franklin Watts, 1997.

Hovannisian, Richard. "Bitter-Sweet Memories: The Last Generation of Ottoman Armenians." In *Looking Backward, Moving Forward: Confronting the Armenian Genocide*, edited by Richard Hovannisian, 113–124. New Brunswick: Transaction Publishers, 2003.

Hughes, Langston. "Southern Gentlemen, White Prostitutes, Mill-Owners, and Negroes." *Contempo*, December 1, 1931.

Hunt, Darnell. *Screening the Los Angeles "Riots": Race, Seeing, and Resistance.* Cambridge: Cambridge University Press, 1997.

Hunt, Darnell. *O.J. Simpson Facts & Fictions: New Rituals in the Construction of Reality.* Cambridge: Cambridge University Press, 1999.

International Labor Defense. *The Story of Scottsboro.* New York, 1933.

Ireland, Marilyn. "Reform Rape Legislation: A New Standard of Sexual Responsibility." *University of Colorado Law Review*, 49 (Winter, 1976): 185–204.

Irwin-Zarecka, Iwona. *Frames of Remembrance: The Dynamics of Collective Memory.* New Brunswick: Transaction Publishers, 1994.

Johnson, Claudia Durst. *To Kill a Mockingbird: Threatening Boundaries.* New York: Twayne Publishers, 1994.

Jordan, Emma Coleman. "The Power of False Racial Memory and the Metaphor of Lynching." In *Race, Gender, and Power in America: The Legacy of the Hill-Thomas Hearings*, Anita Hill and Emma Coleman Jordan, 37–55. New York: Oxford University Press, 1995.

Kelley, Robin D.G. *Race Rebels: Culture, Politics, and the Black Working Class.* New York: The Free Press, 1994.

—— "Rummaging Through 'The Ash Heap of a Bitter Past'." In *Scottsboro Alabama: A Story in Linoleum Cuts*, edited by Lin Shi Khan and Tony Perez, Andrew H. Lee. New York: New York University Press, 2002.

Kellner, Douglas and Steven Best. "Debord and the Postmodern Turn: New Stages of the Spectacle." *Substance*, 90 (1999): 129–156.

Kellner, Douglas. *Grand Theft 2000: Media Spectacle and a Stolen Election*. Lanham, Md.: Rowman & Littlefield Publishers, 2001.

—— *Media Spectacle*. New York: Routledge, 2003.

—— "The Sports Spectacle, Michael Jordan, and Nike." In *Sport and the Color Line: Black Athletes and Race Relations in Twentieth-Century America*, edited by Patrick B. Miller and David K. Wiggins, 63–92. New York: Routledge, 2004.

—— "Media Culture and the Triumph of the Spectacle." In *The Spectacle of the Real: From Hollywood to Reality TV and Beyond*, edited by Geoff King, 23–36. Bristol, U.K.: Intellect Press, 2005.

—— *Media Spectacle and the Crisis of Democracy: Terrorism, War & Election Battles*. Boulder: Paradigm Publishers, 2005.

Kirk, Michael (Director). Michael Kirk and Peter Boyer (writers). May 15, 2001. *Frontline: L.A.P.D. Blues*. Television Documentary. Transcripts of interviews accessed online at http://www.pbs.org/wgbh/pages/frontline/shows/lapd/ (accessed October 6, 2009).

Kitch, Carolyn. "'Useful Memory' in Time Inc. Magazines: Summary Journalism and the Popular Construction of History." *Journalism Studies*, 7 (2006): 94–110.

Kloppenberg, Lisa. *Playing It Safe: How the Supreme Court Sidesteps Hard Cases and Stunts the Development of Law*. New York: New York University Press, 2001.

Landsberg, Alison. *Prosthetic Memory: The Transformation of American Remembrance in the Age of Mass Culture*. New York: Columbia University Press, 2004.

Lapchick, Richard. E. "The Kobe Bryant Case: Athletes, Violence, Stereotypes and the Games We Play." *Center for the Study of Sport in Society*, 2004. http://www.Sport insociety.Org/Rel-Article34.Html (accessed February 21, 2005).

Lawrence, Regina. *The Politics of Force: Media and the Construction of Police Brutality*. Berkeley: University of California Press, 2000.

League of Struggle for Negro Rights. *They Shall Not Die! Stop the Legal Lynching! The Story of Scottsboro in Pictures*. New York: Workers Library Publishers, 1932.

Leonard, David. "Racing Sports." *Popmatters*, 9.11.2003. www.Popmatters.Com/Sports/Features/030911-Kobe.Shtm (accessed February 21, 2005).

—— "The Next M.J. or The Next O.J.? Kobe Bryant, Race, and the Absurdity of Colorblind Rhetoric." *Journal of Sport and Social Issues*, 28 (August, 2004): 284–313.

Lipsitz, George. *Time Passages: Collective Memory and American Popular Culture*. Minneapolis: University of Minnesota Press, 1990.

Lopez, Mark Hugo and Michael Light. "A Rising Share: Hispanics and Federal Crime." Pew Hispanic Center, 2009.

Lotke, Eric. "The Prison-Industrial Complex." In *Multinational Monitor*, 17 (1996). http://multinationalmonitor.org/hyper/mm1196.06.html (accessed March 2, 2009).

Lotz, Amanda. *The Television Will Be Revolutionized*. New York: New York University Press, 2007.

Lowen, James. *Lies Across America: What Our Historic Sites Get Wrong*. New York: The New Press, 1999.

Lubet, Steven. "Reconstructing Atticus Finch." *Michigan Law Review*, 97 (1999): 1339–1362.

Markovitz, Jonathan. *Legacies of Lynching: Racial Violence and Memory*. Minneapolis: University of Minnesota Press, 2004.

—— 2007. "Letters to the Editor." *Chronicle of Higher Education*, September 28, 2007. http://chronicle.com/weekly/v54/i05/05a03901.htm (accessed September 28, 2007).

Maxwell, William. *New Negro, New Left: African-American Writing and Communism Between the Years*. New York: Columbia University Press, 1999.

McChesney, Robert Waterman. *The Problem of the Media: U.S. Communication Politics in the Twenty-First Century*. New York: Monthly Review Press, 2004.

Mcdonald, M.G. "Unnecessary Roughness: Gender and Racial Politics in Domestic Violence Media Events." *Sociology of Sport Journal*, 16 (1999): 111–133.

McKenzie, Jon. "Abu Ghraib and the Society of the Spectacle of the Scaffold." In *Violence Performed: Local Roots and Global Routes of Conflict*, edited by Patrick Anderson and Jisha Menon, 338–356. New York: Palgrave Macmillan, 2009.

Mestrovic, Stjepan. *The Trials of Abu Ghraib: An Expert Witness Account of Shame and Honor*. Boulder: Paradigm Publishers, 2007.

Mezey, Naomi. "Law as Culture." In *Cultural Analysis, Cultural Studies, and the Law: Moving Beyond Legal Realism*, edited by Austin Sarat and Jonathan Simon, 37–72. Durham: Duke University Press, 2003.

Miller, Anita, ed. *The Complete Transcripts of the Clarence Thomas–Anita Hill Hearings: October 11, 12, 13, 1991*. Chicago: Academy Chicago Publishers, 1992.

Miller, James A. *Remembering Scottsboro: The Legacy of an Infamous Trial*. Princeton: Princeton University Press, 2009.

Miller, James, Susan Pennybacker, and Eve Rosenhaft. "Mother Ada Wright and the International Campaign to Free the Scottsboro Boys, 1931–1934." *American Historical Review*, 106 (2001): 387–430.

Mitchell, W. J. T. "The Unspeakable and the Unimaginable: Word and Image in a Time of Terror." *ELH*, 72 (2005): 291–308.

Morris, Errol. "Standard Operating Procedure Discussion Guide." www.takepart.com/SOP (accessed October 20, 2009).

Morris, Errol. "The Most Curious Thing." *New York Times*, May 19, 2008, http://morris.blogs.nytimes.com/2008/05/19/the-most-curious-thing (accessed October 20, 2009).

Morrison, Toni and Claudia Brodsky Lacour, eds. *Birth of a Nation'hood: Gaze, Script, and Spectacle in the O.J. Simpson Case*. New York: Pantheon Books, 1997.

Murray, Hugh T., Jr. "Changing America and the Changing Image of Scottsboro." *Phylon*, 38 (1977): 82–92.

National Association for the Advancement of Colored People. *The Lynching of Claude Neal*. From the NAACP Antilynching Publicity and Investigative Papers. Bethesda, Maryland: University Publications of America, 1937.

—— *Papers of the NAACP. Part 6, The Scottsboro Case, 1931–1950*. Frederick, MD: University Publications of America, 1986.

Nichols, Bill. *Blurred Boundaries: Questions of Meaning in Contemporary Culture*. Bloomington: Indiana University Press, 1994.

Norris, Clarence and Sybil D. Washington. *The Last of the Scottsboro Boys: An Autobiography*. New York: G.P. Putnam's Sons, 1979.

O'Hehir, Andrew. "Interrogating Abu Ghraib." http://www.salon.com/ent/video_dog/ifc/2008/04/25/intv_morris/index.html?source=video (accessed October 20, 2009).

Omi, Michael and Howard Winant. *Racial Formation in the United States From the 1960s to the 1990s*. Second edition. New York: Routledge, 1994.

Patterson, Haywood, and Earl Conrad. *Scottsboro Boy*. New York: Collier Books, 1950.

Pennybacker, Susan. *From Scottsboro to Munich: Race and Political Culture in 1930s Britain*. Princeton: Princeton University Press, 2009.

The People of the State of Colorado v. Defendant: Kobe Bean Bryant, Case No. 04SA200, Supreme Court of Colorado, July 19, 2004.

Perloff, Richard M. "The Press and Lynchings of African Americans." *Journal of Black Studies*, 30 (2000): 315–330.

Pfaff, Daniel W. "The Press and the Scottsboro Rape Cases, 1931–32." *Journalism History*, 1 (1974): 72–76.

Phelan, Peggy. "Afterword: 'In the Valley of the Shadow of Death': The Photographs of Abu Ghraib." In *Violence Performed: Local Roots and Global Routes of Conflict*, edited by Patrick Anderson and Jisha Menon, 372–384. New York: Palgrave Macmillan, 2009.

Philipose, Liz. "The Politics of Pain and the Uses of Torture." *Signs: Journal of Women in Culture and Society*, 32 (2007): 1047–1071.

Pinar, William. *The Gender of Racial Politics and Violence in America: Lynching, Prison, Rape, and the Crisis of Masculinity*. New York: P. Lang, 2001.

Polchin, James. "Not Looking at Lynching Photographs." In *The Image and the Witness: Trauma, Memory and Visual Culture*, edited by Frances Guerin and Roger Hallas, 207–222. New York: Wallflower Press, 2007.

Popular Memory Group, "Popular Memory: Theory, Politics, Method." In *Making Histories: Studies in History-Writing and Politics*, edited by Richard Johnson, Gregor McLennan, Bill Schwartz, and David Sutton, 205–52. London: Hutchinson, 1982.

Pratt, Ray. *Projecting Paranoia: Conspiratorial Visions in American Film*. Lawrence: University Press of Kansas, 2001.

Razack, Sherene H. "How is White Supremacy Embodied? Sexualized Racial Violence at Abu Ghraib." In *Canadian Journal of Women and the Law*, 17 (2005): 341–363.

Reed, Ishmael. "MJ, Kobe, and Ota Benga: Continuing the US War Against Black Men." *Black Renaissance/Renaissance Noire*, 3 (Spring, 2004): 43–59.

Rice, Constance, Jan Handzlik, Laurie Levenson, Stephen Mansfield, Carol Sobel, and Edgar Twine. *Rampart Reconsidered: The Search for Real Reform Seven Years Later*. Los Angeles: Blue Ribbon Rampart Review Panel, July, 2006. http://www.lacp.org/2006-Articles-Main/071506-Rampart%20Reconsidered-Full%20Report.pdf (accessed November 18, 2009).

Riviere, Carole. "Mobile Camera Phones: A New Form of 'Being Together' in Daily Interpersonal Communication." In *Mobile Communications: Re-negotiation of the Social Sphere*, edited by Rich Ling and Per E. Pedersen, 167–185. London: Springer, 2005.

Roberts, Dorothy. "Punishing Drug Addicts Who Have Babies: Women of Color, Equality, and the Right of Privacy." In *Critical Race Theory: The Key Writings that Formed the Movement*, edited by Kimberlé Crenshaw, Neil Gotanda, Garry Peller, and Kendall Thomas, 384–425. New York: The New Press, 1995.

Rogan, Bjarne. "An Entangled Object: The Picture Postcard as Souvenir and Collectible, Exchange and Ritual Communication." *Cultural Analysis*, 4 (2004): 1–27.

Rogin, Michael. "'The Sword Became a Flashing Vision': DW Griffith's The Birth of a Nation." *Representations*, 9 (1985): 150–195.

Romero, Mary. "State Violence and the Social and Legal Construction of Latino Criminality: From El Bandido to Gang Member." *Denver University Law Review*, 78 (2001): 1081–1118.

——— "Racial Profiling and Immigration Law Enforcement: Rounding Up of Usual Suspects in the Latino Community." *Critical Sociology*, 32 (2006): 447–473.

Ross, Felicia G. Jones. "Mobilizing the Masses: The Cleveland Call and Post and the Scottsboro Incident." *The Journal of Negro History*, 84 (1999): 48–60.

Rowe, David, Jim Mckay and Toby Miller. "Panic Sport and the Racialized Masculine Body." In *Masculinities, Gender Relations, and Sport*, edited by Jim McCay, Michael Messner and Donald Sabo, 245–262. Thousand Oaks, CA: Sage Publications, 2000.

Russell, Katheryn K. *The Color of Crime: Racial Hoaxes, White Fear, Black Protectionism, Police Harassment, and Other Macroaggressions*. New York: New York University Press, 1998.

Said, Edward. *Orientalism*. New York: Vintage, 1978.

Said, Edward. *Culture and Imperialism*. New York: Vintage, 1993.

Schechter, Patricia A. *Ida B. Wells-Barnett and American Reform 1880–1930*. Chapel Hill: University of North Carolina Press, 2001.

Schipper, Martin Paul. *Papers of the NAACP. Part 6, The Scottsboro Case, 1931-1950. Guide to the Microfilm Collection*. Frederick, MD: University Publications of America, 1986.

Schlegel, Amy. "My Lai: 'We Lie, They Die' Or, a Small History of an 'Atrocious' Photograph." *Third Text*, Summer (1995): 47–66.

Schlosser, Eric. 1998. "The Prison Industrial Complex." *Atlantic Monthly*, December, 1998.

Schudson, Michael. *Watergate in American Memory*. New York: Basic Books, 1993.

Scifo, Barbara. 2005. "The Domestication of the Camera Phone and MMS Communications: The Experience of Young Italians." In *A Sense of Place: The Global and the Local in Mobile Communication,* edited by Kristof Nyiri, 363–73. Vienna: Passagen Verlag, 2005.

Schwartz, Barry. "The Social Context of Commemoration." *Social Forces*, 61 (December, 1982): 374–402.

Scottsboro Defense Committee. "The Scottsboro Case: Opinion of Judge James E. Horton." New York, 1936a.

Scottsboro Defense Committee. "Scottsboro: The Shame of America: The True Story and the True Meaning of this Famous Case." New York, 1936b.

Scottsboro Defense Committee. "4 Free, 5 in Prison, on the Same Evidence: What the Nation's Press Says about the Scottsboro Case." New York, 1937.

The Sentencing Project. "Reducing Racial Disparity in the Criminal Justice System: A Manual for Practitioners and Policymakers." Second edition. Washington, D.C. (2008). http://www.sentencingproject.org/doc/publications/rd_reducingracialdisparity.pdf (accessed March 12, 2009).

Sexton, Jared. "The Ruse of Engagement: Black Masculinity and the Cinema of Policing." *American Quarterly*, 61 (2009): 39–63.

Simpson, Mark. "Archiving Hate: Lynching Postcards at the Limit of Social Construction." *ESC*, 30 (2004): 17–38.

Small, Sasha. *Scottsboro: Act Three*. New York: International Labor Defense, 1934.

Smith, Shawn Michelle. *American Archives: Gender, Race, and Class in Visual Culture*. Princeton: Princeton University Press, 1999.

Smith, Valerie. *Not Just Race, Not Just Gender: Black Feminist Readings*. New York: Routledge, 1998.

Solomon, Mark. *The Cry Was Unity: Communists and African Americans, 1917–36*. Jackson: University Press of Mississippi, 1998.

Sontag, Susan. "Regarding the Torture of Others." *New York Times Magazine,* May 23, 2004: 24–29.

Spigel, Lynn, and Henry Jenkins, H. (1991). "Same Bat Channel, Different Bat Times: Mass Culture and Popular Memory." In *The Many Lives of the Batman: Critical Approaches to a Superhero and his Media,* edited by Roberta Pearson and William Uricchio, 117–148. New York: Routledge, 1991.

Stein, Mark. *Direct from Death Row The Scottsboro Boys (An Evening of Vaudeville and Sorrow).* New York: Dramatists Play Service, Inc., 1980.

Stocke, Joy, Kim Nagy, and Chris Tiefel. "The Other Side of Abu Ghraib – Part Two: The Yoga Teacher Goes to Istanbul." *Wild River Review,* December (2008), http://wildriverreview.com/essay/politics/other-side-of-abu-ghraib-part-2/nagy-stocke (accessed November 19, 2010).

Sturken, Marita. *Tangled Memories: The Vietnam War, the AIDS Epidemic, and the Politics of Remembering.* Berkeley: University of California Press, 1997.

Sundquist, Eric. "Blues for Atticus Finch: Scottsboro, Brown, and Harper Lee," In *The South as an American Problem,* edited by Larry Griffin and Don Doyle, 181–209. Athens: The University of Georgia Press, 1995.

Supreme Court of the United States, No. 04A73. Associated Press, Et Al. *v.* District Court for the Fifth Judicial District of Colorado. On Application for Stay. July, 2004.

Supreme Court of the United States. *Norris v. Alabama,* 294 U.S. 587, April 1, 1935.

Supreme Court of Alabama. 1932. *Patterson v. State of Alabama.* 141 So. 195 224 Ala. 531. (March 24)

Sussman, Elizabeth, ed. *On the Passage of a Few People Through a Rather Brief Moment in Time: The Situationist International 1957–1972.* Cambridge, MA: MIT Press, 1989.

Tanford, J. Alexander and Anthony Bocchino, A.J. "Rape Victim Shield Laws and the Sixth Amendment." *University of Pennsylvania Law Review,* 128 (1980): 544–602.

Tolnay, Stewart E. and E.M. Beck. *A Festival of Violence: An Analysis of Southern Lynchings, 1882–1930.* Urbana and Chicago: University of Illinois Press, 1992.

Torres, Sasha. *Black, White, and in Color: Television and Black Civil Rights.* Princeton: Princeton University Press, 2003.

Tsing, Anna. "Monster Stories: Women Charged with Perinatal Endangerment." In *Uncertain Terms: Negotiating Gender in American Culture,* edited by Faye Ginsburg and Anna Tsing, 282–289. Boston: Beacon Press, 1990.

Tucker, Bruce and Sia Traintafyllos. "Lynndie England, Abu Ghraib, and the New Imperialism." *Canadian Review of American Studies,* 38 (2008): 83–100.

Tucker, Linda. "Blackballed: Basketball and Representations of the Black Male Athlete." *American Behavioral Scientist,* 47 (November, 2003): 306–328.

United States Senate Armed Services Committee. *Senate Armed Services Committee Inquiry into the Treatment of Detainees in U.S. Custody.* (2008). http://levin.senate.gov/newsroom/supporting/2008/Detainees.121108.pdf (accessed February 12, 2009).

United States Department of Justice, Office of Justice Programs. "National Crime Victimization Survey." (September, 2005). http://www.Rainn.Org/Docs/Statistics/Ncvs2004.Pdf (accessed June 9, 2008).

Waldrep, Christopher. *Racial Violence on Trial.* Santa Barbara: ABC-CLIO, 2001.

Wallis, Brian. "Remember Abu Ghraib." in *Inconvenient Evidence: Iraqi Prison Photographs from Abu Ghraib. Brochure of the Exhibit,* Jessica Gogan, Brian Wallis, and Thomas Sokolowski, curators. (2004). www.museum.icp.org/museum/exhibitions/abu_ghraib/abu_ghraib_brochure.pdf (accessed January 3, 2005).

Wells, Ida B. *Southern Horrors: Lynch Law in All Its Phases*. New York: The New York Age Print, 1892.

West, Heather C. and William J. Sabol. "Prison Inmates at Midyear 2008 – Statistical Tables." Washington, D.C.: Department of Justice Office of Justice Programs. (2009). http://bjs.ojp.usdoj.gov/content/pub/pdf/pim08st.pdf (accessed January 19, 2010).

Willis, Susan. *Portents of the Real: A Primer for Post-9/11 America*. New York: Verso, 2005.

Wilson, Christopher. "'Let's Work out the Details': Interrogation and Deception in Prime Time." *Journal of Criminal Justice and Popular Culture*, 12 (2005): 47–64.

Wood, Amy Louise. "Lynching Photography and the Visual Reproduction of White Supremacy." *American Nineteenth Century History*, 6 (2005): 373–399.

—— *Lynching and Spectacle: Witnessing Racial Violence in America, 1890–1940*. Chapel Hill: The University of North Carolina Press, 2009.

Wright, Richard. "12 Million Black Voices." In *The Richard Wright Reader*, edited by Ellen Wright and Michel Fabre. New York: Harper and Row, 1978.

Wypijewski, JoAnn. "Judgment Days: Lessons from the Abu Ghraib Courts-Martial." *Harper's Magazine*, February, 2006.

Zagorin, Adam. "The Abu Ghraib Scandal You Don't Know." *Time*, February 7, 2005.

Zelizer, Barbie. *Remembering to Forget: Holocaust Memory Through the Camera's Eye*. Chicago: University of Chicago Press, 1998.

—— "Photography, Journalism, and Trauma." In *Journalism After September 11*, edited by Barbie Zelizer and Stuart Allan, 48–68. New York: Routledge, 2004.

NOTES

Introduction

1 *Los Angeles Times*, June 8, 1943. While the main targets were Latinos (many of whom were beaten and humiliated even when they were not wearing zoot suits), the servicemen also went after young African American zoot suiters. See Kelly, *Race Rebels*, for a discussion of the zoot suit as a symbol of resistance for young black men in the 1940s.

2 Debord's understanding of the spectacle bears some resemblance to Jean Baudrillard's notion of "hyperreality," in that both theorists place extreme importance on the realm of imagery and the symbolic. However, despite having been strongly influenced by Debord, Baudrillard would reject the idea that social life had been replaced by its representations, since he argues that the idea of "representation" assumes the existence of a reality to represent. Representations, he says, are judged on the basis of their fidelity to reality, and if there is no original referent outside of representation, if there is instead only hyperreality, then the notion of representation, or, literally, re-presentation, makes no sense. Instead, because "truth, reference, and objective causes have ceased to exist," ("Simulacra and Simulations," 168) it would be folly to see spectacle as distracting from "real world" concerns. Though he does not mention Debord by name, Michel Foucault also was apparently responding to *Society of the Spectacle* when he argued, in *Discipline and Punish*, that a society based on spectacle as a means of projecting power and authority has been replaced by a surveillant society based on disciplinary social norms. Foucault writes that "Our society is one not of spectacle, but of surveillance. . . . We are neither in the amphitheatre, nor on the stage, but in the panoptic machine. . . ." *Discipline and Punish*, 217. For more on Foucault's discussion of "the spectacle of the scaffold" as it relates to Abu Ghraib, see McKenzie, "Abu Ghraib and the Society of the Spectacle of the Scaffold," and my note on McKenzie in Chapter 5.

3 Debord, *Society of the Spectacle*, Section 5. Because *Society of the Spectacle* has come out in many editions, and is widely available on the web in many formats, it has become standard to refer to the numbered sections (or theses) in the text, rather than to page numbers, which vary considerably.

4 Ibid., Section 44.

5 Ibid., Section 5.

6 Ibid., Section 24. This is not to say that Debord rejected the idea of resistance. His theoretical conception of the spectacle did not provide any sense that the spectacle itself might have multiple meanings, or be a site of struggle, but he did think that it was possible to wage a struggle against the spectacle. As the leader of the French political group the Situationist International, Debord advocated for, and created, "critical art" works called "détournements" that were intended to challenge and disrupt the pacification and alienation induced by the spectacle. Détournements worked by reconfiguring existing elements of culture in new and disruptive ways, and they played an inspirational role for the student movement leading up to the events of May and June 1968 in Paris. See Sussman, *On the Passage of a Few People*, for a discussion of détournement and the Situationist International.

7 Some of the most important theorists who have leveled this sort of criticism against Debord include Crary, *Spectacle, Attention, Counter-Memory*; Giroux, *Beyond the Spectacle of Terrorism*; and Kellner, *Media Spectacle*.

8 Kellner, *Media Spectacle*, 2. Kellner has devoted a series of recent books to an examination of "media spectacles" or "megaspectacles" including events as disparate as the O.J. Simpson murder trial, the television show *The X-Files*, the 2000 presidential election, and the ongoing Iraq war. See Kellner, *Grand Theft 2000*; *Media Spectacle*; and *Media Spectacle and the Crisis of Democracy*.

9 Ibid., 11.

10 Ibid., 28.

11 Kellner, "Media Culture and the Triumph of the Spectacle," 32.

12 Kellner, *Media Spectacle and the Crisis of Democracy*, 64.

13 Ibid., 78.

14 Omi and Winant, *Racial Formation*, 55.

15 Ibid., 56.

16 For discussions of groups other than African Americans that were killed by lynch mobs, see Carrigan and Webb, "The Lynching of Persons of Mexican Origin or Descent in the United States"; Gonzales-Day, *Lynching in the West*; and Carrigan, *The Making of a Lynching Culture*. Carrigan presents an especially interesting discussion of the role of collective memory in shaping traditions of vigilante violence that targeted Mexicans, Native Americans, slaves, and white unionists (among others) in central Texas.

17 Smith, *American Archives*, 149.

18 Ibid.

19 "Spectacle lynchings" is Grace Elizabeth Hale's term. See *Making Whiteness*, 201.

20 Hale, *Making Whiteness*, 201. "Spectacle lynchings" were never as common as lynchings by small groups of white men, though their impact as a method of terrorism might have been greater, since representations of these lynchings travelled farther.

21 See Hale, *Making Whiteness*, 204–239 and Markovitz, *Legacies of Lynching*, xxvii for more discussion of the standardization and variations of spectacle lynchings.

22 Ibid., 237.

23 See Markovitz, *Legacies of Lynching* and Schechter, *Ida B. Wells-Barnett and American Reform* for detailed discussions of the strategies of the antilynching movement.

24 Hale, *Making Whiteness*, 209.

25 Ibid., 223.

26 Ibid., 226.

27 Ibid., 227.

28 See Markovitz, *Legacies of Lynching*, and Chapter 1 of this volume for more detailed discussions of anti-racist struggles to debunk the "myth of the black rapist."

29 Markovitz, *Legacies of Lynching*, 140.

30 For a more in-depth discussion of struggles over collective memories of lynching, see ibid.

31 Halbwachs, *On Collective Memory*, 20.

32 It is important to note, however, that some of Halbwachs's most important work focused on "group" memories.

33 Schudson, *Watergate in Collective Memory*, 26. See also Schwartz, "The Social Context of Commemoration," 376. I argued in *Legacies of Lynching* that Schwartz and Schudson appear to be concerned with straw men, since there are, as far as I can tell, no such "radical social constructionists" represented in the collective memory literature. Halbwachs himself addressed a number of ways in which "ancient facts" provided the building blocks for collective memory (Markovitz, *Legacies of Lynching*, 151).

34 Irwin-Zarecka, *Frames of Remembrance,* 4.

35 Popular Memory Group, "Popular Memory: Theory, Politics, Method," 209.

36 Kitch, "Useful Memory," 95.

37 Landsberg, *Prosthetic Memory*, 2.

38 Though, of course, this is true of research into the "minds of individuals" too. Survey data and interviews can be quite useful in helping to gauge knowledge about the past, and to get a sense of how people make use of that knowledge. But surveys that are at all representative cannot begin to capture issues as fraught as the links between knowledge of the past and understandings of the present with any depth or nuance, while the kinds of interviews that might start to capture this kind of complexity cannot be conducted on nearly the scale that could be considered meaningfully representative. This is not to dismiss the value of survey and interview data, but instead, to say that such data should be seen as providing another kind of proxy for collective memory, which is something that can never be assessed directly and comprehensively.

39 Bourdieu, *Language and Symbolic Power*, 229.

40 Ibid.

41 Hunt, *Screening the Los Angeles "Riots,"* 33; Hunt, *O.J. Simpson Facts & Fictions*, 47.

42 Hunt, *O.J. Simpson Facts & Fictions*, 48.

43 Landsberg, *Prosthetic Memory*, 8.

44 Ibid., 9.

45 While there are a few especially well-known racial spectacles that might stand out as particularly glaring omissions for some readers, there is one type of spectacle whose absence in this volume requires explanation. With the partial exception of the Abu Ghraib photographs, none of my case studies involve the victimization, or alleged victimization, of women of color. This is not an accident, nor a reflection of my theoretical or political concerns, but instead a result of mass media priorities. For numerous reasons, the mass media has long been distressingly uninterested in the victimization of women of color, and there have consequently been few mass media spectacles revolving around such victimization. The Duke lacrosse case (discussed briefly in Chapter 2) is one of the few spectacles in recent memory centering around allegations of the sexual victimization of a woman of color, but the bulk of the attention to the case came once the allegations had started to unravel. In this regard, the case is similar to the Tawana Brawley case, in that it is ultimately not really an anti-racist spectacle demonstrating a serious media concern with black women's victimization, but is instead a spectacle that works to reinforce ages-old stereotypes of black women's sexuality. There are other examples of women of color whose victimization has received substantial press coverage, but very few have received the kind of attention that would be needed to rise to the level of a nationally recognizable media spectacle. For an in-depth discussion of the Tawana Brawley case, see Markovitz, *Legacies of Lynching*. I argue there that the mass media tend to display fascination with crimes against women of color only when those crimes are revealed as fabrications. The Duke lacrosse case strikes me as a more recent example of this trend.

46 While racial spectacles have occurred for many decades, most of my case studies address racial spectacles from the late twentieth and early twenty-first centuries. My selection reflects Kellner's observation that we have entered into a new "stage of the spectacle"

characterized by the proliferation of images and information into virtually every aspect of contemporary life, to the point where we are confronted with new forms of spectacle on a regular basis (Kellner, *Media Spectacle*, 94). My hope is that since I have decided to focus the bulk of this study on spectacles of the past twenty years, the kinds of analyses that I offer will be especially well-suited for fostering a better understanding of the contemporary media environment, and will provide useful ways of thinking of racial spectacles still to come.

1 "Exploding the Myth of the Black Rapist"

1 Charlotte Hawkins Brown, speaking in 1920. Quoted in Hall, *Revolt Against Chivalry*, 96.
2 A letter from George Fort Milton, publisher of the Chattanooga News, and Chairman of the Southern Commission to Study Lynching (a commission formed by the CIC), to Judge Fort of the Fort, Beddow & Ray law firm, dated 8/12/1931. Commission on Interracial Cooperation Scottsboro Papers.
3 The quote is attributed to black women members of the Commission. Hall, *Revolt Against Chivalry*, 167.
4 There have been some objections to referring to the defendants as the "Scottsboro Boys," since some of them were over the age of eighteen, and because "boy" has long been used as a term to denigrate and juvenalize African American men. The reference to "boys" becomes particularly problematic as the case progresses through the 1930s and beyond, and as the defendants all emerge from prison as grown men. The "Scottsboro Nine" has been used as an alternative for these reasons. The Scottsboro defense movement's rhetorical choices were not based on an acceptance of racist discourse, but on the strategic decision that "boy" was a useful term for highlighting the youth and innocence of the defendants.
5 Carter, *Scottsboro*, 5.
6 Ibid.
7 See Carter, *Scottsboro* and Goodman, *Stories of Scottsboro*, for the most comprehensive accounts of the case.
8 Goodman, *Stories of Scottsboro*, 5.
9 The only defendant who was not sentenced to death was twelve- or thirteen-year-old Roy Wright. While he was convicted, his case ended in a mistrial, since several of the jurors held out for the death penalty, when the prosecution had requested only life in prison because of his age. Still, he remained in prison as his case went through appeals, until 1937, when the State dropped all charges against him, Eugene Williams, Olen Montgomery, and Willie Roberson.
10 Pinar, *The Gender of Racial Politics*, 771.
11 James Miller, Susan Pennybacker, and Eve Rosenhaft, "Mother Ada Wright," 404.
12 League of Struggle for Negro Rights, *They Shall Not Die!*, 8.
13 See Apel, *Imagery of Lynching*, for a discussion of Scottsboro-related art.
14 See *The History Detectives*, Season 7, Episode 11, 2009, "Scottsboro Boys Stamp" for more information about the stamp. A transcript of the episode is available at http://www.pbs.org/opb/historydetectives/pdf/712_scottsboro.pdf (accessed August 12, 2010).
15 "Sells Juice to Burn Negroes." Editorial Cartoon. *Baltimore Afro-American*, June 6, 1931, 5.
16 See, for example, Scottsboro Defense Committee, "Scottsboro: The Shame of America."
17 League of Struggle for Negro Rights, *They Shall Not Die!* Cover illustration by A. Refregier.
18 Miller, *Remembering Scottsboro*, 47.

19 H.G. Bailey quoted in F. Raymond Daniell, "Inconsistencies Brought Out in Witness' Testimony at Trial of Weems," *New York Times*, July 23, 1937.

20 F. Raymond Daniell, "Scottsboro Case Goes to the Jury," *New York Times*, January 23, 1936.

21 Small, *Scottsboro: Act Three*, 9.

22 Wright, "12 Million Black Voices," 239.

23 *The Crisis*, December, 1934, 364.

24 "Hernond and the Scottsboro Cases." Editorial. *The Crisis*, December, 1935, 369.

25 This was also the date that the antilynching crusader Ida B. Wells-Barnett died. As Patricia Schechter says, her death "marked the beginning and end of an era." *Ida B. Wells-Barnett and American Reform*, 247.

26 Quoted in ibid., 78. See Schechter for a detailed account of the events leading up to this article.

27 Quoted in Wells, *Southern Horrors*, 18.

28 It is not clear if she left town to flee the mob. Schechter notes that, while Wells's autobiography claims that it was simply "fate" that the mob had arrived while she was out of town, she was well aware of the possible consequences of publishing such an inflammatory piece. Wells likely knew the story of another black editor who had been chased out of Montgomery, Alabama after writing a similar editorial a few years earlier, and she had noted that "an antiracist, pro-free speech editor 'might have to be on the hop, skip and jump' in the South." *Ida B. Wells-Barnett and American Reform*, 78.

29 See Markovitz, *Legacies of Lynching*, and Brown, *Eradicating This Evil*, for in-depth considerations of the antilynching movement's strategies and composition. Brown offers a compelling discussion of the Anti-Lynching Crusaders. Schechter notes that some African American leaders saw the effort to expose the myth of the black rapist as potentially incendiary, and instead chose to emphasize the need for better law enforcement as a method of controlling mob violence. *Ida B. Wells-Barnett and American Reform*, 106.

30 The estimate for the number of lynch victims comes from Brundage, *Lynching in the New South*, 8. Tolnay and Beck conclude that 31.1 percent of southern black victims of lynch mobs were charged with rape between 1882 and 1930. *A Festival of Violence*, 49. Because many lynchings went unreported as such, and because many records of lynchings have been lost, no definitive accounting of lynching numbers is possible.

31 For a discussion of the presentation of the myth of the black rapist in *Birth of a Nation*, see Rogin, "The Sword Became a Flashing Vision." For a discussion of the cinematic refutation of this myth in Oscar Micheaux's *Within Our Gates* (1920), see Gaines, *Fire and Desire*, 161–184.

32 Wells, *Southern Horrors*, 14. As I've suggested throughout this discussion, Wells's refutation of the idea that lynching was a response to rape was eventually taken up as a standard part of antilynching activism. In the early 1890s, however, many members of African American communities saw her tactics as potentially incendiary or ineffective. In order to maintain good relations with whites, many African American leaders shied away from exposing the myth of the black rapist in favor of stressing the importance of law enforcement as a method of controlling the mob. Schechter, *Ida B. Wells-Barnett and American Reform*, 106.

33 From an NAACP organizing letter to Youth Council Presidents about the National Youth Demonstration Against Lynching on February 12th, 1937. NAACP antilynching publicity files. For an extended discussion of the antilynching movement's efforts to challenge myths of black rape, see Markovitz, *Legacies of Lynching*. For an early detailed discussion of the "myth of the black rapist," see Davis, *Women, Race & Class*.

34 Tolnay and Beck, *A Festival of Violence*, 29. The first years of the Great Depression saw a spike in lynchings, but the numbers soon began to decline again, until 1940, when the Tuskegee Institute and the Association of Southern Women for the Prevention of

Lynching were finally able to declare the first "lynch-free year," albeit not without controversy.

35 Tolnay and Beck note that "Of course, we cannot know what a similar Gallup poll would have revealed during the height of the lynching era, but it is probably safe to assume that the average southerner was more tolerant of federal intrusion into southern race relations in 1937 than in 1897." *A Festival of Violence*, 202.

36 On lynching in the news media, see Brundage, *Lynching in the New South*, Schechter, *Ida B. Wells-Barnett and American Reform*, and Goldsby, *A Spectacular Secret*.

37 Quoted in Van Doren, "Eight Who Must Not Die," *The Nation*, June 3, 1931, 608. The editorial also ran in the Alabaman paper the *Huntsville Times*, on March 26, 1931. Quoted in Goodman, *Stories of Scottsboro*, 12. The case was national news from the outset, as it was covered by the *Associated Press*, but initial coverage on the new service had a distinctly southern bent, since it was local reporters in Scottsboro, Paint Rock, Huntsville and Decatur, whose reports were picked up by the organization. Goodman, 13.

38 Goodman, *Stories of Scottsboro*, 15

39 See Markovitz, *Legacies of Lynching*, 28.

40 Brundage, *Lynching in the New South*, 224. Brundage argues the lynching of Leo Frank, a Jewish factory owner in Atlanta, prompted national outrage and provided increased incentive for southern urban newspapers to oppose lynching. See also Perloff, "The Press and Lynchings."

41 Quoted in Pfaff, "The Press and the Scottsboro Rape Cases," 73.

42 Quoted in Goodman, *Stories of Scottsboro*, 16.

43 "Who Promote Lynching," *Charleston News and Courier*, March 29, 1931. Editorial included in Commission on Interracial Cooperation Scottsboro papers.

44 Pinar, *The Gender of Racial Politics*, 782. In a 1982 interview, Victoria Price gave a sense of the hostility that Bates had to face when she recanted. Price claims that when Bates "left the courthouse, the bystanders started throwing tomatoes at her. . . . There was three bushels of tomatoes on her face, on her dress and down the front of her. I was standin' in the window watchin' and yellin' 'Hallelujah, Hallelujah.'" Fred Barbash, "Victoria Price; Accuser of the Scottsboro Boys Fights for 40 Years of Forgetting." *Washington Post*. January 4, 1982.

45 Quoted in Goodman, *Stories of Scottsboro*, 198.

46 Solomon, *The Cry Was Unity*, 243.

47 *High Spots*, the Commission on Interracial Cooperation's Department of Women's Work newsletter, April–June 1933. From CIC papers.

48 Jessie Daniel Ames, "Southern Women and Lynching," Atlanta: Association of Southern Women for the Prevention of Lynching, 1936. From ASWPL papers.

49 International Labor Defense, *The Story of Scottsboro*, 7.

50 Goodman, *Stories of Scottsboro*, 150.

51 Pfaff, "The Press and the Scottsboro Rape Cases," 75.

52 Quoted in Carter, *Scottsboro*, 253.

53 Quoted in ibid., 254.

54 Quoted in *Transcript of trial of Clarence Norris, appellant, vs. State of Alabama, appellee, in the Circuit Court of Morgan County, held in December, 1933*, Montgomery, Alabama, certified 5/8/1934, 185.

55 Ibid., 188.

56 *Norris v. Alabama*, 294 U.S. 587, April 1, 1935

57 Quoted in Scottsboro Defense Committee, "4 Free, 5 in Prison," 5.

58 Fletcher, "Correspondence: Is This the Voice of the South?" 735. Fletcher does refer to this position as a "defect" in the southern "system." The editors of *The Nation* write that "Since Mr. Fletcher does not indicate that anything beyond an allegation is necessary, this seems . . . not only shockingly irresponsible but downright unlawful." (736.)

59 Ames, "Editorial Treatment of Lynchings," 84.

60 Ibid., 82.

61 Ibid.

62 Quoted in Goodman, *Stories of Scottsboro*, 326. Ames does not, however, ignore Scottsboro. Instead, she writes that the case

> has become a trifle boring, not only to Alabama but to the larger part of the South. It has done the South no good in many ways but it has proved an asset in one notable way. It has furnished Southern editors a dignified and self-righteous basis for excusing lynchers with a line of argument that the whole country appreciates—delays in court procedure, the uncertainty of punishment, the loopholes in the law—conditions prevalent everywhere and universally condemned.
>
> (Ames, "Editorial Treatment of Lynchings," 83.)

The idea that Scottsboro had provided southern editors with a new method of defending lynching is important, and helps to explain why the ASWPL chose not to take a public stance on the case. Jacquelyn Dowd Hall argues that, while most of the membership of the Association thought that the legal system was weighted against African Americans, they believed that it was a lesser evil than mob justice, and that any efforts to combat racism in the criminal justice system had the potential to undermine the fight against lynching. The Scottsboro case did, however, encourage the Association to more vigorously investigate charges of interracial rape. (Hall, *Revolt Against Chivalry*, 198–202.)

63 Quoted in Goodman, *Stories of Scottsboro*, 167.

64 Quoted in ibid.

65 Quoted in ibid.

66 Ibid., 21.

67 Ibid.

68 Melvin Huston, quoted in ibid., 257. Huston was one of the prosecutors in the third trial of Haywood Patterson.

69 Herndon, "The Scottsboro Boys," 8. Another pamphlet addresses the hypocrisy of presenting Price and Bates as paragons of southern womanhood when they would ordinarily be treated with scorn, referring to "the two white prostitutes," and claiming that "the two white women now ceased to be arrested vagrants and became 'pure' and holy examples of 'outraged white womanhood.'" The implicit claim that Price and Bates had been arrested for vagrancy before claiming rape has not been verified. League of Struggle for Negro Rights, *They Shall Not Die!*, 5.

70 Hughes, "Southern Gentlemen, White Prostitutes," 1.

71 Horton's opinion was reprinted in Scottsboro Defense Committee, "The Scottsboro Case: Opinion of Judge James E. Horton."

72 http://www.law.umkc.edu/faculty/projects/FTrials/scottsboro/HORTONS INSTRUCT.html (accessed June 12, 2009).

73 Judge William Callahan, quoted in Goodman, *Stories of Scottsboro*, 218.

74 *Patterson v. State of Alabama.* 141 So. 195 224 Ala. 531. Supreme Court of Alabama. March 24, 1932.

75 Quoted in Mike Thomas, "The Real-Life Story Behind Harper Lee's Novel," *Chicago Sun-Times*, September 30, 2001.

76 Kelley, "Rummaging Through," xvi.

77 David Oshinsky, "Only the Accused Were Innocent," *New York Times*, April 3, 1994, Section 7, 14.

78 For example, a search in the *New York Times* historical database turns up 737 hits for the keyword "Scottsboro" between 01/01/1931 and 01/01/1939, but only 57 hits for the same search for the dates 01/01/1939–01/01/1947. There are occasional stories that are not related to the Scottsboro case, but, for the most part, the case was the only

reason that "Scottsboro" would turn up in a search of the paper. Search conducted in ProQuest Historical Newspapers, the *New York Times* (1851–2003) database, 7/15/07.

79 Murray, "Changing America," 85.

80 See Goodman, *Stories of Scottsboro*, 287–310 and Carter, *Scottsboro*, 369–398 for detailed discussions of the negotiations over a compromise.

81 Carter, *Scottsboro*, 381.

82 Goodman, *Stories of Scottsboro*, 310.

83 Herndon, "The Scottsboro Boys."

84 The Supreme Court declined to review the convictions of Patterson and Norris in October of 1937. In July of 1938, Governor Graves reduced Clarence Norris's death sentence to life imprisonment.

85 Michael Schudson has argued that there are a series of obstacles confronting anyone who would seek to remake the past, and that chief among them is what he calls "living memory." He argues that "revisionist history, whether it comes from a lone historian or a presidential commission, will have tough sledding if it contradicts the personal memories of persons still living." (*Watergate in American Memory*, 207.) This argument is problematic, since some people who have lived through important historical events have no way to insure that their understandings of those events are heard by mass audiences, and thus do not, at least on their own, pose substantial obstacles to the historical reinventions of people with considerably greater access to the mass media. But, under the right conditions, living memory can work as an important resource for the institutionalization of collective memory. One Holocaust survivor might not have the power to stand in the way of Holocaust denial as a cultural force, but when Holocaust museums or State actors gather survivor testimony, and when policies are enacted on the basis of that testimony, collective memories of the Holocaust are bolstered, and Holocaust denial is marginalized. If Schudson's "obstacles" can be profitably understood as *resources* that are valuable for promoting the institutionalization of collective memory, then the role that obituaries play in refocusing national attention on the Scottsboro case in decades after the 1930s suggests that living memory has a corollary: To Schudson's list of obstacles, I'd like to propose adding the notion of "fatal memory" (or, possibly, "passing memory") as a way of indexing the role that the deaths of key actors in major historical events can play in helping to promote memory of those events.

86 See Patterson, *Scottsboro Boy*, and Norris and Washington, *The Last of the Scottsboro Boys*.

87 By all accounts, *Judge Horton and the Scottsboro Boys* was very well received. It was, however, probably not as widely viewed as Carter suggests. He writes that according to the Nielsen ratings "forty-one million people" viewed the show when it first aired. Carter, *Scottsboro*, 417. If true, that would make it one of the most-watched docudramas of all time, and would mean that it had a larger audience than did the series finales of *All in the Family* and *Dallas*. It was not until 1987 that Nielsen started to collect data on a weekly basis, and apparently the company did not collect data for the week that the show aired. Daniel Bergen, The Nielsen Company, personal correspondence, July 2, 2007.

88 The court found in favor of NBC, since, while the documentary was found to have defamed Price (now named Victoria Street), NBC was not found to have acted with "actual malice." The libel suit is discussed in Carter, *Scottsboro*, 416–462. The Supreme Court's final intervention into the Scottsboro case came in its decision to hear Price's appeal. NBC settled out of court, so the Supreme Court dismissed the case. While terms were not disclosed, the settlement apparently provided Price with enough money to buy a new house shortly before her death. Barbash, "Victoria Price."

89 Mike Thomas, "The Real-Life Story." Writing in 1999, James Lowen referred to the town of Scottsboro's failure to erect a marker about the case as a "particularly outrageous example" of a "landscape of amnesia" that characterizes a broader failure in the United States to come to terms with the nation's history of oppression. Lowen, *Lies Across America*, 249.

90 Murray, "Changing America," 83.
91 Apel, *Imagery of Lynching*, 53, 119.
92 A 2006 feature film about the case, *Heavens Fall*, directed by Terry Green, and starring David Strathairn, Timothy Hutton, Leslee Sobieski, and Anthony Mackie, has not, by the time of this writing, found a distributor.
93 In this lithograph, the Scottsboro defendants are on a box car flat. The telephone wires almost appear to be attached to the defendants, as though the pole, which is shaped like a cross, has become a lynching tree. The image presents the defendants as Christian martyrs, and implicates modern communication and transportation technologies as contributing factors in their martyrdom.
94 Murray, "Changing America," 86.
95 Maxwell, *New Negro*, 133.
96 Claudia Durst Johnson, *To Kill*, 5.
97 Lubet, "Reconstructing Atticus Finch."
98 Sundquist, "Blues for Atticus Finch," 182.
99 Johnson, *To Kill*, 13.
100 Lubet, "Reconstructing Atticus Finch," 1340.
101 The show featured music and lyrics by Kander and Ebb, along with a book by David Thompson. Susan Stroman was the director and choreographer. An earlier play by Mark Stein, *Direct From Death Row, The Scottsboro Boys (An Evening of Vaudeville and Sorrow)* also staged the Scottsboro case as a Vaudevillian production and part-minstrel show. It is not clear if this 1980 production was part of the inspiration for *The Scottsboro Boys*.
102 The show plays around with other stock characters from traditional minstrel shows too. The characters of "Mr. Bones" and "Mr. Tambo" are generally played by white men in blackface, and are used to reinforce racist stereotypes of black men. Librettist David Thompson has said that, in *The Scottsboro Boys*, his goal was to "tip that over and have them play stereotypical white characters." Here, the characters are used to lampoon racist police officers and lawyers. Quoted in Robert Simonson, "Digging Up Mr. Bones: How the Minstrel Show Gave Shape to *The Scottsboro Boys*" playbill.com 6 April, 2010. http:// playbill.com/news/article/print/138406.html (accessed April 17, 2010).
103 One particularly problematic issue involving the show's presentation of the history of the case has to do with the portrayal of Samuel Leibowitz. In real life, the four Scottsboro defendants who were released in 1937 performed in a Vaudeville-style recreation of their trial at the Apollo theater in Harlem. In *The Scottsboro Boys*, Leibowitz enlists the defendants in a vaudeville show, and is held responsible for capitalizing on their fame and turning them into a spectacle. Since the central conceit of *The Scottsboro Boys* is that the real tragedy of the case is precisely that the defendants were turned into symbols and made into a spectacle, Leibowitz is held up here as a uniquely venal figure responsible for a great deal of the defendants' suffering. The real Leibowitz vehemently objected to the defendants' appearance at the Apollo, and "turned down every" commercial opportunity the defendants were offered (Goodman, *Stories of Scottsboro*, 338). It might be reasonable to accuse Leibowitz of having been paternalistic in his dealings with the defendants, but there is no evidence to suggest that he was crassly opportunistic in the ways the play suggests.
104 The *Powell* decision is remarkable partly for the ways that the Court appears to suggest that it is intervening in a distinctly southern practice. The opinion by Justice Sutherland notes that the crime that the defendants were accused of was "regarded with especial horror in the community where they were to be tried" and notes that to try the defendants without adequate counsel is "to go forward with the haste of the mob." *Powell v. Alabama* 287 U.S. November 7, 1932. The opinion is thus perfectly in line with Scottsboro defense movement rhetoric claiming that the trials were "legal lynchings."

105 In 1978, Roy Wilkins, the second editor of *The Crisis*, and the executive director of the NAACP from 1955–1977, has said that "No one who lived through it can forget the Scottsboro case and its effect on the on-going civil rights struggle," and has noted that Judge Horton's death provided a reminder that "the civil rights movement began long before the 1950s and 1960s." Wilkins, 1973, C7. In a discussion of civil rights activism, Ossie Davis said that

> there was a time when the nine Scottsboro boys were about to be executed in Alabama. Everybody black was involved in that. It was such a part of being who you were. Growing up in the thick of it. It was just a way of life. And it followed us through to where we are today.
>
> (Quoted in Marc Warren, "Remembering Ossie Davis." *Afro-American RedStar*, Washington, D.C., February 12–18, 2005.)

Michael Omi and Howard Winant have argued that a key task for civil rights movement leaders was to craft an African American identity based on the belief that meaningful resistance to racist oppression was necessary and possible. *Racial Formation*, 101. Davis's comment suggests that memories of Scottsboro were important elements of this process. By focusing on the criminal justice system as an important source of racism, the Scottsboro defense movement also prefigured the current anti-racist movement directed against the "prison industrial complex." See Davis, "Are Prisons Obsolete?" for a discussion of this movement.

106 Leland Ware, "The Long Legacy of the Scottsboro Case," *St. Louis Post-Dispatch* (Missouri), September 11, 1994, Everyday Magazine Section, 5C.

107 See Cole, *No Equal Justice*, 67–95 for an excellent overview of the trajectory stemming from *Powell*. Gerald Horne notes that the Court has

> slowly but surely retreated from the meaning of *Powell*, narrowly defining what effective representation by counsel means. In *Strickland v. Washington* (1984), the Court ruled that to make a claim that counsel was ineffective the defendant must overcome "a strong presumption that counsel's conduct falls within the wide range of reasonable professional assistance" and demonstrate that the attorney's representation "fell below an objective standard of reasonableness." . . . In a later case from Texas, the Court ruled that a defense lawyer's statement to the jury that the defendant was guilty of murder did not violate the standard in *Strickland*.
>
> (*Powell v. Alabama: The Scottsboro Boys and American Justice*, 104.)

Most recently, the court has come full circle, returning to an Alabaman capital case, and refusing to consider an appeal in *Barbour v. Allen*, ruling that prisoners on Alabama's death row have no right to state appointed attorneys in state post-conviction review. Linda Greenhouse, "Passengers Granted Same Right as Drivers," *New York Times*, June 19, 2007, A12.

108 See Cole, *No Equal Justice*, 109–126 for a discussion of the Court's acceptance of racially based peremptory challenges in jury selection.

109 The progress narrative is also evident in many academic discussions of the case. Christopher Waldrep, for example, writes that while "the Scottsboro Boys case faded from the public's consciousness, the affair still represented a huge stride forward. A case of racial injustice had attracted international attention. Readers around the world learned about the South's criminal justice system." Waldrep, 2001, 74. At times, the mainstream press will acknowledge that progress took time, but while Scottsboro-era racism may have lingered past the 1930s, the implication is generally that we have moved beyond it. Consider, for example, this discussion of the *Norris* decision: "The result of that ruling was that the barring of blacks from jury service became illegal, although the practice persisted for many years in some parts of the country." J.Y. Smith, "Samuel Leibowitz, Noted Judge, Dies," *Washington Post*, January 12, 1978.

110 It is necessary to distinguish here between the northern and southern black press. Northern African American papers felt fairly free to criticize the case openly, while black owned papers in the South had to be somewhat circumspect, since violent reprisals for overt criticism were not at all unlikely. James Goodman provides a fascinating account of Oscar Adams, the editor of the *Birmingham Reporter*. He notes that Adams was cautious about covering the case in its early years, and that he never reported the allegations that Price and Bates were prostitutes, or tried to refute the notion that rape was the explanation for lynchings. Instead, he found ingenious ways to use the paper's layout to call attention to the racism and hypocrisy involved in the case. He ran stories about the Scottsboro case next to stories about white men who were pardoned after rape convictions, or about white women in Virginia who had been indicted for perjury after their testimony had led to a black man being convicted of rape and sentenced to death. The first open criticism of the case in the paper came when some white newspapers started to grow skeptical about the charges, and Adams started reprinting their editorials. *Stories of Scottsboro*, 62–64.

111 Theodore Dreiser, "Lynching," *New York Amsterdam News*, May 27, 1931.

112 The *Portland, Oregon Advocate*, 1931. Quoted in Carter, *Scottsboro*, 81.

113 After the second trial of Haywood Patterson, the *New York Amsterdam News* noted, for example, that

> A jury verdict of more far-reaching importance and consequence to the Negro race in American than any since the Dred Scott decision by the United States Supreme Court, back in 1857, has just been reached in the case of Haywood Patterson . . . on a trumped-up charge of raping two white women in Alabama.
>
> (*New York Amsterdam News*, April 12, 1933.)

The *New York Age* did not limit itself to criticisms of the southern legal system, but also argued that the press was part of the problem:

> The world-at-large is learning many valuable lessons from the Scottsboro case. . . . Usually the public has to depend on information furnished by local representatives of the Associated Press or some other news syndicate who are as narrow and one-sided as their fellow citizens and afraid to be non-partisan even if they desired.
>
> ("The Decatur, Ala. Farce," *New York Age*, April 15, 1933.)

114 Carter, *Scottsboro*, 243.

115 Ross, "Mobilizing the Masses," 56.

116 I discuss the central park jogger case in greater detail in Chapter 2.

117 In its coverage of the Susan Smith case, for example, the *New York Amsterdam News* quotes an attorney named Colin Moore saying that "Smith is no lunatic. She knew full well that America has had a long inglorious history of scapegoating Black men and that her story would be digested by police and the public." The paper goes on to note that

> According to Moore, Smith had seen President Bush get elected by a landslide when he scapegoated a Black man named Willie Horton. "She also knew that 43 years ago [sic] in Scottsboro, Ala., two White prostitutes accused nine Black men of raping them and the men were convicted," he added.
>
> (J. Zamgba, "Blacks Reviled By All Facets of Susan Smith Murder Case," *New York Amsterdam News*, November 12, 1994, 4.)

118 Most recently, the mainstream press has frequently invoked Scottsboro in its coverage of the 2006 Duke Lacrosse case, in which three white members of the university's Lacrosse team were charged with the rape and kidnapping of a black woman. The charges were ultimately dropped, and ethics charges were filed against the prosecutor, who was ultimately disbarred for a variety of offenses, including withholding

exculpatory evidence. When Scottsboro is referenced in coverage of the case, the suggestion is generally that the Duke case was a mirror image of Scottsboro, with some caveats. A piece in the *Wall Street Journal*, for example, says that

> Here is where the real difference between the Scottsboro boys and the Duke boys kicked in: not race but money. The Scottsboro boys were destitute and spent years in jail, while the Duke boys were all from families who could afford first-class legal talent. Their lawyers quickly began blowing hole after hole in the case and releasing the facts to the media until it was obvious that a miscarriage of justice had occurred. (John Gordon, "Racial Role Reversal," *Wall Street Journal*, June 20, 2007, A17.)

Of course, the fact that the Scottsboro defendants were destitute did play a role in the first series of trials. But once the appeals process had started, the defendants had the assistance of some of the best criminal defense attorneys in the country, and they too "began blowing hole after hole in the case." To suggest that the difference was "not race but money" is to ignore that the defendants were nearly lynched, and to discount the mythology of black rape.

119 Thomas, "The Real-Life Story."

120 See Entman, *Democracy Without Citizens*, and McChesney, *The Problem of the Media*, for important critiques of the notion of journalistic objectivity.

121 Curtis Wilkie, "Shades of Black and White: In James Goodman's hands, the Scottsboro Case Becomes a Complex and Subtle Metaphor," *Boston Globe*, March 13, 1994.

122 This divide has been regularly overstated. Public opinion polls suggest that in raw numbers, far more whites thought Simpson was innocent than did blacks. 60 million whites held this view, while only 22 million blacks did. The media generally reported percentages rather than raw numbers, focusing on the fact that 70 percent of blacks thought Simpson was innocent, while 70 percent of whites thought he was guilty. Katheryn Russell argues that "the constant media focus upon those Blacks who thought Simpson was innocent helped create the image the 'The Black Viewpoint' was slightly crazed and fanatical." Russell, *The Color of Crime*, 49–51.

123 Jim Sleeper, "The Simpsons," *New Republic*, October 23, 1995, 17.

124 Jonetta Barras, "My Race, My Gender," *New Republic*, October 23, 1995, 16.

125 In their discussion of the Simpson jury deliberations, Nikol G. Alexander and Drucilla Cornell examine the explanations that jury members offered for their decision. Alexander and Cornell argue that there is substantial evidence that the jury took their responsibilities quite seriously, and that the characterizations of the jurors as "both unreasonable and irrational" were based on "racial fantasies" that, if used as the basis for legal reform, would "legitimate the banishment of African Americans from the body politic." "Dismissed or Banished?" 57.

126 Randall Kennedy, "After the Cheers," *New Republic*, October 23, 1995, 14.

127 Ibid.

128 See Markovitz, *Legacies of Lynching*, for a discussion of a similar mass media presentation of African American collective memory in the Tawana Brawley case.

129 Faulkner, *Requiem for a Nun*, 92.

2 Anatomy of a Spectacle

1 "Sexual assault" is Colorado's legal term for rape. Because this chapter is not concerned with coming to conclusions about the question of Bryant's possible guilt, I do not discuss the alleged rape itself in any detail. I am concerned that providing details about unproven allegations of sexualized violence may encourage a sensationalistic take on the case. The specific allegations are laid out at some length in Alex Markels, "Detective Details Accuser's Case Against Bryant," *New York Times*, October, 10 2003. http://www.

nytimes.com/2003/1010/sports/pro-basketball-detective-details-accuser-s-case-against-bryant.html (accessed October 10, 2003). Additional details are provided in Kirk Johnson, "The Bryant Trial: Anatomy of a Case that Fell Apart," *New York Times*, September 3, 2004, http://www.nytimes.com/2004/09/03/national/03kobe.html (accessed September 4, 2004). Johnson also provides some of the details about aspects of the alleged victim's sexual history that became an issue in the case.

2 Department of Justice, "Growth in Prison and Jail Populations Growing."

3 Lapchick, "The Kobe Bryant Case."

4 Edy, "Journalistic Uses," 73.

5 Ibid.

6 In order to gain a sense of how collective memory might play into public understandings of the Kobe Bryant case, I searched the Lexis/Nexis and Ethnic NewsWatch newspaper and magazine databases using the key words "Kobe Bryant" and "rape." I eliminated all articles with fewer than 250 words because they did not address the case in depth. Still, I was left with over 800 articles from the sports sections, editorial and op-ed pages, entertainment and straight news sections, of local, regional, and national papers and magazines. I conducted a qualitative content analysis coding for recurrent themes, and paying special attention to the ways that the coverage invoked collective memory.

7 Irwin-Zarecka, *Frames of Remembrance*, 8.

8 Crenshaw, "Mapping the Margins"; Roberts, "Punishing Drug Addicts."

9 Kellner, "The Sports Spectacle," 307

10 Boyd and Shropshire, "Introduction," 3.

11 In February of 2004, 77 percent of NBA players were African American, while only 21 percent were white. Lelinwaller, M. "Basketball is flip side of baseball." *Philadelphia Inquirer*. https://web.lexis-nexis.com/universe, July 13, 2004 (accessed November 15, 2004).

12 Alexander, "Can You be Black," 92.

13 Tucker, "Blackballed," 315.

14 Ibid., 322.

15 Banet-Weiser, "Hoop Dreams," 406.

16 Tucker, "Blackballed," 313 . It is worth noting that the one other professional sport that emphasizes all of these things to the same extent as basketball is boxing, and that before the Bryant case, the most widely publicized charges of rape within professional sports involved Mike Tyson. Tucker suggests that the sexuality of the game is part of the appeal, as she quotes a fan as saying that "it's just, you know, bodies on bodies and it's totally erotic." 313.

17 Jessica Johnson, "Bryant's defense team taking big risk if it relies on race card being an ace," *Columbus Dispatch*, January 28, 2004, 11A.

18 E.R. Shipp, "Don't Play Race Card in Kobe Bryant case," *San Diego Union-Tribune*. October 2, 2003, B11. See also Kirk Johnson "In Kobe Bryant Case, Issues of Power, Not of Race," *New York Times*, August 26, 2004, 12.

19 USA TODAY/CNN/Gallup poll results. www.usatoday.com/sports/basketball/nba/lakers/2003-08-07-kobe-usat-gallup.htm (accessed August 7, 2003).

20 Leonard, "The Next M.J.," 292.

21 Ibid.

22 Ibid. The case with the most direct parallels to the Bryant case, but involving a white athlete instead of a black one, is that of Pittsburgh Steelers' quarterback Ben Roethlisberger, who was sued for sexual assault in the fall of 2009, and then, in an unrelated case, investigated for rape in March of 2010. No criminal charges were filed in either case, though the NFL did suspend Roethlisberger for the first six games of the 2010 season. Neither incident received even a fraction of the coverage of the Bryant case, despite the fact that Roethlisberger was arguably at least as famous as Bryant when

the allegations in the first case broke, having won multiple Super Bowls. This could be due, in part, to the lack of criminal charges, but the Bryant case became a media spectacle even before criminal charges were filed, and this is not the case for either Roethlisberger case. The discrepancy in the volume of coverage accorded Roethlisberger and Bryant is one piece of evidence leading Dexter Rogers to conclude that: "The rules aren't the same for African American athletes when compared to their white athletic brethren." "Why has Ben Roethlisberger's rape case disappeared from the news?" *African-American Sports Examiner*, October 15, 2009. http://www.examiner.com/x-17321-AfricanAmerican-Sports-Examiner~y2009m10d15-Why-has-Ben-Roethlisbergers-rape-case-disappeared-from-the-news (accessed November 1, 2009).

23 Leonard, "The Next M.J." writes that "social commentators, from White feminists to conservative pundits, continue to paint the picture of sexual crimes with a Black brush" (304).

24 Ibid.

25 For example, a Nexis search of major papers in 2003–4 yields 812 hits in a search for "catholic church" and "child abuse," while a search in the same time period for "Michael Jackson" and "child abuse" yields 980 hits.

26 Leonard, 2004, 294.

27 Brundage, *Lynching in the New South*; Carrigan and Webb, "The Lynching of Persons." Carrigan and Webb demonstrate that the lynching rates of Mexicans and Mexican Americans after the Mexican war were quite similar to those of African Americans in the post-Reconstruction South, though the raw number of African American lynch victims is still far greater. Carrigan (*The Making*) provides a richly layered account of vigilante violence in Central Texas, involving Mexicans, Native Americans, slaves, white abolitionists, and African Americans.

28 Though Gus never did commit a rape in the film, and in what has been called "the Gus rape scene," he actually assures the woman that he is chasing that he will not harm her. See Gaines, *Fire and Desire*, 239–41 for a discussion of the debates surrounding this scene.

29 Markovitz, *Legacies of Lynching*.

30 Quoted in Miller, 1994, 18.

31 I am following Gramsci's notion of "common sense" here, in that I see common sense as socially constructed, and as the product of discursive battles over hegemony. See Markovitz (*Legacies of Lynching*, 15) for more on this idea. For much more detailed discussions of the Hill/Thomas hearings, see Morrison (*Birth of a Nation'hood*), and Markovitz (*Legacies of Lynching*).

32 On the impact of the Willie Horton ad, see Feagin and Vera (*White Racism*).

33 See Markovitz (*Legacies of Lynching*, 84–90), and Smith (*Not Just Race*, 9–10), for more sustained discussions of these cases.

34 Heller, "Anatomies of Rape," 329.

35 Sydney Schanberg, "A Journey Through the Tangled Case of the Central Park Jogger: When Justice is a Game," *Village Voice*, November 20–26, 2002. www.villagevoice.com (accessed July 25, 2005).

36 In a position paper on the case, the New York Civil Liberties Union argues that

> there is every reason to believe that unreliable confessions are a substantial problem in law enforcement. In the most thorough investigation so far, the *Chicago Tribune* last December reported hundreds of cases in Chicago that involved coerced or otherwise improper confessions since 1991. Earlier this year *The Washington Post* chronicled abusive interrogation practices in Prince Georges County, Maryland that produced false confessions. And state supreme courts in Minnesota and Alaska have ordered that interrogations in those states be recorded to assure that defendants are not being coerced into false confessions. Far too often, cops pressure suspects by lying about evidence or about the statements of supposed accomplices; by making

false promises of leniency; by denying suspects access to lawyers and parents; and by taking advantage of their age, fatigue or simple fear.

(Quoted in Christopher Dunn and Donna Lieberman, "The Lesson of the Central Park Jogger Controversy: Start Videotaping Interrogations," *Newsday*, September 27, 2002. www.newsday.com (accessed January 12, 2005).)

37 Hancock, "Wolfpack."
38 Quoted in ibid., 7. This characterization of the defendants turns out to have been seriously off-base. When the *New York Times* and *New York Newsday* did profiles of the defendants, "Instead of street thugs, reporters found that most of these kids attended decent schools and lived in stable homes with two working parents." Ibid., 8. Not that this information did anything to mitigate the crimes, or the portrayals of monstrosity. Instead "those who believed the boys were rapists saw these details as horrifying. Instead of casting doubt on their guilt, it made them seem even more evil. They had no excuses. No crack-addicted mothers. No blackboard jungle high schools." Ibid., 9.
39 Quoted in ibid., 4. Hancock notes, in fact, that there was no similar predisposition to invocation of stereotypes when it was white teens who were accused of violent crimes. When thirty white teens "cornered sixteen-year-old Yusef Hawkins near a used-car lot and shot him dead . . . New York Newsday referred to those arrested as 'white young men.'" Ibid., 8.
40 Ibid., 5.
41 NBCSport.com. "Attorney: Race Possible Motive in Kobe Accusation: Suggestion Made Amid Dispute Over Notes by Rape Crisis Center," January 26, 2004, http://msnbc.com/id/4031624 (accessed July 25, 2005). At this point in the legal proceedings, Mackey is trying to gain access to notes taken by a rape crisis worker who sat in on a police interview with Bryant's accuser. Her comments come in response to those of a rape crisis attorney who said that "rape reports dropped in Florida after William Kennedy Smith was acquitted, a case in which his accuser's medical background was targeted by defense attorneys." This is the only article that I have found that presents this part of the context for Mackey's comments. The comments are significant, since they demonstrate that Mackey's invocation of the racist history associated with some rape allegations comes in response to an attempt on the part of the prosecution to invoke history for its own purposes. Mackey goes on to say that "I don't think we want to get dragged down into this history any more than we want to get into the history brought up by the rape crisis center," and her argument is *not*, therefore, that the charges need to be understood in historical context, but instead just the opposite: that the case should be understood in isolation, though the clear suggestion is that if the prosecution insists on bringing in historical narratives to help contextualize the charges, then it will not be alone. The vast majority of press accounts of Mackey's comments leave out not only the rape crisis attorney's comments, but also Mackey's claim that she would rather avoid lingering upon the history that she mentions. The result is that it becomes quite easy to portray Bryant's legal team as inappropriately attempting to deflect from the case at hand by putting American race relations on trial in Bryant's stead. A typical example is Jon Sarche's "Kobe Bryant's Defense Team Plays 'Race Card' in Open Court" (Associated Press, January 23, 2004). Sarche refers to "legal experts" as saying that "it was inevitable that race would become a factor in the high-profile case," and he quotes law professor, and former prosecutor Wendy Murphy, as saying "It's incendiary and it will probably stick. . . This is just the beginning, the subtle steps, of what will eventually be a very blatant race-card strategy." The claim that it had been clear that race "would become a factor" in the case is based, of course, upon the premise that race had not been an issue all along, and that it is only relevant now because of an opportunistic invocation of history on the part of the defense team.

42 Maddox, Alton. "Critical Thinking Takes a Hike in the Bryant Case." Editorial. *New York Amsterdam News*, August 26–September 1, 12.

43 Hilliard, L. "The Naked Truth: High Profile Black Stars Undergoing High Tech Lynching," *Mississippi Link*, December 4, 2003, 1.

44 Hobbs, C. "What Kobe Bryant's Rape Charge Dismissal Means," *Capital Outlook*, September 9, 2004. https://web.lexis-nexis.com/universe (accessed July 25, 2005).

45 There are numerous examples of stories seeking to explain support for Bryant by referencing histories of racism. See, for example, comments by Hare in *Ebony*. "Is it open season on black men?" *Ebony*, April, 2004. https://web.lexis-nexis.com/universe (accessed July 25, 2005).

46 Gooding-Williams, "Look: A Negro!"163.

47 Leonard, "Racing Sports," B4.

48 Leonard, "The Next M.J."

49 Pankratz, Howard, and Steve Lipsher. "Lawyers Battle Over T-Shirts, Media Leaks: Judge Wants Names of Seekers of Anti-Kobe Items," *Denver Post* (December 12, 2003), B-04.

50 "Bryant Attorneys Claim Prosecutors Biased Miscellany," *Daily Breeze* (Torrance, CA) December 9, 2003. http://infoweb.newsbank.com/iw-search/we/InfoWeb?p_product =AWNB&p_theme=aggregated5&p_action=doc&p_docid=1124084197D50B30&p_ docnum=9&p_queryname=4 (accessed July 25, 2005).

51 FoxNews. "Kobe T-Shirts Dog Eagle County Prosecutors." December 19, 2003. http://www.foxnews.com/story/0,2933,106247,00.html (accessed November 15, 2003).

52 Indications of a racist climate surrounding the trial do not stop with the Eagle County legal establishment. Leonard notes that white supremacist web sites contained "ubiquitous references to Kobe's large penis and castration" ("The Next M.J.," 294).

53 Rowe, McKay, and Miller, "Panic Sport," 258.

54 Hall, *Revolt Against Chivalry*, 151.

55 Ibid., 153.

56 Apel, *Imagery of Lynching*, 28.

57 Brennan, Charlie. "Bryant Lawyer Kicks Up Ruckus: Attorneys Attack, Defend Mackey's Tactics in Hearing," *Rocky Mountain News*, October 11, 2004: 4A.

58 Justice Bender, joined by Justices Martinez and Rice, dissenting opinion in The People of the State of Colorado v. Defendant: Kobe Bean Bryant, Case No. 04SA200, Supreme Court of Colorado, July 19, 2004.

59 "Bryant's Accuser's Ordeal Shows Limits of Rape Shield Laws," Editorial. *Chicago Sun-Times*, August 16, 2004.

60 Quoted in Reid, T.R. " Some Sexual Details on Accuser Allowed; Judge's Ruling Marks Victory For Bryant," *Washington Post*, July 24, 2004: A2.

61 See "Bryant's Accuser's Ordeal Shows Limits of Rape Shield Law," Editorial, *Chicago Sun-Times* 8/16/04, for an assessment of the ways that the Bryant case is likely to deter rape victims from coming forward.

62 Dahlia Lithwick, "The Shield that Failed," *New York Times*, August 8, 2004. http://www.nytimes.com/2004/08/08/opinion/08lithwick.html (accessed July 25, 2005).

63 Ireland, "Reform Rape Legislation," 189.

64 Tanford and Bocchino, "Rape Victim Shield Laws," 551.

65 Colo. Rev. Stat. § 18-3-407, 1977.

66 *Colorado v. McKenna*, 1978.

67 Recht, D. & Kornfeld, R. "Past Imperfect: Has Colorado's Rape Shield Law Been Violated By Attorney In Kobe Bryant Case? Clearly, No." *Rocky Mountain News*, October 18, 2003: 12C.

68 Bayliff, C. "Past Imperfect: Preposterous, Humiliating Questions About a Victim's Sexual History Are Often Irrelevant." *Rocky Mountain News*, October 18, 2003: 12C.

There are numerous similar examples. See Paulson, A., "Is the Rape-Shield Law Working?" *Christian Science Monitor*, March 25, 2004: 12, and Johnson, K, "Rape Shield Law Becomes Focal Point In Bryant's Case," *New York Times*, March 3, 2004, 14.

69 Henson, S. and Weinstein, H. "Courts Bar Disclosure By Media; Colorado Justices Rule, 4–3, That Documents Accidentally Released in the Bryant Case Cannot Be Published," *Los Angeles Times*, July 20, 2004: D1.

70 Breyer, "Associated Press."

71 Members of the news organizations had said that their interest wasn't so much that they wanted to publish information from the transcripts, but that it was important in principle to fight the prior restraint, so as to avoid the weakening of first amendment principles. The decision not to press ahead after Breyer's refusal to grant a stay must therefore be taken as an indication of concern that the principles they were fighting for could be set back with further action. After all, if the press never really wanted to publish the information from the transcripts, it could hardly have been fully appeased by being given the right to publish only versions of the transcripts that were edited, however lightly. In the end, the trial court's prior restraint was allowed to stand, even if there were hints that it might have been overturned if the process had continued. This outcome was, therefore, far from a clear free speech victory. As Lucy Dalgish, executive director of the Reporters' Committee for Freedom of the Press, explained, "Clearly the prior restraint on the seven news organizations still exists." Quoted in "Edited Kobe Bryant Transcript Released," Associated Press, July 30, 2004.

72 See, for example, Young, C. "Those Accused of Rape Have Rights, Too," *Boston Globe*, October 27, 2003, A13.

73 Luzadder, D. & Siemaszko, C. "Team Kobe Can Fight Privacy Law," *New York Daily News*, January 14, 2004, 20; Lipsher, S., "NBA Defense Tests Rape-Shield Law," *Denver Post*, January 22, 2004, D-4.

74 For example, one article notes that Colorado's rape shield law "says that a woman's prior sexual history is 'presumptively irrelevant.' It was enacted so that women who have been raped would be less reluctant to report the crime to police and take part in a trial. But Ruckriegle [the trial judge] said he will allow defense lawyers to probe any sexual encounters the accuser may have had in the two days before she met Bryant and in the hours after their encounter. Ruckriegle said such evidence is relevant to determine whether Bryant caused the woman's injuries." T.R. Reid, "Some Sexual Details On Accuser Allowed; Judge's Ruling Marks Victory For Bryant," *Washington Post*, July 24, 2004, A2. Because the article does not mention that the rape shield law contains exceptions to the presumption that a woman's sexual history is relevant, the use of "but" in this passage suggests that Ruckriegle is ruling against the use of the statute. And because the headline says that this is a "victory for Bryant," the article implies that Bryant's defense team had successfully challenged the statute.

75 For an example of the press addressing the links between the anti-rape movement and the rape shield laws see A. Markels and A.C. Marek, "A Seismic Shift in Sex-Case Law," *U.S. News and World Report*, October 13, 2003, 45. See also C. Young, "Those Accused of Rape Have Rights, Too," *Boston Globe*, October 27, 2003, A13.

76 The stakes of the case, and the idea that Bryant's defense team was in conflict not only with the accuser in the case, but with a broader anti-rape movement, are also highlighted in a series of articles that quote rape victim advocates and anti-rape organizations expressing concern about the repercussions of the case. See Harden, B., "Bryant Case Is Called A Setback; Recent Rape Victims Cite Confidentiality Breach, Advocates Say," *Washington Post*, September 3, 2004, A08.

77 E.O. Hutchinson, "Race Was Inevitable in Bryant's Case," *Alternet*, 2004. www. alternet.org/story/17723/ (accessed January 12, 2005).

78 Davis, *Women, Race, and Class*, 182. Critiques of the racism of the anti-rape movement, or of the movement's lack of attention to the concerns of women of color, have been centrally important for challenges to the essentialism within much of mainstream feminism. See Crenshaw, "Mapping the Margins" and Harris, "Race and Essentialism" for overviews of these challenges.

79 Reed, "MJ, Kobe, and Ota Benga." See also Alton Maddox, "Critical Thinking Takes a Hike in the Bryant Case." Editorial. *New York Amsterdam News*, August 26–September 1, 12; L. Hilliard, "The Naked Truth: High Profile Black Stars Undergoing High Tech Lynching," *Mississippi Link*, December 4, 2003, 1; C. Hobbs, "What Kobe Bryant's Rape Charge Dismissal Means," *Capital Outlook*, September 9, 2004. https://web.lexis-nexis.com/universe (accessed November 15, 2003). Also I. Reed, "CNN's Ku Klux Feminists Unleashed on Kobe," *Konch Magazine*, July 2, 2003. http://www.ishmael reedpub.com (accessed November 15, 2003).

80 Reed, "MJ, Kobe, and Ota Benga," 45.

81 Kaye, E. "Kobe's Second Act: It All Worked Out For Him: No Shaq, No Phil, No Prison. But Have We Worked Out Our Feelings About Him?" *Los Angeles Times*, October 31, 2004. https://web.lexis-nexis.com/universe (accessed November 15, 2004).

82 Braxton, G., "Torn over Kobe," *Los Angeles Times*, June 12, 2004, E1.

83 Rowe et al., "Panic Sport," 259.

84 Crenshaw, "Color-Blind Dramas,"145.

85 Ibid., 158.

86 McDonald, "Unnecessary Roughness," 128.

87 Crenshaw, "Color-Blind Dramas," 159.

88 Crenshaw, "Color-Blind Dramas," 157.

89 See http://www.harrisinteractive.com/NewsRoom/HarrisPolls/tabid/447/mid/1508/articleId/441/ctl/ReadCustom%20Default/Default.aspx (accessed November 19, 2010).

90 William Rhoden, "Sports of the Times: Its Savior is Kobe; Its Muse, the Dunk." *New York Times*, February 20, 2006. http://query.nytimes.com/gst/fullpage.html?res=9507E2DB113EF933A15751C0A9609C8B63&sec=&spon=&pagewanted=2 (accessed February 21, 2006).

91 See Peter Wallsten, "GOP Attack Ad Draws Heat for Racial Overtones," *Los Angeles Times*, October 24, 2006. http://articles.latimes.com/2006/oct/24/nation/na-ford24 (accessed October 25, 2006). The advertisement included footage of a white woman saying that she'd met Representative Ford at a Playboy party, then winking and asking the candidate to "call me." The ad is available online at http://www.youtube.com/watch?v=1smE1Es-8QA (accessed October 25, 2006).

92 The connection to the World War I-era propaganda poster was first noted by K.R. Kaufman on the "Democratic Underground" website. Rogers Canenhead notes that the poster ("Destroy this Mad Brute," H.R. Hopps, 1917) is thought to have been the inspiration for "King Kong," and he points out a number of similarities between the poster and the Leibovitz photo: "Look at the images side by side and you'll see how many different ways they match: The positions of James and Bundchen, the way he holds his mouth, the color of his clothes, the color of her dress, the curls of her hair, the placement of her feet inside his and his arm around her waist, the basketball in the club hand, and his hunched-over posture." Rogers Canenhead, "Annie Leibovitz Monkeys Around with LeBron James," May 28, 2008. http://watchingthewatchers.org/news/1378/annie-leibovitz-monkeys-around-lebron (accessed June 10, 2008).

93 Irwin-Zarecka, *Frames of Remembrance*, 4.

94 Ibid.

95 Translated by Said, *Orientalism*, 25.

3 Framing Police Corruption

1 See Seth Mydans, "Officer Says Beaten Man Resisted," *New York Times*, March 31, 1991, for early coverage of the King beating. Sergeant Stacey Koon testified during trial that as he ordered officer Laurence Powell to strike King, his intent was that Powell should "cripple" King and "break [King's] bones." U.S. 9th Circuit Court of Appeals, Allen v. City of Los Angeles, No. 95-55475v. D.C. Filed August 7, 1996.

2 Seth Mydans, "Rodney King is Awarded $3.8 Million," *New York Times*, April 20, 1994. http://www.nytimes.com/1994/04/20/us/rodney-king-is-awarded-3.8-million.html (accessed August 12, 2008).

3 Police investigators had been interested in Perez since late in 1997, when a friend of his robbed a bank in South Central, Los Angeles. Perez knew officer David Mack from having worked together in the Rampart district. Mack's robbery of a Bank of America branch netted more than seven hundred thousand dollars. Investigators learned that Mack was celebrating two days later, in Las Vegas, with Rafael Perez. Mack was eventually convicted of the robbery and sentenced to fourteen years in prison. Perez was a suspect in the robbery, as investigators thought that he might have been the getaway driver, but no charges were ever filed against him for this crime. Lou Cannon, "One Bad Cop," *New York Times*, October 1, 2000, Section 6, 32.

4 Rice et al., *Rampart Reconsidered*, 1.

5 Chemerinsky, "An Independent Analysis," 3.

6 One reason that the King beating is better known than the Ovando shooting has to do with the racial backgrounds of the key figures in each case. The King case was literally "black and white," as King was an African American man beaten by white police officers. It was, therefore, easy to represent this as a story about racist police brutality, especially once investigators discovered that officer Powell had referred to a domestic disturbance involving African Americans as "right out of Gorillas in the Mist." (Quoted in Nichols, *Blurred Boundaries*, 153). In contrast, Rafael Perez was Puerto Rican and Nino Durden was black, while Javier Ovando was a Honduran immigrant. Since racism is so often figured as a matter of individual prejudices, it would have been difficult for the mass media to present Ovando as a victim of racism, given that he and one of his assailants were both Latino, while the other assailant was African American. The fact that Ovando's race and ethnicity establishes him as a *typical* Rampart victim is important in establishing the systemic nature of the scandal, but never became a major focus of most news accounts. Still, the bulk of the early coverage of the King beating did not focus on the racist aspects of the brutality, so the races of the officers involved in the two cases do not seem to have been the key factor in determining the amount of coverage each case received.

7 Lou Cannon, quoted in Lori Leibovich, "Rethinking Rodney King," *Salon*, March 13, 1998. http://www.salon.com/news/1998/03/13news.html (accessed August 12, 2008).

8 One partial exception may be a police brutality video that surfaced in the Spring of 2010 that has started to act as a rallying point for anti-racist activists in the Pacific Northwest, and that may eventually garner significant media attention. The video, taken on April 17, 2010, by a freelance videographer named Jud Morris, captures Seattle police stomping on a Latino man's head while one officer threatens to "beat the fucking Mexican piss out of you, homey." Another officer kicks the man's kneecap against the pavement. The officers were responding to a report about an alleged robbery, and let the victim go once they determined he was not involved in the crime. See Dominic Holden, " Did Q-13 Fox Suppress Police Brutality Video?" *The Stranger*, May 7, 2010. http://slog.thestranger.com/slog/archives/2010/05/07/did-q-13-fox-try-to-quash-police-brutality-footage (accessed July 1, 2010).

9 Mike Harvey. "YouTube video fuels US riots over killing of Oscar Grant," *Times Online* (London), January 9, 2009. http://www.timesonline.co.uk/tol/news/world/us_and_americas/article5480713.ece (accessed July 1, 2009).

10 Jesse McKinley. January 8, 2009. "In California, Protests After Man Dies at Hands of Transit Police," *New York Times*. http://www.nytimes.com/2009/01/09/us/09oakland.html?fta=y (accessed July 1, 2009). Mehserle was charged with murder on January 14, 2009, two weeks after the shooting, and after Oakland authorities had allowed him to leave the state. The trial was moved to Los Angeles, and immediately caused a new controversy, as there were no black jury members or alternates. See Julianne Hing, "No Black Jurors In Oscar Grant Trial, But It Might Not Matter Anyway," *Racewire: The Colorlines Blog*, June 9, 2010. http://www.racewire.org/archives/2010/06/no_black_jurors_in_oscar_grant_trial_but_it_might_not_matter_anyway.html (accessed July 1, 2010). In January, 2010, the Bay Area Rapid Transit board agreed to pay $1.5 million to the mother of Oscar Grant's daughter to settle a civil suit filed against the agency. Michelle Quin. January 28, 2010. "BART to Pay $1.5 Million in Grant Case," *New York Times*. http://bayarea.blogs.nytimes.com/2010/01/28/sampler-bart-to-pay-15-million-in-oscar-grant-case-and-mount-reagan-instead-of-mount-diablo/ (accessed July 1, 2010). Mehserle, who claimed that the killing was accidental and that he had intended to shoot Grant with his taser rather than his gun, was convicted of involuntary manslaughter in the case on July 8, 2010, avoiding conviction on more serious murder charges. "Former BART Officer Convicted of Involuntary Manslaughter," *Los Angeles Times*, July 8, 2010. http://www.latimes.com/news/local/la-me-bart-verdict-20100709,0,4753049.story (accessed July 9, 2010). In November, 2010, the presiding judge in the case determined that the jury had erred in adding enhanced gun penalties in their verdict. The enhanced penalties could have resulted in a fourteen year prison term. Instead, Mehserle was sentenced to only two years in jail. With credit for time served, and with reduced prison time due to California prison overcrowding, Mehserle was expected to serve only an additional seven months. The sentencing sparked a new round of protests, some of which involved some degree of violence and were labelled riots by much of the media. See Chris Richardson, "Mehserle Verdict: Johannes Mehserle Sentencing Stuns Oscar Grant Supporters, Sparks Riots in Oakland," *Christian Science Monitor*, November 5, 2010. http://www.csmonitor.com/USA/Justice/2010/1105/Mehserle-verdict-Johannes-Mehserle-sentencing-stuns-Oscar-Grant-supporters-sparks-riots-in-Oakland (accessed November 19, 2010). Shortly after the sentencing was announced, the Justice Department, which had been pressed to open an investigation into the handling of the case and to re-try Mehserle on federal civil rights charges, announced that it had been evaluating the prosecution of the case, and would determine "whether further action is appropriate." Julianne Hing, "DOJ Prepared to Examine Oscar Grant Case," *Colorlines*, November 8, 2010. http://colorlines.com/archives/2010/11/doj_prepared_to_examine_oscar_grants_killing_and_subsequent_prosecution.html (accessed November 19, 2010).

11 This is Benedict Anderson's term. Anderson, *Imagined Communities*.

12 Baudrillard, "Simulacra and Simulations," 173.

13 Key critical works on the "prison industrial complex" include Lotke, "The Prison-Industrial Complex," Davis "Race and Criminalization," Schlosser "The Prison Industrial Complex," and Gilmore, *Golden Gulag*.

14 Prison Policy Initiative, "The Prison Index: Taking the Pulse of the Crime Control Industry," 2003. http://www.prisonpolicy.org/prisonindex/prisoners.html (accessed August 12, 2008). The percentage of African American prisoners has actually declined over the last decade. In the 1990s, African Americans made up over 50 percent of the prison population. See Cole, *No Equal Justice*, 4.

15 Department of Justice, "Growth in Prison."

16 Bonczar and Beck, "Lifetime Likelihood," 1.

17 Cited in Giroux and Giroux, "On Seeing and Not Seeing Race," 174.

18 Amnesty International, "United States of America."

19 Cole, *No Equal Justice*, 142.

20 Christopher Wren, "Less Disparity Urged in Cocaine Sentencing," *New York Times*, November 20, 1996. http://www.nytimes.com/1996/11/20/us/less disparity urged in cocaine sentencing.html?pagewanted=1 (accessed August 12, 2008).

21 "Cocaine Sentencing Bill Advances," *New York Times*, March 17, 2010. http://www. nytimes.com/2010/03/18/us/18brfs-COCAINESENTE_BRF.html (accessed March 18, 2010).

22 This is not to say that it is only recently that racism within the criminal justice system has begun to affect Latinos. Mary Romero notes that Latino youth have been "constructed as inherently criminal" since World War II, and that, aside from gang profiling, Latinos have been regularly targeted for political activity and scapegoated for all sorts of social problems. She writes that state violence against Latino youth was publicly acknowledged during the Chicano movement, when the ACLU filed "174 complaints of serious police brutality against Chicanos" over a two year period. In 1970, "the U.S. Commission on Civil Rights report concluded: 'Mexican American citizens are subject to unduly harsh treatment by law enforcement officers . . . they are often arrested on insufficient grounds, receive physical and verbal abuse, and penalties which are disproportionately severe.'" "State Violence," 1094.

23 Hayden, "LAPD."

24 Ibid.

25 Romero, "State Violence," 449.

26 Arnold, "Racial Profiling," 114.

27 Ibid., 115.

28 Even when local law enforcement agencies are expressly prohibited from engaging with immigration enforcement, there is no guarantee that such policies will be followed. The LAPD prohibits officers from contacting the INS unless an undocumented immigrant is arrested for "multiple misdemeanor offenses, a high grade misdemeanor, a felony offense, or has previously been arrested for a similar offense," but according to the American Civil Liberties Union, this policy is regularly violated. Cafferty and Engstrom, *Hispanics in the United States*, 285. In April, 2010, Arizona passed SB 1070, a new law with a host of draconian anti-immigration measures, that requires police officers who have "reasonable suspicion" that someone is an undocumented immigrant to verify the person's immigration status. Despite protestations to the contrary from the bill's authors and sponsors, the bill appears certain to ensure heightened levels of racial profiling by local police organizations. Immediately after passage of the legislation, the ACLU, the Mexican American Legal Defense and Educational Fund and the National Immigration Law Center announced plans to challenge the measure on the theory that the law interferes with federal immigration enforcement responsibilities. See Teresa Watanabe and Anna Gorman, "Arizona Immigration Fight to Move to the Courtroom," *Los Angeles Times*, April 29, 2010. http://www.latimes.com/news/ local/la-me-arizona-law-20100429,0,7792968.story (accessed April 30, 2010). Perhaps the most interesting lawsuit was filed by Martin Escobar, a Tucson police officer, who argues that the law would compel him to engage in racial profiling. See Randal Archibold and Ana Contreras, "First Legal Challenges to New Arizona Law," *New York Times*, April 30, 2010, A15. Within days of passing the legislation, the Arizona legislature modified the law to require that the police are only required to verify immigration status of people that they stop, detain, or arrest, and not of anyone that they suspect is an undocumented immigrant. The modified law also explicitly bars the police from using race as a factor in determining whether to verify immigration status, though critics argue that if the bill is allowed to be enforced, it will still encourage racial profiling. See Nicholas Riccardi, "Arizona Lawmakers Modify Immigration Law," *Los*

Angeles Times, April 30, 2010. http://www.latimes.com/news/nationworld/nation/la-na-arizona-immigration-20100501,0,2712336.story (accessed April 30, 2010). In July, 2010, a federal judge blocked the most controversial aspects of the law from going into effect. As of this writing, appeals are pending. Randal Archibold, "Judge Blocks Arizona's Immigration Law," *New York Times*, July 28, 2010. http://www.nytimes.com/2010/07/29/us/29arizona.html (accessed July 29, 2010).

29 Lopez and Light, "A Rising Share."

30 Davis, "Race and Criminalization," 271.

31 Ibid.

32 Russell, *The Color of Crime*, 3.

33 The quote is from Perez's statement at the sentencing hearing for his cocaine theft. Quoted in Scott Glover and Matt Lait, "A Tearful Perez Gets 5 Years," *Los Angeles Times*, February 26, 2000. http://articles.latimes.com/2000/feb/26/news/mn-2806 (accessed August 12, 2008).

34 Arendt, *Eichmann in Jerusalem*, 130.

35 Ibid., 139.

36 For a related take on the production of monstrosity in the news, in this case involving coverage of women as violent criminals, see Halkias, "From Social Butterfly."

37 "The Rampart Scandal; Genesis of a Scandal," *Los Angeles Times*, April 25, 2000, 18.

38 For the most comprehensive critique of the LAPD's Board of Inquiry report on the rampart scandal, see Chemerinsky, "An Independent Analysis."

39 Barnhart, "Risk Indicators." The *Los Angeles Times* notes that Rampart officers "systematically circumvented city policy by colluding with a little-known unit of the immigration and naturalization service to deport at least 160 Latino immigrants and deny others citizenship." "The Rampart Scandal; Genesis of a Scandal," *Los Angeles Times*, 25 April, 2000, 18.

40 Chemerinsky, "The Rampart Scandal and the Criminal Justice System," 122.

41 Ibid., 123.

42 Rice et al., *Rampart Reconsidered*, 2.

43 Ibid., 3.

44 Quoted in Chemerinsky, 2000, 125.

45 Chemerinsky, "The Rampart Scandal and the Criminal Justice System," 125.

46 Rice et al., *Rampart Reconsidered*, 51.

47 Ibid.

48 Refusing to spend limited resources following up on Perez's allegations was reasonable to a degree, since there was ample reason to doubt his testimony.

49 Rice et al., *Rampart Reconsidered*, 58.

50 Quoted in Kirk, 2001. District attorney Garcetti echoed this point when noting that

> You simply cannot make successful police corruption cases without police officers working with you . . . the ones that were out there, who we think could have really helped us, could not, or would not, step forward, because they were afraid—fearful of administrative retribution within their own department.

Garcetti argued that officers are in effect told "Fine, step forward. But you will be fired because you did not report it when you should have."(Kirk, 2001.)

51 Rice et al., *Rampart Reconsidered*, 7.

52 Kirk, *Frontline: LAPD Blues*.

53 Perez testified that "everyone" in CRASH kept a drop gun. Peter Boyer, "Bad Cops." *New Yorker*, May 21, 2001. Years later, the Blue Ribbon Rampart Review panel noted that "recent discoveries of replica guns, such as those used by CRASH offenders to frame suspects, suggest that planting evidence is not a thing of the past," adding that a 2006 sting "revealed that such tactics still occur even in the reformed Rampart Division." Rice et al., *Rampart Reconsidered*, 3.

54 Chemerinsky, "The Role of Prosecutors," 2.
55 Rice et al., *Rampart Reconsidered*, 49.
56 Ibid., 3.
57 Lawrence, *The Politics of Force*, 136.
58 Ibid.
59 Ibid., 15.
60 Ibid., 7.
61 Ibid., 98–107.
62 Ibid., 15.
63 Ibid., 32.
64 My analysis of Rampart-related news coverage is based on a content analysis of print journalism. I used a Lexis/Nexis search of "major U.S. and world publications" to examine every article about the scandal, and every article that referenced the scandal, from September 1999 (when the shooting and framing of Javier Ovando came to light) to May 2010 (nearly a year after the federal consent decree was lifted). While there were hundreds of articles, the majority were fairly thin, and since I wanted to address substantial coverage, my analysis centered on articles that were at least 250 words. Since this is a book about media spectacles, it might seem odd that I am focusing on print journalism rather than television or internet news, but one of my contentions is that the Rampart scandal lacked the visual imagery that would elevate it to the level of spectacle until it was appropriated in fictionalized form by popular culture. Consequently, the case was not covered nearly as extensively by television news as it was in the printed press. My decision to focus on print rather than television journalism also follows Lawrence, who notes that newspaper reporters rely on the "police beat" to a much greater extent than do television reporters (*The Politics of Force*, 11). This means that analysis of print journalism can provide much clearer indications of how police sources attempt to frame cases of misconduct, and of when coverage veers from standard journalistic conventions. Television news also generally fails to address public policy issues, including stories of police misconduct, with any depth, so "Analyzing newspaper coverage captures a greater range of news coverage, from daily crime-beat reporting to serious, thematic coverage of policing problems" (11). Just as important, print journalism still plays a central role in setting the agenda for television news, so the importance of major newspapers and, I would add, news magazines "extends beyond their own readership to the content of other news media" (11).
65 "The Rampart Scandal; Genesis of a Scandal," *Los Angeles Times*, April 25, 2000, 18.
66 Interestingly, "bad apple" explanations for Rampart did start to emerge more frequently in the later years of the scandal. The key events legitimizing this kind of explanation seem to have been the decision by a trial court to throw out the convictions of three officers tried for Rampart-related crimes, along with a 2006 civil jury's decision to award the officers a total of $15 million for false arrest and malicious prosecution. This decision was upheld by the 9th Circuit Court of Appeals in July, 2008. For a discussion of this case, see Rice et al., *Rampart Reconsidered*. Some journalists and commentators have argued that the problems in the prosecutions of these three officers provide evidence that the entire scandal was overblown, and that a gullible press and legal system was all too willing to take a corrupt cop's words at face value. These claims neglect the fact that much of Perez's testimony was corroborated, and that investigations revealed many other Rampart-related problems. I would suggest, though, that the emergence of a "bad apple" explanation for Rampart is conditional above all upon a collective amnesia about aspects of the scandal that never received much attention. As I argue in my discussion of filmic and televisual representations of Rampart, a collective memory of the systemic nature of the scandal was never firmly established in popular culture.
67 Robert Lopez and Rich Connell, "Targets of Gang Injunctions Were Named by Officers in Police Probe," *Los Angeles Times*, September 23, 1999, 19.

68 Nita Lelyveld, "LAPD Feels Heavy Toll of Corruption Scandal Fallout: Lost Cases. Disgraced Officers. Hostility. Lawsuits," *Philadelphia Inquirer*, April 25, 2000, A1.

69 Andrew Murr and Ana Figueroa, "L.A.'s Dirty War on Gangs." *Newsweek*, October 11, 1999, 72.

70 Ibid.

71 Lawrence, *The Politics of Force*, 15.

72 Jane Fritsch, "Squads That Tripped Up Walking the Bad Walk," *New York Times*, March 5, 2000, Section 4, 6.

73 William Booth, "LAPD Admits Poor Management; Lax Supervision, Culture of Mediocrity Blamed for Police Corruption." *Los Angeles Times*, March 2, 2000, A3.

74 The city council and mayor agreed to the consent decree in November, 2000, though it was not formally approved by the federal district court until June, 2001. See *Consent Decree Overview*, Los Angeles Police Department, 2001. http://www.lapdonline. org/search_results/content_basic_view/928 (accessed May 12, 2010).

75 Steve Yagman, "Perspective on Rampart Scandal," *Los Angeles Times*, January 25, 2000, 7. Yagman sums up the stakes of the public defender's inaction thus: "perhaps thousands of potentially wrongly convicted felons, serving long terms in state prisons, don't know their cases might be tainted. If Judge [the public defender] won't tell them, who will?"

76 Steve Lopez, "Shifting the Blame in Rampart Scandal," *Los Angeles Times*, November 21, 2001, B1.

77 Erwin Chemerinsky, "To Prevent a Repeat of Rampart, Fix More than the LAPD," *Los Angeles Times*, April 25, 2003.

78 Connie Rice, "The Story of LAPD Reform is Never-Ending," *Los Angeles Times*, January 22, 2001, B7.

79 Daniel Wood, "Undoing the Wrongs of L.A.'s Rogue Police." *Christian Science Monitor*, May 23, 2000, 1.

80 Samuel Pillsbury, "Perspective on Justice: Even the Innocent Can be Coerced into Pleading Guilty," *Los Angeles Times*, November 28, 1999, 5.

81 Lou Cannon, "One Bad Cop,"*New York Times*, October 1, 2000, Section 6, 32.

82 Tamar Toister, "Rampart Hasn't Changed How Criminal Courts Do Business," *Los Angeles Times*, September 21, 2000.

83 Andrew Gumbel, "How the LAPD's Gangbusting Division Became a Death Squad," *The Independent* (London), February 11, 2000, 16. For more details about the shooting of Juan Saldana, see Lou Cannon, "One Bad Cop," *New York Times*, October 1, 2000, Section 6, 32.

84 David Hirst, "LA Confidential," *The Australian*, March 6, 2000.

85 Tim Cornwell, "Stench of Corruption Chokes City of Angels," *The Scotsman*, February 11, 2000.

86 Scott Glover and Matt Lait, "LAPD Misconduct Cases Rarely Resulted in Charges," *Los Angeles Times*. October 22, 2000. Apparently, this "immunity" is not in place for other police departments. A recent *New York Times* article noted that "From 1992 to 2008, nearly 2,000 New York Police Department officers were arrested, according to the department's own annual reports of the Internal Affairs Bureau, an average of 119 a year." The article notes that officers were investigated for crimes involving

> drugs, theft or crimes like fraud, bribery or sex offenses, on and off the job. . . . Officers rob banks. They collude with drug dealers. They pilfer credit cards from prisoners to buy groceries, and they take payoffs from street peddlers as protection money. Sex is often at the center of their sins.
> (Al Baker and Jo Craven McGinty, "N.Y.P.D. Confidential,"
> *New York Times*, March 26, 2010.)

87 Duncan Campbell, "Dirty Cops 'Rob' LA of $125 million," *The Observer*, February 27, 2000, 22.

88 Earl Ofari Hutchinson, "A Kinder, Gentler LAPD?" *Los Angeles Times*, August, 12, 2008.

89 Mark Rosenbaum and Peter Bibring, "LAPD – It's Not Quite Reformed," *Los Angeles Times*. June 4, 2009, A 27.

90 Tom Hayden, "Chief Concerns," *Los Angeles Times*, August 13, 2009, A. 25.

91 Joel Rubin, "U.S. Ends Oversight of L.A. Police," *Los Angeles Times*, July 18, 2009, A1.

92 Elizabeth Armet, "Poll Analysis: Rampart Scandal Affecting the State of the City," *Los Angeles Times*, April 9, 2000.

93 Patt Morrison, "Rampart Scandal Colors Jury Deliberations," *Los Angeles Times*, December 10, 1999, 1.

94 Nita Lelyveld, "LAPD Feels Heavy Toll of Corruption Scandal Fallout: Lost Cases. Disgraced Officers. Hostility. Lawsuits," *Philadelphia Inquirer*, April 25, 2000, A1.

95 Cited in ibid.

96 Public disapproval of the LAPD was still quite strong when the *Los Angeles Times* conducted a survey in 2005, but had taken a dramatic turn by the time their next poll (occasioned by the lifting of the consent decree) was conducted in June, 2009. By this time, nearly 80 percent of respondents, including 68 percent of black respondents, approved of LAPD performance. Joel Rubin, "Approval of LAPD Spans Race, Ethnicity," *Los Angeles Times*, June 22, 2009, A1.

97 Elizabeth Armet, "Poll Analysis: Rampart Scandal Affecting the State of the City," *Los Angeles Times*, April 9, 2000.

98 Lawrence, *The Politics of Force*, 6.

99 Of course, none of these terms are unproblematic, and none can capture the complexity of the aftermath of the first trial of the officers who beat Rodney King. "Riots" suggests chaos and unthinking violence. While there were surely some people who acted brutally, the term does not explain the actions of people who stole milk or diapers to meet the needs of their families during blackout conditions. The term also divorces anger from any kind of legitimate grievance, about the verdict itself, about police brutality more broadly, or about underlying social conditions. In doing so, use of the term can all too easily play into long histories of representing people of color as unthinking in their violence and rage. "Uprising" and "rebellion," on the other hand, imply that participants' actions were sparked by oppressive social conditions, and were organized and clearly targeted. It's true that some of the people who responded to the verdict did so in ways clearly intended to make a political point, but neither of these terms can explain the motivations or actions of most of the people that have been labeled "rioters" by much of the mass media. Acknowledging that each of these terms is problematic does not mean that they must be rejected, but that they need to be used advisedly, with knowledge of their connotations and with attention to relevant context.

100 Javier Ovando was shot in 1996, and we might mark July, 2009, when the federal consent decree was lifted, as the end of the scandal.

101 Lawrence, *The Politics of Force*, 64.

102 Ibid., 93.

103 Ibid., 135.

104 Ibid., 136.

105 Ibid., 135.

106 One of the most telling indications that systemic critiques of police misconduct may have become the norm is the fact that Rampart has become a standard reference point in stories about other cases of police brutality and corruption, since this means that these cases are not being considered as isolated events. The Rampart case is mentioned in virtually every substantial story about police misconduct in Los Angeles, but perhaps more interesting is the fact that it has also become a common reference point for police

misconduct cases in other areas. For example, an article about an Oakland, California officer who alleged that corruption and brutality were rife in his department refers to the case as "almost a replica of the scandal which gripped the Los Angeles Police Department this year when three officers from the inner-city Rampart Division were found guilty of planting evidence and filing fake crime reports against gang members." Darrell Giles, "Police Face Corruption Charges," *Sunday Telegraph* (Sydney, Australia), December 17, 2000, 93. Similarly, when a massive police scandal erupted in Toronto, and the Chief of Police tried to blame the problems on a few "bad apples" the *Toronto Star* brought in Erwin Chemerinsky saying that this was precisely the strategy used by the Chief of Police to explain away misconduct in the Rampart case. Maureen Murray, "Police Scandals Often More than 'Bad Apples'," *Toronto Star*, May 8, 2004, A1. One indication that the Rampart scandal may be changing the ways that police misconduct cases are reported on is that, throughout the duration of the scandal, the press regularly turned to prominent critics of, and experts on, the scandal in order to help explain other examples of brutality and corruption. An article about an officer who pushed a suspect into a squad car and then sprayed him in the face with pepper spray before shutting the door, for example, noted that Constance Rice, who is cited as "chairwoman of the Police Commission's Blue Ribbon Rampart Review Panel," was concerned about the case and had referred it to the LAPD for investigation. Patrick McGreevy and Richard Winton, "LAPD Officials 'Livid' Over New Arrest Videotape," *Los Angeles Times*, November 14, 2006.

4 Reel Bad Cops

1 Debord, *The Society of the Spectacle*, para 4.
2 The Chicago police torture scandal is one of the most startling police scandals in modern U.S. history. From 1972–1991 at least 135 African American men, women, and boys were subjected to forms of torture including "electric shock to the ears and genitalia, mock executions, suffocation, and burning." See "Human Rights At Home: The Chicago Police Torture Archive," http://humanrights.uchicago.edu.chicagotorture (accessed May 12, 2010). In May, 2010, the city of Chicago agreed to a $16.5 million settlement in a class action lawsuit alleging that an "institutionalized system of police torture" existed in the department. "Illinois: Chicago Reaches Deal in Lawsuit Claiming Police Abuse," *New York Times*, May 12, 2010. http://www.nytimes.com/2010/05/13/us/13brfs-CHICAGOREACH_BRF.html (accessed May 12, 2010). In June, 2010, John Burge, the former commander who is accused of having presided over and participated in the torture, was convicted of perjury and obstruction of justice for lying about the case. He was not tried for the torture itself, since the statute of limitations had passed for any possible charges. A lawyer representing men who reported being abused under Burge's leadership claims that twenty people who were convicted on the basis of coerced confessions remain in prison. Monica Davey and Emma Fitzsimmons, "Officer Accused of Torture is Guilty of Perjury," *New York Times*, June 28, 2010. http://www.nytimes.com/2010/06/29/us/29burge.html (accessed June 28, 2010). The Philadelphia scandal involved officers who framed suspects, conducted illegal searches, regularly lied under oath, and were accused of a "historic pattern of police abuse" targeted against African Americans and Latinos. Michael Janofsky, "Philadelphia Police Scandal Results In a Plan for a Suit Claiming Racism," *New York Times*, December 12, 1995. http://www.nytimes.com/1995/12/12/us/philadelphia-police-scandal-results-in-a-plan-for-a-suit-claimingracism.html (accessed August 12, 2008). The New Orleans case is particularly interesting not only because of the depth of the corruption and the sheer number of people unjustly killed by police officers, but also because it is a rare case in which a city's mayor actually *requested* a consent decree with the federal government. See "A New Chance in New Orleans," *New York Times*,

May 19, 2010, A24. These are just a few of the notable recent scandals. Judith Grant has argued that police "scandals" are so common that "what has heretofore been termed 'scandalous' behavior may in fact be part and parcel of the very structure of police practices in America." "Assault Under Color," 387.

3 Bandes and Beermann, "Lawyering Up," 1.

4 Quoted in Mezey, "Law as Culture,"52.

5 Ibid.

6 A recent high-profile attempt to weaken the *Miranda* decision came in May, 2010, as Attorney General Eric Holder advocated for an exception to the warnings for terrorism suspects. Charlie Savage, "Holder Backs a *Miranda* Limit for Terror Suspects," *New York Times*, May 9, 2010. http://www.nytimes.com/2010/05/10/us/politics/10holder. html (accessed May 9, 2010). In June, 2010, the Supreme Court ruled, in a 5–4 decision, that criminal suspects must explicitly invoke their *Miranda* rights in order to exercise them. Remaining silent for hours after having been read the *Miranda* warnings can no longer be taken as evidence that a suspect has invoked the right to remain silent, and anything that a suspect says while in custody after having been read the warnings can now be taken as an indication that the suspect has agreed to waive their right to silence. In her dissent, Justice Sotomayor noted that the decision "turns *Miranda* upside down" and "bodes poorly for the fundamental principles that *Miranda* protects." Quoted in Adam Liptak, "Mere Silence Doesn't Invoke *Miranda*, Justices Say," *New York Times*, June 1, 2010. http://www.nytimes.com/2010/06/02/us/02scotus.html?ref=miranda_ warnings (accessed June 1, 2010).

7 Grant, "Assault Under Color," 389.

8 Torres, *Black, White, and in Color*, 71.

9 Grant, "Assault Under Color," 389.

10 Ibid.

11 Ibid.

12 Ibid. The examples that Grant provides of this type of film include *Cop Land* (James Mangold, 1997), *The Negotiator* (F. Gary Gray, 1998), and *Robocop* (Paul Verhoeven, 1987).

13 This is how Ray Pratt summarizes the conclusion that the protagonist of *The Big Heat* has come to by the film's conclusion. *Projecting Paranoia*, 198.

14 Henry Weinstein, "Rampart Probe May Now Affect Over 3,000 Cases," *Los Angeles Times*, December 15, 1999, 1.

15 Todd S. Purdum, "Los Angeles Police Scandal May Soil Hundreds of Cases," *New York Times*, December 16, 1999, A16.

16 District Attorney Steve Cooley, quoted in Matt Lait and Scott Glover, "The Rampart Scandal: LAPD Probe Fades Into Oblivion," *Los Angeles Times*, August 11, 2003, A.1.

17 Samuel Pillsbury, "Perspective on Justice: Even the Innocent Can be Coerced into Pleading Guilty," *Los Angeles Times*, November 28, 1999, 5.

18 Goldman, *The Crucial Decade*, 198.

19 Halberstam, *The Fifties*, 191.

20 Goldman, *The Crucial Decade*, 194.

21 Ibid., 195.

22 Quoted in Halberstam, *The Fifties*, 192.

23 Pratt, *Projecting Paranoia*, 197.

24 Pratt notes that the Kefauver hearings led to the "Confidential" series of films that focused on supposedly corrupt cities, including *Kansas City Confidential* and *New York Confidential*. These films served "as early models for *L.A. Confidential*." *Projecting Paranoia*, 197.

25 See the Rockstar games homepage for information about the game: http://www.rock stargames.com/sanandreas/ (accessed August 12, 2008).

26 Just before completing the manuscript for this book, *Variety* announced that production was to begin in the summer of 2010 on a film called "Rampart," based on a James Ellroy screenplay about the scandal, starring Ice Cube, Woody Harrelson, and Ben Foster. The film was to be directed by Oren Moverman. Dave McNary, "'Rampart' Cops a Trio: Cube, Harrelson, Foster to Star in Police Drama." *Variety*, April 28, 2010. http://www.variety.com/article/VR1118018420.html?categoryid=1236&cs=1 (accessed May 5, 2010). Moverman received an academy award nomination for *The Messenger* (2010) for best writing, while Harrelson was nominated for best supporting actor for the same film. Given the fame of the director and cast, this is likely to be one of the highest profile fictionalized versions of the scandal. At the time of this writing, very little information about the film was available, but earlier comments from James Ellroy about the scandal suggest that the film is likely to take a "bad apple" approach. In an interview with the *National Review Online* in 2005, Ellroy claimed that

> Rampart is another of these misperceived criminal conspiracies. It's really the story of a handful of rogue, criminal cops who ratted out a wider number of untainted cops to save their own skins. And the entire event blew out of proportion into a media event that most people took to represent large-scale endemic corruption in the LAPD. In reality it wasn't that. Cops are afraid to do their jobs now. There are nuisance suits filed routinely on officers who bruise the pinkies of violent street suspects, and they all have to be dealt with through the civilian complaint process. This wastes time and diverts energy from the real business of police work.
> (See Jack Dunphy, "Ellroy Confidential: A conversation with the Demon Dog of American letters," *National Review Online*, November 15, 2005. http://old.nationreview.com/dunphy/dunphy200511150827.asp (accessed June 3, 2010).)

Ellroy and David Ayer (the screenwriter for *Training Day*) have been at the center of a mini industry of Rampart-inspired films. Ellroy was one of the screen writers for *Street Kings*, a 2008 corruption film starring Keanu Reeves and Forrest Whittaker and directed by Ayer. The film had a somewhat bigger budget than the intended-for-DVD Rampart-related films, but had limited marketing and never received much critical attention or audience support. Ayer and Ellroy had teamed up earlier to write the screenplay for Ron Shelton's *Dark Blue* (2002), which was one of the intended-for-DVD Rampart-related films. Plans for an earlier film titled *Rampart Scandal*, to be written and directed by Sylvester Stallone, were dropped when Stallone became concerned about potential lawsuits. See "Stallone's Biggie/2Pac Movie On Hold," *HHNLive.com* December 11, 2006. http://hnnlive.com/news/more/700 (accessed June 3, 2010).

27 Paul Haggis and Matt Dillon also received Academy award nominations for the film, for best director and best supporting actor, respectively.

28 David Ayer, "A Story From the Streets," *Los Angeles Times*, September 9, 2001. http://articles.latimes.com/2001/sep/09/entertainment/ca-43657/2 (accessed August 12, 2008). Ayer elaborated on this position to another reporter, noting that "the scandal really helped me sell the script, because it made it topical." Quoted in Rene Rodriguez, "Training Day a New Take on the Nasty Cop," *Ottawa Citizen*, October 4, 2001, G10.

29 Quoted in John Horn, "'Day' of Reckoning," *Newsweek*, October 4, 2001.

30 http://www.imdb.com/title/tt0139654/ (accessed August 12, 2008).

31 What appears to be a genuine 1999 version of the script, revised just as the Rampart scandal was starting to make headlines, can be found online at http://sfy.ru/sfy. html?script=training_day (accessed August 12, 2008). It is quite close to the film that was shot, but key plot points, and apparent references to the Rampart scandal that I discuss below, do not yet appear here. One such apparent acknowledgement of the scandal that I do not address in the body of this chapter comes about halfway through the film, when Jake Hoyt expresses his concerns about having been involved in an illegal

search and seizure with Alonso Harris by saying that "With the scandals and whatnot it is open season on misconduct. They will nail us to the wall."

32 The fact that Rafael Perez and Alonso Harris both have problems stemming from trips to Las Vegas has been noted by other people writing about the film, including Aaron Baker, who refers to Harris's trip as a "specific reference to Perez and Mack [Perez's bank-robbing friend with whom he was celebrating in Vegas]" ("Beyond the Thin Line," 56). This seems unlikely to be the case, since Harris's Vegas trip appears in the 1999 draft of the script, which was written before many details of the Rampart scandal had come to light. Still, regardless of whether this part of the story was borrowed from Rampart or is just coincidental, the parallel certainly helped to ensure that *Training Day* would be understood as a fictionalized version of the scandal.

33 Matt Lait and Scott Glover. "Insignia of Rampart Anti-Gang Unit Raises Concerns; Police: Some officers had tattoos of the grinning skull. Critics say such menacing symbols show vigilante mentality," *Los Angeles Times*, February 8, 2000, B.1.

34 Coleman and Cobb note that the tattoos might also have been inspired by "the Oakland Riders," a group of four officers who were charged with a variety of crimes in the San Francisco Bay area at about the same time that Rampart-related cases were starting to come to trial. "*Training Day* and *The Shield*," 104.

35 Ibid., 105.

36 In a deleted scene, Harris again emphasizes his virility, and links it to his power as a police officer. He yells at two women who are walking past him that "You're under arrest. I'll put the handcuffs on you. I'm a have to spank you. Hey Baby, I give you ten sons, baby, ten."

37 Sexton, "The Ruse of Engagement," 53.

38 Sharon Waxman, "Back in the 'Hood: The Filmmakers Knew There Was Only One Place to Shoot Their Movie," *Washington Post*, October 6, 2001, C1.

39 Ibid.

40 Ibid.

41 Kloppenberg, *Playing it Safe*, 67.

42 Quoted in Rene Rodriguez, "Training Day a New Take on the Nasty Cop," *Ottawa Citizen*, October 4, 2001.

43 Lou Cannon, *Official Negligence*, 95.

44 Kloppenberg, *Playing it Safe*, 67.

45 Ibid. Kloppenberg notes that this decision effectively meant that the Court had decided that there was no one who had standing to sue to stop the practice: "if Mr. Lyons, who was nearly choked to death, cannot seek injunctive relief, who can? As a young African American man living in Los Angeles, he was more likely than most others to encounter the use of an LAPD choke hold in the future" (70).

46 Ibid., 73.

47 Quoted in Bernard Weintraub, "Police Show Has Humans, Not Heroes: In FX's Hit 'The Shield,' Means Justify Ends," *New York Times*, March 3, 2002. http://www.nytimes.com/2002/04/03/arts/police-show-has-humans-not-heroes-in-fx-s-hit-the-shield-means-justify-ends.html (accessed August 12, 2008).

48 Lotz, *The Television Will Be*, 226.

49 Quoted in Rene Rodriguez, "Training Day a New Take on the Nasty Cop," *Ottawa Citizen*, October 4, 2001, G10.

50 www.fxnetwork.com/shows/originals/the_shield (accessed August 12, 2008).

51 Bernard Weintraub, "Police Show Has Humans, Not Heroes: In FX's Hit 'The Shield,' Means Justify Ends," *New York Times*, March 3, 2002. http://www.nytimes.com/2002/04/03/arts/police-show-has-humans-not-heroes-in-fx-s-hit-the-shield-means-justify-ends.html (accessed August 12, 2008).

52 Coleman and Cobb, "*Training Day* and *The Shield*," 102.

53 John Sumser, quoted in Chopra-Gant, "The Law of the Father," 659.

54 Torres, *Black, White, and In Color*, 77.

55 Chopra-Gant, "The Law of the Father," 668. See also Fuchs, "Terrordome."

56 See Chopra-Gant, "The Law of the Father," for an extensive list of examples (668).

57 *The Shield*, Season 1, Episode 8, "Cupid & Psycho" Air Date 4/23/2002.

58 *The Shield*, Season 3, Episode 14, "All In" Air Date 6/8/2004 and Episode 15, Air Date 6/15/2004.

59 *The Shield*, Season 1, Episode 8, "Cupid & Psycho" Air Date 4/23/2002.

60 *The Shield*, Season 1, Episode 6, "Cherrypoppers" Air Date 4/16/2002.

61 *The Shield*, Season 1, Episode 6, "Cherrypoppers" Air Date 4/16/2002.

62 *The Shield*, Season 1, Episode 8, "Cupid & Psycho" Air Date 4/23/2002.

63 *The Shield*, Season 1, Episode 6, "Cherrypoppers" Air Date 4/16/2002.

64 *The Shield*, Season 1, Episode 5, "Blowback" Air Date 4/9/2002.

65 Julien is portrayed as a "basically good cop" despite the fact that he almost kills the drag queen that he brutalizes. The beating is sickening, and is portrayed as a savage act, but the camera lingers on Julien's enraged facial expressions, rather than the suffering of his victim. The point of the beating seems to have been to clarify the extent of Julien's self-loathing (he might be seen as engaged in a metaphorical attempt to beat the homosexuality out of himself, and, indeed, in the following episodes he joins a support group meant to convert him to heterosexuality), and not to offer any kind of detailed examination of homophobic hate crimes, since the act of brutality does not become a substantial issue in the remainder of the series. The drag queen is fairly one-dimensional, not much more than a prop whose victimization merely serves to further develop Julien's characterization, and the beating never becomes an issue in its own right.

66 Torres, *Black, White, and In Color*, 85.

67 These are not the first popular culture productions to feature "bad cop" protagonists, but I am not aware of any earlier productions that place such protagonists at the center of similar investigations into the nature of police corruption. *Bad Lieutenant* (Abel Ferrara, 1992) and *Bad Lieutenant: Port of Call, New Orleans* (Werner Herzog, 2009) feature dirty cops, but these films are really extended character studies of individual officers who have gone over the brink, rather than meditations on the workings of corruption itself.

5 Racial Spectacles under an Anti-Racist Gaze

1 I discuss Copwatch briefly in Chapter 3.

2 I discuss some recent examples, including the 2009 New Year's Day killing of Oscar Grant by a Bay Area Rapid Transit (BART) police officer, in Chapter 3. Also notable is a one week period in November of 2006 in which three separate incidents of apparent police brutality that were captured on cell-phone video dominated the news in southern California. While none of the footage was taken by professional journalists, the mainstream media provided extensive coverage of each of these cases, though viewers who wanted to see the videos in their entirety often had to turn to the internet. (As noted in Chapter 3, YouTube.com has become a particularly important site for archiving and discussing videos of police brutality.) The videos in each of these cases provided the impetus for official investigations and sparked far-ranging discussions of proper policing techniques and policies. See Chapter 3 for greater discussion of some of these issues.

3 Amy Harmon, "Improved Tools Turn Journalists Into a Quick Strike Force," *New York Times*, March 24, 2003, Section C.

4 Television was in its infancy during the Korean War, though the U.S. Army Pictorial Center did produce a weekly series about the war during 1951, which was broadcast on CBS. See Bernhard, *U.S. Television News*, 142. Television provided a modest supplement to newsreel footage of the war that was screened in movie theaters.

5 Sturken, *Tangled Memories*, 125.
6 See, for example, Baroody, *Media Access*, 18.
7 Sturken, *Tangled Memories*, 127.
8 Bolter and Grusin, *Remediation*, 19.
9 Sturken, *Tangled Memories*, 126.
10 Barton Gellman, "Allied Air War Struck Broadly in Iraq; Officials Acknowledge Strategy Went Beyond Purely Military Targets," *Washington Post*, June 23, 1991, A1.
11 Riviere, "Mobile Camera Phones," 171.
12 Scifo, "The Domestication," 367.
13 Mestrovic, *The Trials*, 91.
14 Wypijewski, "Judgment Days."
15 Baudrillard, "War Porn."
16 Freud, *On Creativity and the Unconscious*, 123.
17 See, for example: Apel, "Torture Culture"; Carby, "A Strange and Bitter Crop"; Philipose, "The Politics of Pain"; Razack, "How is White Supremacy Embodied?"; Sontag, "Regarding the Torture."
18 Zelizer, *Remembering to Forget*, 15.
19 Sontag, "Regarding the Torture."
20 Feldman, "Abu Ghraib."
21 Luc Sante, "Tourists and Torturers," *New York Times* op-ed, May 11, 2005.
22 Allen, *Without Sanctuary*.
23 Wood, "Lynching Photography," 375. Wood also cautions, however, that we have access to only a small number of lynching photographs, so claims about standardization are somewhat problematic: "thousands of images could have been lost or destroyed, or have not yet been recovered." Nevertheless, she argues that "the apparent consistencies among the photographs that do exist . . . suggest that certain kinds of images were either more likely to be captured or more likely to be developed, sold, and preserved." *Lynching and Spectacle*, 80.
24 Ibid., 382.
25 Quoted in http://mediamatters.org/items/200405050003 (accessed September 12, 2007).
26 Said, *Orientalism*, 3.
27 Tucker and Traintafyllos, "Lynndie England," 97.
28 Hersh, "The Grey Zone," 38.
29 Wypijewski, "Judgment Days," 12.
30 Razack, "How is White Supremacy Embodied?" 347.
31 Ibid.
32 The conviction, of Lt. Col. Steven Jordan was overturned in January, 2008. Eleven low ranking soldiers were convicted in military courts in connection with the torture at Abu Ghraib, while two other officers faced military disciplinary measures, but not criminal charges or dismissal. "General Clears Army Officer of Crime in Abu Ghraib Case," *New York Times*, January 11, 2008.
33 Danner, *Torture and Truth*, 42.
34 U.S. Senate Armed Services Committee. *Inquiry into the Treatment*, xii.
35 Ibid., xxix.
36 "Abu Ghraib Swept Under the Carpet," Editorial. *New York Times*, August 30, 2007.
37 "On Torture and American Values," Editorial. *New York Times*, October 7, 2007.
38 Scott Shane, David Johnston and James Risen, "Secret U.S. Endorsement of Severe Interrogations," *New York Times*, October 4, 2007.
39 Sheryl Gay Stolberg, "Bush Says Interrogation Methods Aren't Torture," *New York Times*, October 6, 2007.
40 Gooding-Williams, "Look, A Negro!," 165.
41 Apel, "Torture Culture," 89.

42 Hamilton, "Image and Context," 173.

43 Ibid., 177.

44 'The Nation: My Lai: An American Tragedy', *Time*, vol. 49, no. 23, December 5, 1969, 29. Quoted in Schlegel, "My Lai," 54.

45 The photographer who took the shot of General Loan was upset that the photo had become understood as an anti-war photo. He saw the photo as having played a "very detrimental" role as "perfect propaganda for North Vietnam." Eddie Adams, quoted in Hamilton, "Image and Context,"178.

46 Wallis, "Remember Abu Ghraib."

47 It is worth noting that even the phrasing in this passage provides only a fairly muted critique: the photos are said to offer a picture of "war" in very generalized terms as a form of "systematic cruelty." If this reading is correct, then there is nothing *specifically* troubling about the ways in which this particular war is being waged.

48 Danner, *Torture and Truth*, 28.

49 Philipose, "The Politics of Pain," 1053.

50 Ibid., 1063.

51 One possible indication of the continuing power of Orientalist discourse as the Abu Ghraib photographs are circulated in contexts that are, to varying extents, critical of U.S. foreign policy is that, despite the fact that the names of many of the victims photographed at Abu Ghraib are a matter of public record, those names have almost never been mentioned in the American press, and remain unknown to most of the American population. This remains true even as "Lynndie England" has become a household name. Even if the only reason that the media has provided the torturers with clear identities is to better single them out as "bad apples," they have been represented as full human beings, while their victims have been, at best, reduced to images of pure and anonymous suffering. Two of the most famous victims of Abu Ghraib have been given nicknames (either by soldiers at Abu Ghraib, or by the American media) that involved a process of metonymic substitution in which the nature of their suffering was made to stand in for any kind of meaningful knowledge about their identities: Perhaps the most iconic Abu Ghraib photo is of a hooded and robed man, standing on a box with outstretched arms, and wires attached to his fingers and genitals, who had been told that he would be electrocuted if he fell off the box. The victim, regularly referred to in the press as "Hooded Man," and by his torturers as "Gilligan" was Abdou Hussain Saad Faleh. See Kate Zernike, March 18, 2006, "Cited as Symbol of Abu Ghraib, Man Admits He Is Not In Photo," *New York Times*. Similarly, "Ice Man" (Manadel al-Jamadi) died during interrogation by a CIA officer, and photos were taken of Charles Graner and Sabrina Harman posing with "thumbs up" signs over his corpse, which was packed in an open body bag filled with ice. (Zagorin, 2005.) To support my suggestion that the media's willingness to rely upon nicknames when referring to these men, or its lack of interest in their actual names, is indicative of Orientalist dehumanization, I would simply pose the rhetorical question of whether it is conceivable that, had international audiences been repeatedly exposed to images of two Americans subjected to similar treatment, and had the names of those Americans been made public, the press would have failed to publicize those names? If these were lives that mattered to the press in any substantial way, is it conceivable that their names would be any less recognizable than that of Daniel Berg, or that there would be no widely distributed stories about the victims' personal lives and backgrounds? The lack of publicity accorded the available names of the Abu Ghraib victims is indicative of an unwillingness to address the humanity of the victims in any meaningful sense.

52 I am borrowing here from Gooding-Williams, whose analysis of the trial of the officers who beat Rodney King discusses a "storehouse of interpreted images of black people that American jurors, lawyers, and media pundits have available to them as elements of the culture they have in common." "Look, a Negro!,"163.

53 Though Jon McKenzie makes a similar point. He argues that the proliferation of new communication technologies and networks means that the ability for the public display of punishment to act as a disciplinary mechanism has increased dramatically. McKenzie sees the "spectacle of the scaffold" that Foucault defined as characteristic of pre-disciplinary society as a defining feature of a new media age in which "the spectacle of the scaffold has become networked and screenal: satellites, televisions, security cameras, facial and gestural recognition software, cell phones, Blackberrys, iPods, YouTube, Google Maps, The Memory Hold—all become means for capturing or being captivated by spectacles." McKenzie, "Abu Ghraib and the Society of the Spectacle of the Scaffold," 340. The idea that the circulation of the Abu Ghraib photos was *intended* as a way of projecting U.S. disciplinary authority finds some support in former General Janis Karpinski's suggestion that the Bush administration may have encouraged the circulation of some of the photographs as a way of countering the ways that images of Jessica Lynch had feminized representations of the Iraq war. See Phelan, "Afterword: 'In the Valley of the Shadow of Death,'" 378.

54 Butler, "Endangered/Endangering," 17.

55 Butler has since written about the Abu Ghraib photos directly, arguing in two articles ("Photography, War, Outrage" and "Torture and the Ethics") that the photographs, and photographs in general, provide interpretations in the ways that they frame their subject matter. Of the Abu Ghraib photos specifically, she writes that "The camera angle, the frame, the posed subjects all suggest that those who took the photographs were actively involved in the perspective of the war, elaborating that perspective and even giving it further validity." ("Photography, War, Outrage," 822). Butler's argument is not that photographs do not require further interpretation, but that when we interpret photographs, we are interpreting interpretations, since we never have transparent access to the "reality" that they represent.

56 Andén-Papadopoulos, "The Abu Ghraib Torture Photographs," 13. See also Bennett, et al., "None Dare Call."

57 See Bennett et al., *When the Press Fails*, 100–103 for a discussion of the ways that the Bush administration capitalized upon CBS's willingness to delay broadcasting the photographs.

58 Gourevitch and Morris, *Standard Operating Procedure.*

59 www.takepart.com/SOP (accessed September 12, 2007).

60 Errol Morris, "Standard Operating Procedure Discussion Guide."

61 Errol Morris, "The Most Curious Thing."

62 Errol Morris, "Standard Operating Procedure Discussion Guide"

63 O'Hehir, "Interrogating Abu Ghraib."

64 Heath, "The Great Interrogator."

65 The quote is from Special Agent Brent Pack, the lead forensic examiner in charge of examining the CDs containing the photographic evidence to be used in the Abu Ghraib trials. Quoted in *Standard Operating Procedure* (Errol Morris, Sony Pictures, 2007) and in Gourevitch and Morris, *Standard Operating Procedure*, 267.

66 Both versions of *Standard Operating Procedure* and Morris's *New York Times* blog present fairly detailed and compelling explanations of the killing of al-Jamadi, relying upon Morris's own interviews, and upon testimony provided for the official investigation into his death. On the day he died, Manadel al-Jamadi was first captured by Navy Seals who suspected him of providing explosives that had been used in an attack on offices of the Red Cross that killed two Iraqi civilians in October, 2003. Al-Jamadi was beaten by the Seals, who broke several of his ribs, but he was soon turned over to C.I.A. interrogators who questioned him at an air force base in Baghdad, before torturing him at Abu Ghraib. By the time that Harman and Graner first entered the shower room where al-Jamadi was killed, he had been dead for more than sixteen hours. The C.I.A. interrogators, along with some M.P.s, had decided to place al-Jamadi's body in a body

bag and cover it with ice to slow the decomposition while deciding what to do with the corpse. Harman and Graner decided to check out the shower room because the ice had started melting and was leaking under the door, and they wanted to know where the water was coming from. Morris, who doesn't use the word "torture" notes that al-Jamadi was put in a stress position called a "Palestinian hanging," which he describes as "a low-budget crucifixion without the nails." He further explains that "His arms were handcuffed behind him and then the handcuffs were suspended from a window frame. (As a prisoner becomes weaker and weaker, greater and greater pressure is put on the arms, potentially pulling them out of the sockets.)" According to the military's medical investigation, al-Jamadi's death was ultimately caused by a combination of the stress position (which made it difficult to breathe, given internal injuries that had been caused by "the 'slow deliberate application of force,' such as would have resulted from someone kneeling on his chest, or holding al-Jamadi down by placing the heels of someone's boots on his chest"), and being hooded, which exacerbated his respiratory problems. Morris, "The Most Curious Thing."

67 Morris, "The Most Curious Thing."

68 Quoted in Gourevitch, *Standard Operating Procedure*, 180.

69 Still, they are a distraction that might make it quite difficult to sympathize with Harman. After all, the fact that Harman didn't kill al-Jamadi doesn't mean that she wasn't gloating over his death. To address this issue, Morris enlisted the aid of an expert on facial expressions named Paul Ekman, an emeritus professor of psychology at the University of California, San Francisco. Ekman examined many photographs of Harman in Iraq, and concluded that her smile betrayed no genuine enjoyment, but was instead just a "say cheese" smile, provided as a kind of automatic response, "doing what people always do when they pose for a camera." Quoted in Morris, "The Most Curious Thing." Of course, it is not at all clear that genuine emotion is necessary to justify a comparison with lynching photography, or to see this as a trophy photo. After all, if the intent is to convey pleasure, it makes sense to read the photo as a display of dominance, regardless of whether that pleasure is genuine.

70 Quoted in Mestrovic, *The Trials*, 90.

71 Ibid.

72 Ibid., 91.

73 Ibid., 4. See also the interview with Mestrovic by Richard Bryne in Richard Bryne, "Rejecting the 'Rotten Apple' Theory of Abu Ghraib Abuse," *Chronicle of Higher Education*, September 7, 2007. http://chronicle.com/weekly/v54/i02/02a02002.htm (accessed September 12, 2007).

74 Mestrovic, *The Trials*, 31.

75 Bryne, "Rejecting the Rotten Apple Theory."

76 Quoted in "Errol Morris Discusses 'Standard Operating Procedure,'" www.washingtonpost.com, April 14, 2008 (accessed November 19, 2010). Morris focuses on Harman's documentary impulses to the exclusion of any substantial discussion of her crimes. For example, he has written that "Sabrina wasn't involved with al-Jamadi's death, and she wasn't part of the cover up. Nevertheless, she was accused of several crimes." Morris, "The Most Curious Thing." The problem with this statement is that the crimes that Harman was not only accused of, but convicted for, had nothing to do with al-Jamadi's death. Instead, she was found guilty of conspiracy to maltreat detainees, maltreating detainees, and dereliction of duties. The specific offenses included a failure to report abuse, posing in photographs with detainees, scrawling "rapeist" on a prisoner's body during the night of the naked pyramid, and attaching wires to a prisoner's hands and threatening him with electrocution as he stood in a stress position on a box (this is the famous "hooded man" photo that has become an icon of Abu Ghraib). "Soldier is found guilty in abuse case," Associated Press, *New York Times*, May 17, 2005.

http://www.nytimes.com/2005/05/17/national/17abuse.html (accessed August 12, 2008). See also Mestrovic, *The Trials*, 138.

77 Notably, Philip Gourevitch is somewhat less convinced of Harman's documentary intent than is Morris. Writing about her letter home, Gourevitch says that

> her reactions to the prisoner's degradation and her part in it—ricocheting from childish mockery to casual swagger to sympathy to cruelty to titillation to self-justification to self-doubt to outrage to identification to despair—she managed gradually to subtract herself from the scenes she sketched. By the end of her outpourings she had repositioned herself as an outsider at Abu Ghraib, and observer and recorder, shaking her head, and in this way she came clean to her wife. In this way she preserved her innocence. . . . Harman said she wanted to be there to get pictures, and she imagined herself producing an exposé—to "prove that the U.S. is not what they think." The idea was abstract, and she had only a vague notion of how to see it through, or what its consequences might be. She said she intended to give the photographs to CNN after she got home from Iraq and out of the army. But.
>
> (*Standard Operating Procedure*, 112.)

78 Morris's attempts to humanize the Abu Ghraib soldiers have convinced me to reassess my own stance. In response to an interview with Mestrovic that was published in the *Chronicle of Higher Education*, I wrote that Mestrovic's "efforts to draw attention to the 'contaminated orchard' are laudable, but attempts to make the 'rotten apples' smell better are unwarranted." Markovitz, "Letters to the Editor." While I stand by my argument that there is no reasonable basis to conclude that the soldiers who were court-martialed at Abu Ghraib should be seen as whistle-blowers, and that it is necessary to hold them accountable for the crimes that they carried out, I now accept that the notion of bad (or rotten) apples is not just isolating but also dehumanizing. Efforts to highlight the soldiers' humanity are necessary not only because it is all too easy to judge and impossible to know how we might have acted in their place, but also because such efforts can begin to make it possible to understand the social forces that helped produce their actions.

79 One of Harman's letters home does mention the idea of turning the photos in, but this is a letter written once the photos have *already* become the subject of investigation, and she never says *who* she was planning to turn them in to: "Well sweetie you married a criminal. Yup, the pictures are out and I am under investigation as of 10:00am this morning. So much for turning those pictures in when I come home cause they're already out." Quoted in Gourevitch, *Standard Operating Procedure*, 246. Because Harman has discussed vague documentary intentions in earlier letters, it might not be fair to read this letter entirely as a self-serving justification after the fact. But the fact that the first mention of anything approaching a declaration of whistle-blowing intent comes only once such intent has been effectively pre-empted certainly makes the declaration appear somewhat hollow.

80 Quoted in Gourevitch, *Standard Operating Procedure*, 112.

81 Ibid., 112. Gourevitch rejects Mestrovic's position, noting that Harman "did not pretend to be a whistle-blower-in-waiting; rather, she wished to unburden herself of complicity in conduct that she considered wrong, and in its cover-up, without ascribing blame or making trouble for anyone in particular." 112.

82 Quoted in ibid., 108.

83 This is not the only time that Harman took pictures for her own amusement. She explains the shots of herself and Sgt. Graner posing and grinning with their thumbs up over the corpse of al-Jamadi by saying that "I guess we weren't really thinking, Hey, this guy has family, or Hey, this guy was just murdered . . . . It was just—Hey, it's a dead guy, it'd be cool to get a photo next to a dead person." Quoted in Gourevitch, *Standard Operating Procedure*, 178.

84 Quoted in ibid., 247.

85 Quoted in ibid., 236.

86 Quoted in ibid., 134.

87 Quoted in ibid., 200.

88 Morris is discussing the iconic photograph of Lynndie England, apparently holding a leash and dragging a prisoner, but his comments provide a good sense of his assessment of all of the Abu Ghraib photographs: in his eyes, the photographs should be seen as an indictment of U.S. foreign policy, not of the actions of low-level soldiers. Quoted in Croce, "Nonstandard Operating Procedure."

89 This is *not* true of Gourevitch's book version of *Standard Operating Procedure*, which does focus on broader issues of U.S. foreign policy.

90 Polchin, "Not Looking," 216.

91 Much of this artwork has been discussed at length elsewhere (see, for example, Apel, "Torture Culture"; Mitchell, "The Unspeakable"), and my goal here is not to present a comprehensive overview of this artwork, but to assess a few examples of particularly potent "aggressive readings" of the Abu Ghraib photos.

92 Mitchell, "The Unspeakable," 302.

93 "Hooded Man" has become perhaps the most iconic Abu Ghraib photograph. The photo shows a hooded and robed man, standing on a box with outstretched arms, and wires attached to his fingers (and, we know from the victim's testimony, to his genitals), who had been told that he would be electrocuted if he fell off the box. The victim, regularly referred to in the press as "Hooded Man," and by his torturers as "Gilligan" was Abdou Hussain Saad Faleh (Zernike, "Cited As"). I discuss his case in more detail below. On Sallat's mural see, for example, Apel, 2005; Mitchell, 2005; Andén-Papadopoulos, 2008. Noting that Sallat has said that he chose the location based on the fact that "everyone can see it," Apel writes that "Here Sallat makes clear his understanding that the mere act of rendering the images visible to the public begins their undoing." It is not clear, however, what kind of critique Sallat's mural would have provided had it merely brought the images to public visibility without actively yoking them to one of the most recognizable icons of American national identity. Wendy Hesford notes that a photograph of a mural of the Abu Ghraib torture in Tehran was included in the *Inconvenient Evidence* exhibit discussed above, and suggests that the point of including the mural, as well as the actual Abu Ghraib photographs, is to ask American audiences to bear witness to the torture. But Hesford asks whether the notion of bearing witness might "distance American viewers from recognizing their own relationship to the trauma depicted?" ("Staging Terror," 32). If we see ourselves as witnesses to atrocity, how likely are we to also see ourselves as responsible for the events that we are bearing witness to? It is difficult to be confident that this kind of visibility alone is part of the process of "undoing" the destructive qualities of the photographs.

94 Sallat's decision to so explicitly link the "Hooded Man" icon to the Ku Klux Klan as a symbol of American national identity draws out associations that others have noted when considering the relationship between the Abu Ghraib images, lynching, and lynching photography. Susan Willis, for example, draws upon Baudrillard's suggestion that the "Hooded Man" image is akin to a "photographic negative" of an image of a Klansman, "where the robe is black unlike the Klansman's white." Willis sees Baudrillard's rendering of U.S. history as somewhat flat, failing to account for complexities as he reads the photograph as a sign. She argues that reading "history back into the sign" puts us "in a position to grasp the image as an icon that conflates the history we repress (lynching) with the history we disavow (torture)" (*Portents of the Real*, 120). Willis goes on to argue that the core values and ideas of the Klan, including nativism, xenophobia, and heteronormative masculinity, "saturate our military," (124) and that all of the Abu Ghraib photos "should be read as documents of lynching" (123).

95 Di Bella's actions have apparently raised the ire of British and American authorities. According to Di Bella, a shipment of the artwork that was sent to the United States was intercepted by the police and then by a British anti-terrorist agency, in order to investigate "the content of the parcel for alleged 'anti-American documentation'." Di Bella was informed by an agent from the courier company that he had used that the British authorities had deemed the work "offensive," though the package was eventually sent on to American authorities for additional inspection before ultimately being released to Di Bella's American associate, who was subsequently questioned by the FBI about the artwork and about Di Bella. (Di Bella, "The Story Behind the Abu Ghraib Series.")

96 Di Bella, "The Story Behind the Abu Ghraib Series."

97 Ibid.

98 Simpson, "Archiving Hate," 19. On postcards, commodification, and consumer culture see Rogan, "An Entangled Object."

99 Di Bella, "The Story Behind the Abu Ghraib Series." Di Bella notes that he affixed regular postage stamps alongside the Abu Ghraib stamps, so as to ensure that he could not be charged with any form of mail fraud.

100 National Association for the Advancement of Colored People, *The Lynching of Claude Neal*; also see Markovitz, *Legacies of Lynching*, 27–28.

101 Barbie Zelizer makes a similar point about Holocaust atrocity photographs. She writes that the power of these photos

> derived from a lesser, rather than greater, degree of explicitness about [their] details. Faces were blackened or obscured by shadows. Names—identified on uniforms—were smudged from view. . . . But there was a broader significance to these images of violence. The photos offered broader parameters for visualizing atrocity that were beyond the explicit details of a given instance of death or mutilation. They linked with the broader interpretive themes that justified the war effort. The potency of these images thus derived from their invocation as symbols—from representational strategies connected with generic representation, anonymity, connotation, generalizability, and universality.
>
> (*Remembering to Forget*, 34.)

102 Ali Shalal Qaissi's business card was reproduced in a *New York Times* article about his efforts on the part of people imprisoned by American occupation forces around the world, but the paper issued a correction to the article when it became clear that he was not, as the article reported, the iconic "Hooded Man." I sought permission from the *Times* to reproduce the photograph of the business card in this book, but was told that, since the article was retracted, they could not provide permission for reproduction in any form. When I contacted the photographer who had taken the photograph of the card that the *Times* used, he confirmed that he held the copyright to the photo, but wrote that "Unfortunately the story in the Times was retracted so I'm afraid I can not give you permission to use the photograph." (Email correspondence with Shawn Baldwin, April 15, 2010.) It is unclear why inaccuracies in the story should lead to diminished public access to the *Times*' archival holdings, and the paper's position strikes me as akin to an attempt to consign their journalistic failures to an Orwellian "memory hole." Still, as of this writing, the *Times* has not obliterated all traces of its lack of due diligence, as an image of the card can still be found accompanying the original article on the paper's website. See Hassan M. Fattah, "Symbol of Abu Ghraib Seeks to Spare Others His Nightmare," *New York Times*, March 11, 2006. http://www.nytimes.com/2006/03/11/international/middleeast/11ghraib.html (accessed August 12, 2008).

103 Ali Shalal Qaissi now admits that he is not the person who is in the widely circulated "Hooded Man" photograph, but he insists that he believed his initial claims to the

media. He told the *New York Times* that "I know one thing. . . . I wore that blanket, I stood on that box, and I was wired up and electrocuted." Quoted in Zernike, "Cited As." In fact, Qaissi's claims suggest more severe victimization than what the military has acknowledged in Faleh's case, since the military's position all along has been that the wires that were attached to Faleh were not live, and that the threats of electrocution were empty. In contrast, Qaissi claims that he *was* shocked, to the point where "It felt like my eyeballs were coming out of my sockets." The *Times* notes that Qaissi's legal case was not based on the iconic photograph, and that court documents allege that "he was punched, kicked, hit with a stick and chained to his cell while his captors poured cold water over his naked body." Zernike, "Cited As."

104 Quoted in Jim Gladstone, "Beyond the Hoods: The Abu Ghraib Images of Daniel Heyman," *Smith Magazine*, June 6, 2007. http://www.smithmag.net/2007/06/06/beyond-the-hoods-the-abu-ghraib-images-of-daniel-heyman/ (accessed July 7, 2007).

105 Quoted in ibid. Heyman has also commented on Fernando Botero's paintings of Abu Ghraib, noting that, while they are powerful,

> They continue to deny the individuality and the full life stories of the former detainees. . . . These paintings make a strong political point, but they don't go any further. They make a generalized point about human suffering, but they don't say anything particular about the individuals who suffered.
>
> (Quoted in Feffer, "Interview With Daniel Heyman.")

106 Stocke et al., "The Other Side of Abu Ghraib."
107 Hesford, "Staging Terror," 35.
108 Though the anti-war movement had peaked a full year earlier, and it is interesting to speculate about the possible reception that similar photos might have generated had they been released in the early months of 2003, as tens of millions of people protested the Iraq war around the globe.
109 Bennett, Breunig and Givens, "Communication and Political Mobilization,"269.
110 Gunthert, "Digital Imaging Goes to War," 107.

Conclusion: Lessons from a Campus Movement

1 The invitation is included in "UCSD Frat Denies Involvement In 'Ghetto-Themed' Party," 10News.com, February 17, 2010. http://www.10news.com/news/22588063/detail.html (accessed February 18, 2010).

2 The racist incidents were not confined to the UCSD campus, as graffiti of swastikas and nooses were found at UC Davis, UC Santa Cruz, and California State University, San Marcos. (Nor was the hatred confined to issues of race or ethnicity, as the campus center for lesbian and gay students at UC Davis was vandalized.) While most of the racist episodes were clustered around February and March, there have been subsequent incidents. In May, 2010, a group of students dressed in mock Native American attire and performed pseudo-Native American rituals during the University's annual "Sungod" festival (a festival centered around a sculpture by Niki de Saint Phalle titled "Sun God"). For details about this incident, see the UCSD Native Student Alliance press release on file at http://stopracismucsd.wordpress.com/ (accessed August 10, 2010). The site also contains the most comprehensive archive of information about responses to all of the racist incidents at UCSD during this time period.

3 For example, Jorge Mariscal argued in 2009 that UCSD "is a public university in name only with only 6% of its budget coming from the state." Jorge Mariscal, "How Will the University of California Survive?" *La Prensa San Diego*, July 17, 2009. http://laprensa-sandiego.org/editorial-and-commentary/how-will-the-university-of-california-survive/ (accessed August 12, 2009).

4 Alvarez et al., *Another University is Possible*, xii. The acceptance rate of African American students has actually been much higher in recent years, though relatively few African

Americans who are accepted agree to enroll at UCSD. "Sorting Through Race
Relations at UCSD," interview with Sara Clarke Kaplan, Andrea Guerrero and
Glynda Davis. *These Days*, KPBS, February 25, 2010.

5 A female student who identified herself as a member of a minority group turned herself
into the campus police for having left the noose in the library. Her identity has not
been revealed to the campus community, but she did confess to the crime in a letter
to the main student newspaper. The student was suspended for her actions, but she has
claimed to have had no racist intent. Anonymous, "Noose in Geisel Was Not Intended
as a Threat," *UCSD Guardian*, March 1, 2010. http://www.ucsdguardian.org/feature-
on-slider/noose-in-geisel-was-not-intended-as-a-threat/ (accessed March 10, 2010).

6 Photographs of the noose were fairly widespread on the internet, though I am not aware
of any existing photographs of the Klan's hood. Discussions of the hood are part of the
broader spectacle, though images of it are not.

7 Though some of those concessions may have been short-lived. Jorge Mariscal, a professor
of Literature at UCSD, reports that "Promises about hiring more U.S. minority faculty
began to unravel as powerful disciplines such as management and engineering dispatched
their deans to lock up limited funding for their already well-endowed coffers." Jorge
Mariscal, "Trouble in Paradise: Welcome to Post-Racial California," *Counterpunch*,
March 12–14, 2010. http://www.counterpunch.org/mariscal03122010.html (accessed
March 20, 2010).

8 A typical example is a comment attributed to "Sam Beau" on the 10news.com website
saying "just T.N.B. everyone knew it was a spook that put that noose up."
http://www.10news.com/news/22682950/detail.html (accessed July 20, 2010).
According to the top ranked definitions on urbandictionary.com, "T.N.B." is an
acronym for a racist piece of pseudo-folk wisdom. http://www.urbandictionary.
com/define.php?term=TNB (accessed July 20, 2010).

9 Quoted in http://www.10news.com/news/22682950/detail.html (accessed July 20,
2010).

10 Mark Yudof and Russell Gould, "Statement of Mark G. Yudof, President, University
of California Russell Gould, Chair, UC Board of Regents," February 26, 2010.
http://battlehate.ucsd.edu/docs/Yudof_UCSD_statement_2-26-10.pdf (accessed July
20, 2010).

11 Mary Anne Fox and Penny Rue, "Condemnation of Off-Campus Party and Affirma-
tion of Principles of Community," *Campus Notice*, February 16, 2010. http://battlehate.
ucsd.edu/docs/President_and_Chancellors_responses.pdf (accessed July 20, 2010).

12 Judy Piercey, "UC San Diego and Black Student Union Sign Agreement, Announce
Common Goals."

13 "Sorting Through Race Relations at UCSD," interview with Sara Clarke Kaplan,
Andrea Guerrero and Glynda Davis. *These Days*, KPBS. February 25, 2010.
http://www.kpbs.org/news/2010/feb/25/sorting-through-race-relations-ucsd/
(accessed July 20, 2010).

14 City News Service, "Another Noose Found on UCSD Campus," July 29, 2010.
http://www.kpbs.org/news/2010/jul/29/another-noose-found-ucsd-campus/
(accessed August 5, 2010).

15 American bombing campaigns during the Gulf War destroyed much of the electrical
grid, along with water-pumping and sanitation systems. David Cortright, "A Hard
Look at Iraq Sanctions," *The Nation*, November 15, 2001. http://www.thenation.com/
article/hard-look-iraq-sanctions?page=0,2 (accessed July 20, 2010).

16 http://www.iraqbodycount.org (accessed July 20, 2010). By some estimates, the war
has already resulted in over a million violent deaths. See Project Censored, "Over
One Million Iraqi Deaths Caused by US Occupation," 2009. http://www.project
censored.org/top-stories/articles/1-over-one-million-iraqi-deaths-caused-by-us-
occupation/ (accessed July 20, 2010).

INDEX

Abu Ghraib photographs: as anti-racist spectacle 135; and art 150–156; legacies of 136; migration of 137, 138; and Orientalism 133, 140, 212 n. 51; and social movements 158; and torture 136; and U.S. foreign policy 135; and viewer complicity 129

Adams, Oscar 191 n. 110

Afghanistan 127, 165, 168

African American press 8, 21, 53; as part of the Scottsboro defense movement 43–48, 191 n. 110; and racialized collective memory 48

Alabama Supreme Court 23, 35

Albert, Marv 57

Alexander, Nikol G. 192 n. 125

Al-Jamadi, Manadel 143, 144, 212 n. 51, 213 n. 66

American Civil Liberties Union (ACLU) 36, 87, 88, 92, 95

Ames, Jessie Daniel 30, 31, 187 n. 62

Amnesty International 78, 169

Andén-Papadopoulos, Kari 141, 169, 216 n.93

anti-rape movement see rape

Apel, Dora 216 n.93

Arendt, Hannah 81

Artest, Ron 55

Association of Southern Women for the Prevention of Lynching 30, 187 n. 62

Ayer, David 102, 108, 111, 112, 208 n. 26

Bad Lieutenant 210 n. 67

Baker, Aaron 209 n. 32

Banet-Weiser, Sarah 55

Barbour v. Allen 190 n. 107

Bates, Ruby 19–21, 24, 27–36, 186 n. 44, 187 n. 69; see also Scottsboro

Baudrillard, Jean 78, 82, 128, 129, 181 n. 2, 216 n. 94

Beck, E. M. 185 n. 34, n.35

Bin Laden, Osama 133

black rapist, myth of the 9, 15, 26, 28, 30, 33, 35, 165; see also lynching; see also Scottsboro

black women: and rape 35; and sexist stereotypes 35

Bolter, David 126

Bourdieu, Pierre 12

Bratton, Chief William J. 83

Brawley, Tawana 46, 183 n. 45

Breyer, Justice Stephen 66, 197 n. 71

Brown v. Board of Education 42

Brownmiller, Susan 68

Brundage, W. Fitzhugh 186 n. 40

Bryant, Kobe (rape case): accuser tried for sexuality, 63; and clash of discourses, 51, 67, 69, 73, 197 n. 76; and collective memory 60–68, 196 n. 45; exposes limits of rape shield statutes 64, 66; and hangmen t-shirts 62; impact on public attitudes about rape 64; and intersectional politics 69; misrepresentations of rape shield

statutes 67; mug shot 49; and
Olympics 70; and racism 61, 195
n. 41; and sexism 63
Butler, Judith 141, 213 n. 55

Callahan, Judge William *see* Scottsboro
Cannon, Lou 109
Carrigan, William 182 n. 16, 194 n. 27
Carter, Dan 36, 38, 45, 188 n. 81
Central Park jogger 44; and coerced
confessions 59; news coverage of 59;
and racist stereotyping 60, 194 n. 36
Chamberlain, Wilt 55
Chamura, Mark 57
Chemerinsky, Erwin 83, 84, 89, 90
Chiklis, Michael 96, 111, 112
Chinatown 100
choke-holds: as racist policing tactic 108;
in *Training Day*, 108
Chopra-Gant, Mike 115
Christopher Commission report 84
Civil Rights act of 1964 42
Civil Rights Movement 1, 9, 15, 36, 42,
125, 165
Cobb, Jasmine 106
Cole, David 190 n. 107
Coleman, Robin 106
collective memory: of anti-rape
movement 64; construction of 12;
and contemporary racial spectacles 51;
and credibility 46; differences in 52;
encoded in legislation 65; and identity
12, 14; institutionalized in the law
65; and journalism 52; as "lens," 51,
61; and "memory projects" 53;
multiplicity of memories 12, 51;
"prosthetic memory" 12; and public
opinion 12; and racial formation 14;
racialized 13, 46–48, 52, 61; and racial
spectacles 14, 73; as shared resources
52, 71; and skepticism 60; and survey
data 183 n. 38; and understandings of
the present 50
Colorado Coalition Against Sexual Assault
see Bryant, Kobe
Commission on Interracial Cooperation
19, 26, 172
common sense 3, 4, 58, 62, 68, 69, 97;
see also Gramsci, Antonio
Communist Party 21, 22, 30, 164
"Compton Cookout" 159–163; *see also*
University of California, San Diego

Copwatch 76, 124
Cornell, Drucilla 192 n. 125
Crary, Jonathan 182 n. 7
Crash 102
CRASH (Community Resources Against
Street Hoodlums) *see* Rampart
Crenshaw, Kimberlé 69, 70
criminal justice system: and false
confessions 194 n. 36; in film and
television 97; public perceptions of
16; racial disparities within 78; as site
of racialization 16; and systemic
inequities 85
"Crisis, The" *see* National Association for
the Advancement of Colored People;
See also African American Press
Critical Race Theory 53

Danner, Mark 134, 140, 142
Davis, Angela 68, 80
Davis, Ossie 190 n. 105
Debord, Guy 4–6, 12, 96, 168, 181 n. 2,
181 n. 3, 182 n. 6
detournements 182 n.6 *see also* Debord,
Guy
Department of Justice: and immigration
law 79
Di Bella, Giuseppe 151–156, 217 n.95,
n.99
Dogg, Snoop 104
Dos Passos, John 21
Dreiser, Theodore 21
Dukakis, Michael 59
Duke Lacrosse case 71, 183 n. 45; 191
n. 118
Durden, Nino *see* Rampart Scandal

Ebb, Fred 40
Eichmann, Adolph 81
Einstein, Albert 21
Eisenhower, President Dwight D. 42
Ellroy, James 208 n. 26
England, Lynndie 148
Eyreman, Ron 11

F/X network 17, 112
Fair Sentencing Act of 2010 78
Faleh, Abdou Hussain Saad 154, 155,
216 n. 93
Feagin, Joe 194 n. 32
Feldman, Allen 131
Ford, Senator Harold 71, 198 n. 91

Foucault, Michel 133, 181 n. 2, 213
n. 53
Fox, Mary Anne 162
Fuchs, Cynthia 115
Fuqua, Antoine 102, 108, 110

Gaines, Jane 185 n. 31
gang profiling 79; *see also* racial profiling
Garcetti, Los Angeles District Attorney
Gil 84, 100
Geneva conventions 135
Gideon V. Wainwright 20, 43
Giroux, Henry 182 n. 7
Gold, Russell 162
Gonzales-Day 182 n. 16
Gooding-Williams, Robert 61, 136, 139,
212 n. 53
Goodman, James 33, 38, 43, 45
Gourevitch, Philip 142, 146, 148
Gramsci, Antonio 73, 194 n. 31
Grand Theft Auto: San Andreas 101
Graner, Charles 143, 148, 213 n. 66
Grant, Judith 99, 206 n.2
Grant, Oscar 77, 200 n. 10
Griffith, D.W. 26, 58
Grusin, Richard 126
Guantánamo Bay 135
Gulf war: coverage of 126, 127; toll on
Iraq 127, 219 n.15

Haggis, Paul 102
Halbwachs, Maurice 10, 11, 183 n. 32,
183 n. 33
Hale, Grace Elizabeth 8, 9, 182 n. 16,
182 n. 20
Halkias, Alexandra 202 n. 36
Hall, Jacquelyn Dowd 187 n. 62
Harman, Sabrina 143–148, 213 n. 66,
214 n. 69, 214 n.76, 215 n.77, 215
n. 79, 215 n. 83
Hawke, Ethan 104
Hayden, Tom 79, 84, 92, 174
Heavens Fall 189 n. 92; *see also*
Scottsboro
Hersh, Seymour 134, 141
Hesford, Wendy 156, 216 n.93
Heyman, Daniel 155, 156, 158, 218
n. 105
Hill, Anita 36, 58, 68
Holder, Attorney General Eric 158
Holliday, George 1, 74, 76, 80, 124
Holocaust, the 130, 180, 188 n. 85

"Hooded Man" 150, 216 n. 93; *see also*
Abu Ghraib photographs
Horton, Judge James, Jr. 34, 38, 42, 190
n. 105
Horton, William ("Willie") 59
hyperreality 181 n. 2; *see also* Baudrillard,
Jean
Hughes, Langston 34, 38
Hunt, Darnell 13
Huntington, Samuel 133
Hussein, Saddam 133
hyperreality *see* Baudrillard, Jean

ILD *see* International Labor Defense
Immigration: and law enforcement 201
n. 28; and racial profiling 79; SB 1070
(Arizona) 201 n. 28
International Center of Photography
139
International Labor Defense 21
Iraq war: invasion of Iraq 5; and possible
revival of Al Qaeda 5; "shock and
awe" 5; toll of 166, 219 n.16; *see also*
Gulf war
Ireland, Marilyn 64
Irwin-Zarecka, Iwona 11, 71, 73, 183
n. 34
Iverson, Allen 55

Jace, Michael 120
Jackson, Michael 57
James, LeBron *see* Bryant, Kobe
Jet magazine, 1
Johnson, Claudia Durst 40
Johnson, Earvin "Magic" 55, 57, 62
Jordan, Michael 54–56

Kander, John 40
Kaplan, Sara Clarke 162
Kefauver hearings 101, 207 n. 24
Kelley, Robin D.G. 36, 181 n. 1
Kellner, Douglas 5, 8, 16, 54, 182 n. 7,
182 n. 8, 183 n. 46
Kennedy, Randall 47
Kennedy, Rory 155
King Kong 71, 198 n. 92
King, Martin Luther, Jr. 65, 125
King, Rodney 1, 14, 46, 47, 74–77, 80,
84, 87, 88, 93–97, 109, 122, 124, 136,
141, 199 n. 6
Kitch, Carolyn 12
Kloppenberg, Lisa 109, 209 n. 45

Koch, Mayor Edward 60
Koon, Stacey 74, 199 n. 1
Korean war 210 n. 4
Ku Klux Klan 26, 160, 216 n.93

L.A. Confidential 100, 108
Landsberg, Alison 12, 13
Latinos: as targets of criminal justice
    system 78, 201 n. 22; stereotypes of,
    80
Lawrence, Regina 86- 88, 93, 94, 203
    n. 64
Lee, Harper 40
Leibovitz, Annie 198 n. 92
Leibowitz, Samuel 39, 189 n. 102; *see also*
    Scottsboro
Leonard, David 57, 61, 194 n. 23
Limbaugh, Rush 132
Lopez, Steve 89
Los Angeles Lakers *see* Bryant, Kobe
Los Angeles Police Department: and
    public opinion 205 n.96; *see also* King,
    Rodney; *see also* Rampart scandal
Louima, Abner 102
Lowen, James
Lynch, Jessica 133, 213 n. 53
lynching: antilynching legislation 10;
    antilynching movement 6, 8–10,
    25–28, 32, 58, 149, 185 n. 29;
    as anti-racist spectacles 8; extent of
    185 n. 30, 185 n. 34; of latinos 182
    n. 16, 194 n. 23; "legal lynching" 21,
    43, 44; as "lens" 6 ; and the myth
    of the black rapist 26; narratives 58;
    of Native Americans 182 n. 16;
    photographs of 130, 137, 149; public
    support for 10; rates decline 26;
    as reference point 10; as spectacle 6;
    spectacle lynchings 7–10, 15, 27, 58,
    131, 161; as terrorism 8

Mack, David 104, 199 n. 3
Mackey, Pamela 195 n. 41; *see also* Bryant,
    Kobe
Maddox, Alton 46
Mankiewicz Don 39
Mann act 20
Mann, Thomas 20, 21
Martinez, Benito 116
McDonald, M.G. 69
McKay, Jim 62, 69
McKenzie, Jon 213 n. 53

Mehserle, Johannes *see* Grant, Oscar
Meili, Trisha *see* Central Park jogger
Memphis Free Speech see African American
    Press
Mestrovic, Stjepan 144–146, 215 n. 78
Mezey, Naomi 98
Miller, Toby 62, 69
minstrel shows 40
Miranda v. Arizona 20, 43, 98–99, 207
    n.6
Mississippi Link, The 61
Mitchell, J.T. 150, 172, 176
Montgomery, Olen 24, 37, 184 n. 9;
    see also Scottsboro
Morris, Errol 142–149, 216 n. 88
Morris, Jud 199 n. 8
Murray, Hugh T., Jr. 36
My Lai massacre 138, 156; *see also*
    Atrocity photographs
myth of the black rapist 58

NAACP 8, 9, 23, 26, 36, 137, 149,
    154
National Basketball Association: as racial
    spectacle 55; *see also* Bryant, Kobe
NBA *see* National Basketball Association
Neal, Claude 8, 10, 154
Nelson, Lemrick 46
new media: and Abu Ghraib, 17;
    in anti-racist struggles 168; and
    counter-surveillance 124; and coverage
    of war 126; and identity 127; and
    immediacy 127
New York Amsterdam News 60
Newspapers: white southern 15; *see also*
    African American Press
Nguyen Ngoc Loan *see* Atrocity
    photographs
Norris v. Alabama 20, 43
Norris, Clarence 20, 23, 24, 31, 36, 38,
    42–45
NYPD Blue 98

Obama, President Barack 136, 158,
    165
objectivity, journalistic 192 n. 120
Omi, Michael 190 n. 105; *see also* racial
    formation
O'Neal, Shaquille *see* Bryant, Kobe
Orientalism *see* Abu Ghraib photographs
Ovando, Javier 74–77, 81, 82, 87–90, 93,
    102–105, 167, 199 n. 6

Parker, Mack Charles 67
Parks, Chief Bernard 84, 85, 87, 89
Parks, Rosa 65
Patterson, Haywood 22, 24, 34, 36, 38, 44, 45
Pennybacker, Susan 176, 177
Perez, Raphael 74, 75, 81–89, 102–105, 120–123, 199 n. 3
Philipose, Liz, 140
Phuc, Kim 137; *see also* Atrocity photographs
plea bargain: and unjust sentencing 86; *see also* criminal justice system
Polchin, James 149
police brutality 1; and Chicago torture scandal 97, 206 n. 2; *see also* King, Rodney; *see also* Rampart scandal
police corruption: and the Justice Department 97; in New Orleans 97, 206 n.2 ; in New York 204 n.86; in Philadelphia 97; in Seattle 199 n. 8
popular culture: and the *Miranda* decision 98; and views of police corruption and brutality 98, 122
Popular Memory Group, the 12
Pounder, CCH 116
Powell v. Alabama 20, 189 n. 104, 190 n. 107
Powell, Laurence 74, 199 n. 1
Powell, Ozzie *see* Scottsboro
Price, Victoria 20–22, 27–38, 187 n. 69, 188 n. 85, *see also* Scottsboro
prison industrial complex 16, 76–79, 95, 110, 122, 168, 199 n. 13; and racialization 79

Qaissi, Ali Shalal 154, 155, 217 n. 102, n.103

racial formation 3, 6, 10, 14, 15, 24, 122
racial profiling: *see* immigration
racial project 6–8, 10, 13; *see also* Racial Formation
racial spectacles: anti-racist racial spectacles 15, 18; and collective memory 10–14; and credibility 24; importance of 1–3; and lynching 6–10; political potential of 164–168; and racial formation 4–6; and socialization 2; and women of color 183 n. 45

Rampart scandal: as "accidental event" 94; appropriation within popular culture 101; and "bad apple" explanations 86, 203 n. 66; and changing journalistic conventions in coverage of police misconduct 94, 205 n. 106; and "code of silence" 84, 85, 97, 120, 121, 167; and consent decree 82, 89, 92, 93, 95, 165; and coverage of LAPD reforms 92; extent of 75, 82, 85; and film noir 100; and immigration policy violations 201 n. 38; impact on coverage of police misconduct 91; impact on popular culture 122; impact on understandings of race and crime 92; as indicative of systemic problems 88; limited "systemic" critique of 88; and mistrust of the police 93; news coverage of 87; obstruction of investigation 84; and racialized gap in public perceptions 93; and systemic inequities 82
rape: and professional sports 49; anti-rape movement 51, 52, 62; rape reform legislation 53; rape shield laws 35, 53, 62, 197 n. 74; sexist rape myths 64
Razack, Sherene 134
Reed, Ishmael 68
Rice, Constance 83, 84, 89, 90
"riots": and racial stereotyping 205 n.106
Roberson, Willie 24, 37
Rodman, Dennis 55
Romero, Mary 79, 201 n. 22
Rosenbaum, Yankel 46
Rosenhaft, Eve 176
Roethlisberger, Ben 193 n. 22
Rowe, David 62, 69
Rue, Penny 162
Russell, Katheryn 80, 192 n. 122
Ryan, Shawn 102, 112–114

Said, Edward 133
Saldana, Juan Manuel 90; *see also* Rampart Scandal
Sallat, Salaheddin 150, 216 n.93
Sante, Luc 131
SB 1070 (Arizona) *see* immigration
Schechter, Patricia 182 n. 16
Schudson, Michael 183 n. 33, 188 n. 85
Schwartz, Barry 183 n. 33
Scifo, Barbara 127

Scottsboro: and Civil Rights Movement 42; and collective memory 38, 46; and contemporary racial spectacles 46; and credibility 45; and narrative of racial progress 43, 190 n. 109; release of defendants 23, 37; and sexist rape mythology 33; as source of embarrassment for Alabama 32; Scottsboro Defense Committee 36
"Scottsboro Boys": as patronizing label 184 n. 4
Sharpton, Reverend Al 46
Simpson, O.J. 2, 13, 14, 16, 36, 44, 46, 49, 55, 57, 69, 182 n. 8, 192 n. 122, 192 n. 125
Sinclair, Upton 21
Sleeper, Jim 46
Smith, Susan 44, 59, 191 n. 117
Smith, William Kennedy 57
socialization narratives: in "Bad Cop" films 108
Society of the Spectacle see Debord, Guy
Sontag, Susan 131
Southern Christian Leadership Conference 125
Southern Horrors see Wells, Ida B.
southern press 22, 27, 28; as extension of the mob 27; changing views of race 28, 32
"southern womanhood": and Scottsboro case 22
spectacle: contested 5; defined 4; reversal of 5, 9; see also racial spectacles
Sprewell, Latrell 55
Standard Operating Procedure 142–143, 146, 149
Strickland v. Washington 190 n. 107
Stuart, Charles 44, 59
Sturken, Marita 11, 127
Supreme Court 3, 15, 20, 31, 38, 42–44, 58, 65, 66, 98, 109
Sussman, Elizabeth 182 n. 6

Taliban 133
Taylor, Prentiss 189 n. 93; see also Scottsboro
terrorism: and Abu Ghraib 140; and "gang profiling" 79; and Orientalism 140; lynching as form of 7–9, 25, 27
Tet offensive 138
The Big Heat 100

The Birth of a Nation 26, 58
The Shield 17, 96, 102, 111–123
Thomas, Clarence 23, 24, 36, 38, 45, 57, 58, 68
Thomas, Hank Willis 56
Thompson, David 189 n. 102
Till Bradley, Mamie 1, 166 see also Till, Emmett
Till, Emmett 1, 14, 32, 36, 42, 46, 47, 65, 67
To Kill a Mockingbird see Lee, Harper
Tolnay, Stewart 185 n. 34, n.35
Torres, Sasha 99, 114, 121
Training Day 17, 96, 102–123
Traintafyllos, Sia 134
Trump, Donald 60
Tucker, Linda 55, 193 n. 16
Tucker, Bruce 134
Tyson, Mike 55, 57, 62

UCSD. See University of California, San Diego
United States Department of Justice 75
University of California: privatization of 166, 218 n. 3
University of California, San Diego: and institutionalized racism 160, 218 n. 4; anti-racist protest movement 161; Black Student Union 159–163, 166; MECHA 160; racist incidents at 159, 218 n. 2, 219 n. 5

Vietnam war: coverage of 126; see also My Lai massacre
Voting Rights Act of 1965 42

Wallace, George 23
"War on Drugs": and racial disparities 78
Warhol museum 139
Warhol, Andy 151
Washington, Denzel 96, 102–103, 114
Webb, Clive 182 n. 16, 194 n. 27
Webber, Chris 55
Weems, Charlie 24
Wells, Ida B. 25, 26, 182 n. 16, 184 n. 25; 184 n. 28; 185 n. 32
Wexley, John see Scottsboro
white southern press: 58; and changing views on lynching 27
white women: and sexist stereotypes 63; "purity" of 25

whiteness: made visible 125
Whittaker, Forrest 119
Williams, Eugene 24, 37
Willis, Susan 56, 216 n.94
Winant, Howard 190 n. 105; *see also* racial
    formation
Without Sanctuary postcard exhibition
    see lynching photography
Wolf, Naomi 68
Wood, Amy Louise 131, 211 n. 23

Wright, Ada 21
Wright, Andy 24
Wright, Richard 23, 39
Wright, Roy 24, 37, 45, 184 n. 9
Wypijewski, JoAnn 128

Yudof, Mark 162

Zelizer, Barbie 11, 130, 217 n. 101
Zoot Suit Riots 1, 181 n. 1